4156

The Commonwealth armies

Also in the series

The army, politics and society in Germany, 1933–45
Klaus-Jürgen Müller

Troubled days of peace: Mountbatten and SEAC, 1945–46
Peter Dennis

The politics of manpower, 1914–18
Keith Grieves

The Commonwealth and the Korean War
Jeffrey Grey

F. W. Perry

The Commonwealth armies

Manpower and organisation
in two world wars

Manchester University Press

Copyright © F. W. Perry 1988

Published by Manchester University Press
Oxford Road, Manchester M13 9PL

Distributed exclusively in the USA and Canada
by St. Martin's Press, Inc., 175 Fifth Avenue,
New York, NY 10010, USA

British Library cataloguing in publication data
Perry, F. W.
    The Commonwealth armies: manpower and
    organisation in two world wars.—
    (War, armed forces and society).
    1. World War, 1914–1918—Campaigns
    2. Commonwealth of Nations—Armed Forces
    3. World War, 1939–1945—Campaigns
    4. Commonwealth of Nations—Armed Forces
    I. Title II. Series
    940.3'32   D547.C/

Library of Congress cataloging in publication data applied for
ISBN 0 7190 2595 8 *hardback*

Typset in Hong Kong by Best-set Typesetter Ltd
Printed and bound in Great Britain by
Biddles Ltd, Guildford and King's Lynn

Contents

Acknowledgements

Thanks are due to the directors, librarians and staff of the following institutions for their friendly and willing production of documents and publications: the Public Record Office, the Imperial War Museum library, the National Army Museum library, the India Office library, the library of the Office of Population Censuses and Surveys, the Ministry of Defence library (Central and Army). The staffs of the Gloucestershire and Hertfordshire Library Services and of the library of the City of London Polytechnic cheerfully sought and found many obscure titles. Information was readily given by: the Director, Australian War Memorial, Canberra; the Director, Directorate of History, National Defence Headquarters, Ottawa; the Secretary of Defence, Defence Headquarters, Wellington; the Officer in Charge, Central Army Records, Melbourne. My thanks are due to Brian Bond for his patience, helpful advice and criticism when acting as adviser for the original research on which the book is based. Finally, as always, my thanks to Hilary and Philippa for their proof-reading skills and to Ian, who drew the graphs.

Introduction

In February 1918, on the eve of the German offensive, British divisions in France were reduced from twelve battalions to nine. Earlier, in November and December 1915, two Indian divisions were transferred from the Western Front to what was hoped would be a less demanding theatre. In the Second World War, as British troops broke out of the Normandy bridgehead in 1944, divisions in France were being disbanded and further reductions followed in Italy in the winter of 1944/45. For the Commonwealth, as early as mid-1940 it was estimated that the establishment of the proposed South African Field Force of two divisions was 26,000 more than the expected number of volunteers. In Australia the disbandment of formations commenced in August 1942, before the repulse of the Japanese thrust on Port Moresby. In all of these cases the reason for the reductions is said to be manpower shortage. Yet if one examines the manpower figures for the respective armies it is apparent that the reductions took place against a background of rising numbers of men. The examination of this paradox is the purpose of the present study.

There is ample evidence that the armies experienced manpower problems during the two World Wars. It is, however, unclear whether or not the apparent manpower shortages were real in the sense of there being an absolute shortage of men at national level, or unreal in the sense of there being men available to the armies but being employed wastefully. On the other hand one can invert the problem and simply assert that the organisations of the armies were expanded to a level at which it became impossible to sustain them.

Should a field army be over-expanded, more divisions and brigades being created than can be kept up to strength with the manpower available, a number of consequences inevitably follow. First, the large number of formations initially available may inspire over-ambitious strategic and tactical plans, with unfortunate results. Second, as front-line forces waste away due to shortage of rein-forcements, ad hoc arrangements will be needed to transfer troops from other arms, troops who will require re-training for their new role and whose absence will be regretted in their old. Third, the initially over-large number of formations will require a corres-pondingly over-large production of munitions and other supplies and excess manpower will have to be allocated to this purpose. This will effectively reduce the strength at which the army could be maintained throughout the time that the munitions industries are over-producing and over-manned until redundant workers can be re-deployed from industry to the army.

Under conditions of national emergency, when a government has secured control over the deployment of the civil population, allo-cation of men and women to the Armed Services is subject to central decision. It may then arise that one Service is treated more or less generously than others, with the deficient Service suffering from a shortage of manpower. Similar considerations may arise under conditions of voluntary enlistment when service in one force is seen to be more or less attractive than service in others. To some extent, therefore, it is impossible to examine the manpower prob-lems of one Service in isolation. However in both wars it is not apparent that the sea and air forces suffered overall manpower shortages, although suffering at times from shortages of men and women with specific skills. In the first half of the twentieth century the sea and air Services were essentially Services dedicated to the operation of machines tended by men, whilst in the land Services operations were conducted by men assisted by machines. This points to a difference in kind between the sea and air forces on the one hand and the armies on the other, the one being 'capital intensive', the other 'labour intensive'. It is therefore accepted that, for much of the periods under consideration, the absolute strength of the armies was subject to external control to a greater or lesser degree. Whilst to some extent the three Services were competitors for manpower the principal subject under consideration is the number of men made available to the armies and the use made of them.

Manpower problems can, of course, arise at several levels. At the operational level the problems may be due to the methods used to expand the army and train and deploy those recruited. Legislative and constitutional limitations may be laid on the raising of forces and their deployment. Finally, manpower problems may be due to the overall concept within which the forces are being raised and lie in the realm of strategy and policy.

Within the overall problem of recruiting and organising large numbers of men for war there are many subsidiary problems. Although subsidiary many of these can acquire great, perhaps overriding, importance at certain stages of expansion or in the provision of reinforcements. Examples of this type of problem are the recruitment of men with special skills and the recruitment of officers. Although the existence of these problems has been noted in the following pages no attempt has been made to discuss them in detail. Some of them are extremely complex, that of officer selection and training, for example, including the definition of what constitute 'officer-like qualities', how these may be recognised, and how they can be cultivated during a training programme.

The initial task in the following pages is to outline the organisation of the pre-war armies of the various Commonwealth countries since these provided the base from which the war-time armies grew and to a large extent moulded the form of that growth. The underlying question to be answered for both World Wars is, 'Was the contribution which Britain and her allies were attempting to make to the land war within the capabilities of those countries?'.

Chapter 1
The British Army 1907–18

i *Before the war*

At the beginning of this century the role of the British Army was defined by the Stanhope Memorandum which had been published in June 1891 but which had been in effect since 1882. This gave first priority to support of the civil power in the United Kingdom and to garrison India and the colonies, second priority to the mobilisation of two corps for home defence and lowest priority to finding two corps for service abroad. This simple, not to say simplistic, arrangement began to find little favour in the years immediately following the Boer War. The relative decline in British economic strength, growth of German naval power and recurrent fears of invasion made the British feel increasingly alone in an unfriendly world. The time was ripe for change.

The first evidence of Britain's desire to seek friends abroad is, perhaps, to be found in the Anglo-French Entente of 1904. Although founded in a settlement of colonial differences the agreement soon led to implications nearer home. The Moroccan crisis of 1905, and the Algeciras conference which followed it, for the first time found France and Britain facing Germany and Austria. In the shadow of the crisis consultations between the Staffs of Britain and France were commenced, although these were not pursued vigorously once the crisis was past. British military thinking, too, was turning away from an India-centred strategy from 1904. That strategy made demands upon the Army which it was unable to meet. A European strategy provided an attainable role.[1]

Against this background the reorganisation of the Army had been an active issue from 1901. Under the Cardwell system of linked units, one at home and one abroad, the Army had become

little more than a colonial gendarmerie and, as such, it had failed
miserably when tested in South Africa. After more or less abortive attempts by Broderick and Arnold-Foster it fell to Haldane to
carry through the reforms which now bear his name. Essentially
Haldane's plans produced an expeditionary force, with reserves,
and a force for home defence. Although after the event Haldane
was to claim that his scheme had European war in mind issues were
not so clear cut at the time and Haldane himself, at a CID meeting
in February 1907, acknowledged that the size of his Regular force
was fixed by the peace requirements of India and the colonies.[2]

The expeditionary force proposals were presented to the House
of Commons in July 1906. Six divisions and four cavalry brigades
were proposed, the latter to be formed into a cavalry division on
mobilisation. In all the force would consist of 150,000 men of
whom 100,000 would have to be found from the reserves or auxiliary forces. Compensatory reductions would be made in overseas
garrisons and eventually nine battalions were disbanded. Interestingly, no higher level of organisation than the division was
envisaged. The Commander-in-Chief would have to directly control the operations of his formations in addition to his many other
duties, both military and diplomatic, as the Commander of an
independent force on foreign soil. In addition to the expeditionary
force units were also earmarked for a seventh division and a fifth
cavalry brigade as an imperial policing force.

The most difficult task in the reorganisation of the army was the
reorganisation of the auxiliary forces into a coherent whole. In
1906 these consisted of three distinct groups; Militia, Yeomanry
and Volunteers. The Militia, the 'constitutional force', was a
voluntary home service force jealous of change but serving best as a
means of recruitment to the Regular Army rather than as a home
defence army. The Yeomanry was another voluntary home service
force, liable for service under the Militia Acts. The Volunteers were
liable for service in Great Britain in the event of actual or
apprehended invasion.[3] The reorganisation of the auxiliary forces
had been the subject of two investigations prior to the Haldane
reforms. The first of these, by the Norfolk Commission, reported in
1904 with conclusions strongly in favour of universal service. The
second was by the Territorial Force Committee which looked at
alternative schemes of reorganisation before ending its meetings
in July 1906. The real problem was the place of the Militia in any

new scheme but in the event the reforms went through with the exclusion of the Militia, which became moribund and faded away. Although to a limited extent it might be true to say that the Militia 'became' the new Special Reserve, it is clear that the old Militia, the historic defence force of the country, had passed away.

The Territorial and Reserve Forces Act of 1907[4] authorised the reorganisation of the auxiliary forces. Henceforward the Army Reserve would consist of two classes of men. On the one hand there would be the existing men who transferred to the Reserve on completion of their colour service, on the other there would be men who enlisted directly into the Special Reserve and who, after completing an initial training period of six months, would be liable for four weeks of Reserve training each year. For individuals who enlisted in the 101 Special Reserve battalions conditions of service were onerous and could not appeal to a man in regular employment or to his employer. The Special Reserve would appeal, as had the Militia before it, mainly to the casually employed.

Elsewhere in the Act the conditions of service of the new Territorial Force were outlined. The basic term of enlistment was for four years with an annual training liability. The Yeomanry would become part of the TF and the whole would be administered by County Associations. The fourteen Territorial Divisions and fourteen Mounted Brigades were liable only for home service but the Act authorised individuals and units to opt for overseas service liability and in presenting the Army Estimates in February 1907 Haldane expressed his confidence in that taking place at a time of national emergency.[5]

The establishment of the Force was 302,199 all ranks and, to the disappointment of Haldane, this strength was never achieved in peace-time. A peak of 276,000 was reached in 1910 but strength thereafter was of the order of 250,000.[6] To improve the strength situation a National Service (Territorial Force) Bill was introduced before the Commons in April 1913. This would have introduced elements of compulsion into recruitment but in face of widespread opposition the measure was withdrawn before comng to a vote.[7]

On the international scene the years following the Haldane reforms were marked by increasing tension and renewed alarm at German naval expansion was soon followed by the Agadir crisis of 1911. At a special meeting of the CID on 23rd August the outline proposals of the military and naval Staffs were presented. The

Army view, presented by the Director of Military Operations, Major-General Wilson, outlined a German thrust through Belgium and envisaged the deployment of the British Expeditionary Force on the French left. The whole of the expeditionary force would be needed, perhaps supported by two or three divisions from India and the seventh division from the colonies.[8] The suggestion is of particular interest as being the first occasion on which the use of troops from India was mentioned, as well as the remarks concerning the unformed seventh division. The naval proposals envisaged a maritime strategy with military action confined to landings on enemy coasts. Although the crisis was soon over the difference in view between the Staffs persisted, until overtaken by events in 1914, and underlay much of the subsequent dispute between 'easterners' and 'westerners' throughout the Great War. The meeting may also be regarded as the first intimation that contact between the French and British Staffs had been revived. Indeed, mobilisation plans worked out during the early months of 1911 included plans for the embarkation of the BEF, whilst a memorandum signed by Wilson and Dubail on 20th July provided for the deployment of the British force and a timetable for its concentration in northern France. Although not binding on the British Government the agreement had a moral weight to which regard had to be given in August 1914.

The following years saw refinement and completion of the Staff plans but the possibility of a protracted war on a massive scale was never envisaged. In 1914 Britain had been free of involvement in a major European war since 1815. The pattern of modern war in Europe appeared to be short and sharp and in a complex industrial society it was believed that a prolonged conflict would bring economic collapse to both sides. There was no need to plan the creation of new forces which would only appear after peace was signed. Both sides marched to war in 1914 in the confident expectation of being 'home by Christmas'.

ii *Creating a continental army*

On 1st August 1914 the strength of the Regular Army was 247,432. Twelve out of thirty-one cavalry regiments and seventy-four out of 157 infantry battalions were abroad. Recruits in the main enlisted for nine years with the colours and three with the reserve. In the infantry a recruit was first posted to the Regimental Depot for training before passing to the home battalion of his regiment, becoming eligible for transfer to the overseas battalion on reaching the age of twenty. Strengths of home battalions were low and variable, while on mobilisation under-age soldiers would have to be returned to the Depot. To bring units up to a war establishment of 1002 the 209,280 Reservists and Special Reservists would be needed. Indeed of the first six divisions which landed in France some 60% of the strength came from the reserves.

The 268,777 Territorials were in fifty-five Yeomanry regiments, 208 infantry battalions and other supporting units but of these only 18,683 men and five complete units had taken the General Service obligation.[9] Behind these lay a Territorial Reserve of only 2082.

On 5th August, on the first morning of the war, an ad hoc council of war consisting of Asquith, Grey, Churchill, Haldane, Kitchener and the principal Service chiefs met to consider policy and plans. Kitchener attended the meeting with no official status, having been summoned back to London as he was about to embark for Egypt, but later that same day he was appointed Secretary of State for War.[10] As to the business of the meeting, it was decided that fearing invasion and, perhaps, civil unrest only four divisions of the Expeditionary Force would initially embark for France. Decisions were also taken to bring home certain colonial garrisons as soon as they could be relieved and the Indian Government was to be asked to provide two divisions for Egypt. Although not confirmed by the Minutes, Haig is said to have raised three points; first, that a long war should be planned for; second, that a force of a million men should be aimed for immediately; third, that officers and NCOs should be withdrawn from the Expeditionary Force to act as instructors.[11] The first offers of help had already arrived from the Dominions and although there was a proposal that their troops would best serve as overseas garrisons it was finally decided that they should come to England. Concurrently, the Commons was authorising an extra 500,000 men for the Regular Army.

The first call for volunteers by the War Office came on 7th August when 100,000 men aged 19–30 were invited to enlist for three years or the duration of the war. These men were to form a New Army of six divisions and the call was shortly followed by others. The same day Canada and Australia each offered 20,000 men with a further 8000 from New Zealand. Attending his first Cabinet meeting as War Minister Kitchener asserted that Britain's contribution to the war could not be limited in any way. He proposed to plan for a war lasting at least three years and to build an army of at least a million men.[12]

It is generally accepted that Kitchener had in mind the formation of about seventy divisions but this is to over-simplify what became a long drawn out evolutionary process. On 25th August the House of Lords was told that thirty divisions were contemplated[13] and by 17th September this had become about fifty.[14] By January 1915 the number had become twenty-five Army Corps or fifty divisions including Indian but excluding Canadian and other Dominion troops, plus the army at home.[15] Such an expansion was not unattended by criticism from those who believed that such an enlargement was impracticable.[16] It was not until August 1915 that the proposed strength of the army was considered by a Cabinet Committee. Then Kitchener revealed that his current intentions were for seventy divisions. In fact plans for the ultimate expansion of the army did not exist. The seventy divisions were a declaration of intent rather than a planning target. In the event the short term problems of maintaining the BEF in the field, with expenditures of military stores vastly greater than any imagined, with demands for weapons and equipment not previously dreamed of, and at the same time attempting to equip such new forces as were raised, outweighed the long-term problems produced by the lack of a concrete plan. The heavy casualties in France, with the need for reinforcement and replacement, threw further heavy burdens on the task of producing new units and formations with the available manpower. Again short-term problems over-rode any disadvantages which might have arisen from the lack of an overall plan. The expansion of the army thus took place as an improvised process through a series of relatively small steps but by the standards of the pre-war army they were very large steps indeed.

There remains the question of why seventy divisions was chosen as the intended size of the army. There is no direct evidence on this point but pre-war forces of major European countries, based on compulsory service, were of this order and by implication any country which wished to influence the course of events would have to produce forces of similar magnitude. Kitchener himself is reported to have observed that the British forces would not reach their maximum strength until 1917 by which time, as a result of attrition, the British Army would be the largest in the field with all of the advantages, military and political, that would flow from that position.[17]

In terms of manpower it was noticed earlier that Parliament authorised an increase in the strength of the army by half a million men on the outbreak of war. A further half million was added on 9th September and another million on 12th November. For 1915/16 the strength of the army was taken as three millions and on 21st December 1915 an increase to four millions was sought. Finally, on 20th December 1916, an additional million was approved to legitimise forces raised in the colonies. The authorised strength of the army remained at five millions until the end of the war.

One of the outstanding features of the expansion of the British armies and the BEF in 1914 is the variety of measures used to provide that expansion. It was noticed earlier that considerable forces were serving in overseas garrisons and that on 5th and 6th August decisions were taken to bring home such as could be relieved. On 4th August the South African Government offered to relieve British forces in the Union and shortly the Canadian Government undertook to replace the British battalion in Bermuda. Further, to anticipate later discussion, units and formations of the Territorial Force were used to relieve the Regular garrisons of Malta, Gibraltar, Egypt and much of that in India. Indian units were used to relieve other colonial garrisons. By early 1915 fifty-six infantry battalions and three cavalry regiments had been made available to form 7, 8 and 27–9 Divisions and a cavalry brigade for France. In addition to these movements a further six battalions and six regiments returned to Europe as part of Indian formations.

On 7th August the War Office made its first call for 100,000 men to form the First New Army (9–14 Divisions) and this was followed by further calls on 11th and 13th September for the Second (15–20 Divisions) and Third (21–6 Divisions) New Armies. It is interesting to note that, at least at this early stage, it was apparently intended that the New Armies would fight as such and not be integrated into existing formations. The flood of recruits resulting from these calls passed all expectations and in an attempt to control the flow a scheme of deferred enlistment was introduced early in

September under which a man would be paid a retainer whilst remaining at his work until called for.[18] With the 11th September call the height standard for recruits was raised from the usual five feet four inches to five feet six inches but by the end of October the flood was declining and the height standard was lowered again, the age limit being raised to thirty-eight. Early in November the regulation height was lowered to five feet three inches and, in July 1915, to five feet two inches when the age limit was raised to forty. The need to reduce standards was evidence of how difficult recruiting was becoming but in the first four months of the war alone over a million men had volunteered for service.

In the early days of the expansion men were posted to Regimental Depots for clothing, equipping and initial training but these were soon overwhelmed and recruits were then posted directly to New Army battalions. The new battalions were formed on very small cadres of Regular officers and NCOs supplemented by retired officers and by Indian Army officers who had been on leave and detained. To these were added in due course other officers from the Reserve of Officers, a limited number of newly-promoted Warrant Officers and NCOs and newly gazetted officers who had been trained in school and university OTCs. The OTC had been formed as part of the 1908 reforms and from the beginning of the war to March 1915 20,577 former members were commissioned.[19] Perhaps the greatest difficulty was experienced in finding trained NCOs and men to train the recruits. Here recourse was often made to the promotion of men who were themselves but partially trained. This difficulty was somewhat eased later by the return from the Front of men who had been wounded but who were again fit for duty.

Overlying all the difficulties of organising the new units were those related to the lack of physical resources. By clearing married quarters barrack accommodation could be found for 262,000 men. For the rest buildings had to be hired and as many as 800,000 were billeted before permanent camps and hutments could be provided. Similar difficulties were met in clothing. The output from cloth and clothing manufacturers was limited and as an interim measure half a million blue serge suits were made up from Post Office stocks of material. A similar number of civilian overcoats was purchased and issued and recruits with serviceable clothing of their own were required to continue wearing it until uniform supplies became available. The question of weapons was even more difficult since, even for rifles, pre-war manufacturing capacity was merely 6000 per month. On 10th August contracts were placed for equipping and arming the First New Army but many months would elapse before the material was seen. Some rifles were obtained from naval stocks but the only significant result of a world-wide search for ready-made weapons was a supply of 0·275″ Japanese rifles which were used to equip Territorial units in 1915. A Cabinet Committee on Munitions was formed on 12th October to coordinate munitions supply and sanction was given for the expenditure of large sums on the expansion of factories at home and for placing contracts in Britain and the United States. As Kitchener told the House of Lords on 17th September, 'Our chief difficulty is one of material rather than of personnel'.[20]

Turning to the Territorial Force, which had been embodied on 4th August, the first recognition accorded to it by the new War Secretary on 7th August was unfavourable. A circular to the County Associations prohibited enlistment except to replace men who had joined the New Armies. Second thoughts soon followed, though, since on the 10th Kitchener enquired of the Director-General of the Force as to what parts of the Force would be prepared to serve overseas. With the Expeditionary Force's departure the TF, with the Special Reserve, became the principal home defence force and the transfer of units and formations to other theatres could only take place at the expense of depleting the home defence organisation. However, concurrently with the expansion of the New Armies, enlistment in the TF was soon proceeding rapidly in spite of difficulties in the provision of clothing and equipment. The County Associations were responsible for the maintenance of the Force but found that orders with their suppliers were subordinated to orders placed by the War Office. Theoretically the maintenance of the Force devolved upon the War Office from mobilisation but the War Office, faced with all of the problems of raising the New Armies, was quite unable to provide supplies from its own resources. The Force was further handicapped by the withdrawal of Regular instructors, diverted to meet the needs of the new units and formations. Thus, in practice, the expansion of the Territorial Force was accorded a lower priority than that of the new Regular units and its progress was inhibited accordingly.[21]

Following the War Secretary's enquiry on 10th August the TF

was canvassed to promote volunteering for overseas service, instituting a procedure which was to be repeated with increasing vigour until 1916. The immediate priority was to find reliefs for overseas garrisons and in September the first TF units and formations to serve abroad left Britain. 7 and 8 Middlesex Regiment went to Gibraltar, 1 London Brigade to Malta and 1 East Lancashire (later 42) Division, with two Yeomanry units, to Egypt. The first formal step in the expansion of the TF took place on 15th August when County Associations were authorised to form new units to replace those volunteering for general service and this became general from 21st September when what was effectively a duplication of the Territorial Force was authorised.[22] The duplicate or 'second line' units were composed of home service men transferred from the 'first line', together with surplus general service men, and, as canvassing continued, the number of general service men in the 'second line' rose steadily. Meanwhile the flow of Territorial units overseas continued. In September the first three units crossed to France and by the end of the year twenty-three infantry battalions, six Yeomanry regiments and other units had joined the BEF. In October Wessex and Home Counties Divisions sailed for India and these were followed in December by 2 Wessex Division, the first 'second line' formation to serve overseas.

The next stage in the expansion of the TF commenced on 24th November with an instruction that when a 'first line' unit proceeded overseas a 'third line' unit should be raised in its place. This too became general in March 1915. A significant change in policy emerged in April 1915. In light of the heavy casualties in France a reserve and replacement organisation was needed for any unit or formation on active service and this became the role of the Territorial 'third line' units. Home service men were now posted away to what were designated 'Provisional' units. In the infantry there were sixty-eight Provisional Battalions, although as men in them opted for overseas service the number was reduced until by the end of 1916 only forty remained, composed of men unfit for front-line duties.

Concurrently with the expansion of the New Armies and the TF a Fourth New Army (30–5 Division) was formed in November from battalions of the Special Reserve. In April 1915 these divisions were broken up to form a training and reserve organisation for the first three New Armies.[23]

A fourth main thread of expansion took place by local initiative when units were raised by individuals and local organisations. This form of expansion received a considerable impulse through the work of the Parliamentary Recruiting Committee which promoted enlistment by publicity methods, often based on the local party organisations. The units formed in this way at first held local titles, as for example the 1–4 Salford Battalions raised by Mr Barlow, MP, and the Salford Brigade Committee. Units were housed, clothed and fed by their sponsors until the War Office took them over in 1915, refunding their organisers' expenditure.[24] These units formed the Fifth and Sixth New Armies. Particular note should be made of 36 (Ulster) Division, based on the Ulster Volunteer Force, and 38 (Welsh) Division formed under the auspices of the Welsh National Executive Committee. That this form of recruitment might not be entirely in the national interest is shown by the fate of 18–21 Royal Fusiliers and 16 Middlesex Regiment. Composed largely of better educated men and containing many potential officers, they were taken out of the line in France in February 1916 for the removal of those suitable for commission. Three of the battalions were then disbanded.

Altogether 142 battalions were raised through local sponsorship, each with a depot company, and in 1915 these companies were grouped to form sixty-eight Local Reserve Battalions to supply reinforcements to their service battalions.

The expansion of the army thus took place in four distinct forms; Regular Army, Territorial Force, the New Armies and the privately raised forces. To a great extent it would appear that each was competing with the others for the men who were willing, or who could be persuaded, to come forward. In the long run the total number of men who enlisted was probably little affected but there was undoubtedly a great waste of effort in the duplication. Further, it became difficult to control the rate of expansion and relate it to the housing, equipment and training facilities available. In the expectation of a short war of limited liability there were no plans for the expansion of the army at the beginning of the war and the rate of expansion became to a large extent controlled by pressures outside the War Office. The lack of planning extended to the mobilisation of the country's industrial resources and manpower and the expansion of the army itself made a contribution to the munitions shortages under which it was shortly to labour. Perhaps in the context of 1914 the form which the war would take and the country's part in it could not have been predicted but the lack of even an outline plan was unfortunate.

A lot of criticism has been directed at Kitchener's decision to expand the army through the formation of New Armies rather than through the medium of the Territorial Associations. Haldane himself expressed the thought that Territorial line after line could have been formed, each stepping into the place of the other as it moved forward. Much of this criticism arose, however, in the 1920s, long after the event.[25] To some extent the criticisms are fair, but they miss the essential point that the TF was a home service force. To make it liable for overseas service would have entailed recourse to Parliament and, even if successful there, changing pre-existing conditions of service would be of dubious legality. Such a measure could only be introduced in conjunction with the implementation of compulsory service, a much more contentious issue. Short of conscription, the availability of the TF for employment overseas had to be decided at the level of the individual. This was, in fact, the procedure followed. Implicitly, however, what was being undertaken was the division of the TF into two parts. Units and formations which had undertaken liability for general service had to be used piecemeal in 1914 and 1915. Under this procedure Highland, West Lancashire and 1 London Divisions were broken up, their units being used individually. Although in the end almost all of the old TF accepted overseas liability the time needed to complete this cannot be considered to be over until the last of the broken-up divisions was reconstituted in February 1916. For the 'second line' formations, eventually eight out of fourteen divisions served abroad, but a strong home service element persisted until the introduction of conscription. The sixty-eight home service Provisional Battalions compared with the pre-war 208 Territorial Battalions is an illustration of how strong that element was. It is clear, therefore, that the TF was in practice a very imperfect instrument for expansion due to the restrictive nature of its constitution. That the Force provided, in spite of its defects, a valuable reinforcement for the BEF is not to be denied but the limited effective duplication actually attained demonstrates that other machinery was needed to achieve the 70-division target. Perhaps the principal criticism that can be levelled at the formation of the New Armies is that the diversion of resources to them extended the time needed to prepare the pre-war TF for active service. This was, however, part of the price to be paid for expansion on the scale needed.

iii *Conscription*

The expenditure of material in France and the need to equip the expanding forces in the United Kingdom produced an unprecedented demand on the industrial capacity of the country. At the same time the indiscriminate acceptance of volunteers for the army, with the acceptance of skilled workers from heavy industry, was a significant factor in reducing potential industrial capacity. The first measures to passively check indiscriminate enlistment were taken early in 1915 when the Admiralty and War Office began to issue war service badges to workers whose services were considered essential, the workers being identified by their immediate employers. A Ministry of Munitions was formed in June 1915 and the following month this became the sole badging authority. At this stage a principal difficulty was the identification of skills which really were essential and in general the Ministry was forced to rely on the information provided by employers who had their own individual standards as to what was, or was not, essential work. Thus the munitions industries and the army became competitors for the supply of men, particularly since the first flush of enthusiasm for enlistment was now spent. The scene was thus set for the introduction of compulsion, on the one hand to secure the number of men needed for war purposes and on the other to secure a proper distribution between the armed forces and essential industries.

Compulsory service may be said to have been a live issue in British politics from 1902, championed by the National Service League of which Lord Roberts became President in 1905.[26] The Norfolk Commission reported in 1904 with a strong recommendation in favour of universal military training but both major parties reached 1914 believing themselves committed to opposing conscription. There was some awareness that with the adoption of a continental strategy an increase in forces was needed and an active lobby pressed for conscription but such an expansion was unacceptable in peacetime.[27] Views as to how the country would have responded to compulsory service in August 1914 are divided. In practical terms such an introduction was impossible. There was no machinery to implement the measure, not even a registration of all able-bodied citizens. The imposition of conscription could only have been achieved at the cost of considerably delaying the expansion of the army. Even the carrying out of a National Registration was delayed until July 1915. Curiously, no provisions were made for up-dating the Register until 1918.[28]

As early as October 1914 there were signs that voluntary recruiting might not be able to supply all of the men required and in the early months of 1915 disquiet began to be expressed by public figures and in the press. Although in general the Conservative Party advocated and the Liberals opposed conscription there were many individual differences. The result was that Cabinet discussions on the subject were lengthy, inconclusive and lacking clear leadership.[29] In August 1915 a War Policy Committee was set up to investigate the case for conscription in relation to the country's resources. Those appearing before the Committee gave evidence both of the diversity of view on conscription and of the practicable size of the army. The view of Lloyd George, Minister of Munitions, was that if Germany forced Russia out of the war many more than seventy divisions would be needed. The President of the Board of Trade demonstrated that not more than thirty-five divisions could be supported. The Chancellor stated that the country lacked the financial resources to support seventy divisions. Kitchener stated that although he would like to see a hundred divisions, seventy were probably all that could be attained.[30] Not surprisingly the Committee was unable to reach a conclusion although a dissenting Supplementary Report favoured both the introduction of conscription and a target size for the army of 100 divisions. No further action was taken but on 8th October Kitchener presented a memorandum to the Cabinet outlining a quota system for recruitment, supported by a ballot.[31] The proposal failed to receive support but it led to a last trial of the voluntary system in the shape of the Derby Scheme. Lord Derby was appointed Director General of Recruiting and under his scheme men aged 18–41 were invited to attest; i.e. to be ready to enlist when called upon. Men attesting were grouped according to age and marital state with the declared intention of calling upon the young before the old and the single before the married. By the middle of December some two million men had attested but only a quarter of a million were available for

immediate service. In consequence a Military Service Act received
Royal Assent before the end of January 1916 applying conscription
to all single men and childless widowers aged 18–41.[32]

According to the wording of the Act men were deemed to be
enlisted in His Majesty's forces and placed in the Reserve to be
called upon when required. Applications to Local Tribunals for
certificates of exemption were authorised, these being issued to
those in war industries. The perhaps over-generous use of this
facility was such that in March 1916 the War Office found it
necessary to call up some of the Derby Scheme's younger married
groups. Generally, however, the initiative for call-up was in the
hands of the War Office which could summon men who did not
hold exemption certificates. Meanwhile a Cabinet Committee
reported on 4th February in favour of a force of sixty-two divisions
as a field force, with a further five divisions at home, and on 18th
April the CIGS reported that a scheme of fifty-seven divisions
abroad and ten at home was being applied.[33] It was thus becoming
apparent that the continuing manpower shortage had no prospect
of alleviation, while the political will to apply total conscription
was still lacking. Discussions inside and outside the Cabinet were
extensive but it was the pressure inside the House as a whole which
resulted in the withdrawal of a compromise Government Bill and
the passing of a measure to bring in universal service.[34]

The Military Service (2) Act of 1916 went much further than the
previous Act in extending the concept of compulsory service. The
age limit for overseas service was reduced from the ruling twenty to
nineteen and the Act also retained soldiers who had completed their
engagement period. Indeed until now some 2000 soldiers had been
leaving the army each month on completion of their contractual
service, leaving their units in France and elsewhere with due
ceremony.[35] The Act also provided that men of the TF could be
transferred to other corps or to the regular forces. Thus in effect the
Territorial Force became absorbed into the Regular Army for the
remainder of the war. One of the incidental effects of these changes
was that men who had not hitherto accepted the general service
obligation became liable to serve overseas and the former Provisional units were shortly disbanded.

After all the press and Parliamentary disputation which led up
to the later Military Service Act the results were disappointing.
There was little increase in the number of men enlisting and the

War Office was driven to the bizarre expedient of conducting 'round-ups', sealing off football matches, railway stations and so on to screen the crowds for men without exemption certificates. The future manpower position looked bleak.

iv   Training and home defence

The introduction of conscription, with the prospect of the army being able to receive recruits in an orderly manner instead of irregularly as individuals joined up, instigated a reorganisation of the system under which recruits were trained and drafted. Hitherto the system had been an ad hoc one; henceforward some degree of regularity would prevail.

Under pre-war arrangements the Regimental Depots had been responsible for recruit training. On the outbreak of war they were rapidly overwhelmed by the vast numbers enlisting and responsibility then devolved upon the units themselves. Indeed the first Army Order authorising the expansion of the army included training syllabuses to be completed in six months.

Pre-war planning was that the Special Reserve battalions would provide drafts for the Regular Army and, with some modifications, these arrangements were retained to the end of the war. The battalions also had to provide for coast and harbour defence, tasks which interfered with their training role but which were eased at a later date by the formation of units specifically for local defence. Until September 1916 the Special Reserve battalions received men who had been enlisted and equipped at the Depots and gave individual and sub-unit training for a period which depended to some extent on the need for drafts but which was usually considered complete after about eight weeks. After September 1916 responsibility for initial training was allocated elsewhere and sub-unit training was then the principal activity. The through-put of men in these units was very high and 3 Border Regiment is recorded as having posted 600 officers and 47,000 men during the war.[36]

One of the features of Great War enlistment much commented upon is the emphasis that was placed upon locally-based recruiting and the adverse social consequences which resulted when a locally-raised unit suffered heavy casualties. While this was true for the Territorial units and those of the Fifth and Sixth New Armies, mostly made up of locally-raised units, and was an incidental factor

in the formation of the other New Armies when friends and work-
mates joined up together, it became less true as time went on and
reinforcement replaced wastage. The local nature of battalions was
diluted from an early stage and, taking 3 Norfolk Regiment as an
example, in 1915 nearly half of this unit's drafts were for units
other than the Norfolk Regiment. Destinations were as diverse as
the Essex and Border Regiments and the Royal Dublin Fusiliers.[37]

The Irish regiments found particular difficulty in maintaining
strength after the first flush of enthusiasm for recruiting in 1914,
when units were formed for the First and Second New Armies. As
early as 5th December 1914 it was necessary to disband the Regular
2 Connaught Rangers because of lack of men. The internal situation in Ireland militated against further recruiting and the Statutes
which applied conscription to Great Britain did not do so to Ireland. In consequence the war-formed Irish units tended to waste
away.

The evolution of the Territorial 'third line' units into a training
system was remarked on earlier and in 1916 these units became
Reserve battalions, providing the same functions for serving units
of the TF as did the Special Reserve for the Regular. At the same
time the small depots which had been formed in 1914 by Territorial
units were grouped into general TF Depots, paralleling those of the
Regular regiments.

From the outbreak of war to the end of November 1914 the BEF
in France suffered casualties totalling 3627 officers and 86,237
other ranks, mostly falling on the infantry of the seven Regular
divisions who numbered only 84,000.[38] It was in the face of such
unprecedented demands for replacements that the Fourth New
Army was broken up in April 1915 to provide a training organisation for reinforcements for the first three New Armies. This organisation was joined later in the year by units formed from the depot
companies raised with the privately formed battalions. All of this
was superceded from 1st September 1916 when the Training
Reserve was formed.

Under the Training Reserve organisation 112 Training Reserve
Battalions provided individual and sub-unit training for recruits,
after which they were transferred to Special Reserve or Territorial
Reserve units for further training and to await drafting to
battalions on active service. Further changes took place from May
1917 when initially fourteen TR Battalions were designated Young

Soldier Battalions to give individual training to the eighteen-year-olds now being conscripted. After basic training the recruits were posted, by companies, to one of twenty-eight Graduated Battalions to complete a total of one year's training before being posted overseas on reaching the age of nineteen. From July 1917 Graduated Battalions were posted to Home Service Divisions, most of which had been Territorial 'second line' Divisions not selected for overseas service. From October 1917 Young Soldier and Graduated Battalions were affiliated to the line regiments and other portions of the TR reduced to half-a-dozen Recruit Reception and Distribution Battalions. In summary, a recruit would pass successively through Distribution, Young Soldier and Graduated Battalions before going to a Special or Territorial Reserve Battalion for posting overseas. If the number of unit transfers appears excessive the system at least promised that training would be orderly and progressive and was a far cry from the improvisations of the Kitchener Armies of 1914.

Concurrently with the mobilisation and improvisation of field armies the National Reserve mobilised in 1914 to supplement the Special Reserve's guard tasks and to provide guard detachments for vulnerable points. The National Reserve, 215,451 strong in October 1913, had been formed in 1910 from volunteers with former service in one or other of the armed forces.[39]

The Territorial Force also mobilised supernumerary companies for similar tasks, sometimes incorporating National Reserve detachments. From the summer of 1915 Garrison Battalions were formed from over-age and lower medical category men who had enlisted. These were intended for garrison and lines of communication duties at home and overseas. Since local defence troops at home were by now rather a heterogeneous collection, the various guard sub-units were gathered into a Royal Defence Corps in March 1916 and the rationalisation was taken a step further in August 1917, when the home-service Garrison Battalions joined the Corps.

From the summer of 1915 a number of Transport and Labour Battalions were formed in the line regiments. The former were mainly employed on dock work in the home ports and their formation was inspired by a desire to have a nucleus of men under military discipline, available to move from port to port as needed. The demand for the Labour Battalions came from the insatiable need for labour in France for all sorts of construction work in the field and on the lines of communication. All of these battalions were absorbed into the Labour Corps when it was formed in February 1917.[40]

A further thread in the tangled skein of the home defence forces remains to be noticed. From August 1914 a number of local volunteer corps were organised by those who were unable or unwilling to accept an obligation for full time service. In the November a measure of official approval was granted and a Central Association of Volunteer Training Corps was set up to administer the units. In April 1916 the Corps was officially recognised under the Volunteer Act of 1863, although a limitation on use was recognised in that under the Act men could only be required to serve in the event of invasion. A new Volunteer Act and subsequent regulations prescribed drills and provided for wider service.[41] A boost to membership came when Tribunals made the granting of exemption certificates conditional upon memership of the Corps. Administration was now transferred to the TF Associations which remained responsible for the 300,000 members of the Corps to the end of the war.

v *Cavalry and mounted troops*

Only passing reference has been made previously to cavalry and mounted units of which at the beginning of the war there were thirty-one Regular, three Special Reserve and fifty-five Yeomanry regiments. One Cavalry Division crossed to France in August 1914 with an independent brigade and later other brigades were formed from units withdrawn from colonial garrisons, divisional cavalry squadrons and elsewhere so that by April 1915 there were three Cavalry Divisions.

In August 1914 seventeen Reserve Cavalry Regiments were formed to provide drafts for the Regular regiments. The three Special Reserve Regiments duplicated themselves in 1914 and early 1915, each forming a Reserve Regiment. As in the case of the other units of the TF, Yeomanry Regiments formed 'second' and 'third line' units with similar functions.

With the limited tactical opportunities available for cavalry action, the development of the mounted forces during the war was particularly complex and, perhaps, could only be completely described by narrating developments at squadron level. Indeed for much of the war the mounted troops found themselves in the position of a force looking for a role to play. The six Special Reserve and twelve Yeomanry Regiments went to France between 1914 and 1916 to serve as divisional cavalry squadrons. From May 1916 they were regrouped as Corps Cavalry Regiments and most were absorbed into infantry units in 1917.

For the Yeomanry, 1 and 2 Mounted Divisions were formed in August 1914 from seven of the original fourteen brigades. 2 Mounted Division was sent to Egypt in April 1915 and later served as infantry at Gallipoli, together with another six independent brigades which were sent there. These, together with a further three brigades which had arrived in Egypt, were reorganised early in 1916 into four Dismounted Brigades, organised as infantry, and four Mounted Brigades. At this time the Military Service (2) Act of 1916 had not reached the Statute Books and men of the TF could not be required to change their corps. The fine distinction between dismounted yeomanry and infantry had to be preserved – for the time being. The Dismounted Brigades became 74 Division in March 1917. Three of the Mounted Brigades became the Yeomanry Division three months later and were further reorganised in April 1918 when 1 and 2 Mounted Divisions (later 4 and 5 Cavalry Divisions) were formed from Yeomanry and Indian units. Nine surplus Yeomanry units then went to France as Machine-gun Battalions.

In the United Kingdom 1 Mounted Division was joined by 3 and 4 Mounted Divisions by 1916, formed from 'second line' units. There was thus at this time a mass of mounted troops at home, expensive in men and horses, and with little prospect of employment. Contraction shortly followed when 1 and 4 Mounted Divisions became Cyclist Divisions, only to be broken up in November 1916. 3 Mounted Division eventually became The Cyclist Division, remaining as such until the end of the war. As well as The Cyclist Division there were, at the end of the war, nine Cyclist Brigades serving on garrison duties in Britain and Ireland.

vi   *Manpower problems in 1917 and 1918*

The passing of the second Military Service Act of 1916, together with the formation of the second coalition Government under Lloyd George on 7th December 1916, may be regarded as marking a change in phase in the manpower problems of the Great War. Before, the main problem had been the provision of men for the army in competition with industry. After, the men needed by the army could only be found from the youngsters coming within the provisions of the Military Service Act or by the withdrawal of men from essential occupations. It will be recalled that the initiative in the granting of exemption certificates was in the hands of the Ministry of Munitions, acting on the advice of industry. Effectively the Ministry was able to establish its own priorities in the recruitment and retention of labour. At the same time the Trade Unions were apprehensive that under the existing system the employers had considerable powers over their employees in the issuing of certificates, whilst dismissal could immediately imply a loss of exemption and then conscription. Industrial unrest thus became established as part of the background against which the army's manpower needs were being considered. Advisory bodies, such as the Manpower Distribution Board and the Reserved Occupations Committee, were all reporting to the Cabinet at about this time, whilst the War Committee was considering the introduction of full industrial conscription for men up to the age of sixty.[42] It was decided to go ahead with a Schedule of Protected Occupations which would give varying degrees of protection to workers according to occupation, age and medical category. How the scheme was to be implemented remained in abeyance since there was no mechanism for the withdrawal of exemption certificates once issued so long as a man remained in the same employment. Without assurance of support from the country the Government continued to rely on voluntary methods for the deployment of its industrial force, establishing a National Service Department, with Mr Neville Chamberlain as Director, in December 1916. The Department was to provide a focus for voluntary effort and to prepare systems for industrial compulsion.[43]

So far as the army was concerned the period was one of continuing shortage of men. Meeting on 5th February 1917 the Cabinet had before it a Memorandum from the Army Council which stated that if heavy fighting was renewed in April the strength of the army in the field could not be maintained no matter what steps were taken. The Cabinet agreed in principle to release men from munitions work and an Act was passed in April which, at last, allowed for the withdrawal of exemption certificates under certain circumstances.[44] The War Office was asked to look into reducing the number of battalions in a division from twelve to nine. This step had recently taken place in the armies of France and Germany, although in the latter case the move had been made to provide cadres for new formations. No reorganisation was made at that time but the question arose again later. Preliminary enquiries were also made regarding the possible replacement of British troops in outer theatres by Indian. The shortages continued and in October Lieutenant-General Wilson was referring to a net monthly deficit of 25,000 men for the army in France, mostly infantry.[45]

In August 1917 the Department of National Service was re-formed as a Ministry under Sir Auckland Geddes and given full control over the allocation of manpower, whether for the forces or for industry. It was authorised to prepare lists of reserved occupations, to arrange for the transfer of men from less important to more important jobs and to secure the enlistment of such men as could be spared. All this, however, would have to be done on the basis of existing legislation. By November 1917 the Adjutant-General's accumulated manpower deficit since the beginning of the year and amounted to 437,095, three quarters of them men in the highest physical categories.[46] The Minister now proposed that all fit men should be de-certified and after negotiations with the principal Trade Unions the necessary Act was passed in February 1918, although not without further labour unrest.[47]

A Cabinet Manpower Committee, with the Prime Minister in the Chair, was set up on 6th December to examine the manpower shortages. Although the Committee did not report until March 1918, by which time other events held pride of place, decisions by the Cabinet in light of the interim workings of the Committee had considerable impact.[48] In a draft report on 13th December manpower shortages for the armed services were estimated at between 500 and 600 thousand men and for industry 100,000 immediately and 400,000 in future. Drastic measures, such as lowering the age for overseas service, raising the upper age limit for conscription and extending conscription to Ireland were seen as last resorts. The measures recommended were that the Command in France should conduct operations in such a way that casualties were reduced and that the twelve battalions in a division should be cut to nine.

The application of conscription to Ireland had been under discussion since the introduction of that measure in Britain in 1916.

The Easter rising of 1916 deferred serious consideration to the following year, when Irish conscription appears to have been regarded as a bargaining counter in Home Rule questions, perhaps in conjunction with the granting of amnesties for Irish Republican prisoners.[49]

While the Cabinet debate was continuing the Adjutant-General was estimating that as well as reducing the divisional establishments it would be necessary to reduce the number of divisions in France from fifty-six to forty-four in July 1918 and then to thirty in the following winter.[50] In the event the reduction in divisional establishments was ordered by the Cabinet on 10th January 1918. The reduction in the number of battalions would allow the creation of a pool of 22,000 men who would be employed on the construction of defence lines pending their utilisation as reinforcements. The strength of a division would be reduced from 18,825 to 16,035 men.

As can be seen from Figure 1.1 the strength of the British Army towards the end of 1917 approached four million men from which one might legitimately ask if the shortages were so acute that the strength of the BEF had to be reduced. The argument was bitter at the time and spilled over into the memoirs of the principal participants in the post-war years. So far as the Government was concerned the army in France had suffered very heavy casualties in 1915, 1916 and 1917 in offensive campaigns which had had little result. A consequence was a loss of confidence in the military leadership by many of the political figures in Britain. In the post-war battle of the memoirs Churchill accused the Prime Minister of unnecessarily retaining troops in Britain as a reserve instead of sending them to France where there was a risk of them being squandered in fruitless offensives.[51] The Prime Minister's response was that the army had ample troops and all that the High Command had to do was make the best use of them.[52] Certainly there is no evidence in the Cabinet papers that that body formally influenced the flow of drafts to the BEF. Such control as was exercised was in the regulation of the flow of men from civil life to the army as a whole.

The extent to which the manpower shortage in France was real or apparent is unlikely ever to be resolved. Surviving statistics are confused and to some extent contradictory and depend for interpretation on whether or not Dominion troops are included and

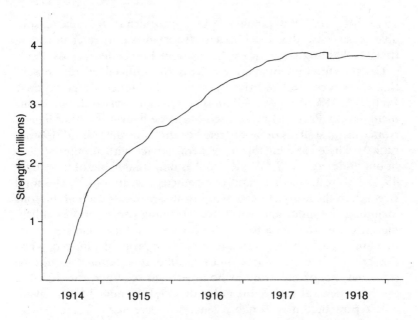

Figure 1.1. British Army Strength: 1914–18. Source: *Statistics of the Military Effort of the British Empire*, H.M.S.O., 1922, pp. 228–31.

whether or not labour troops are included and, indeed, on which labour troops are included and which not. If an overall shortage of manpower was to be established there still remains the question of whether or not the shortages could have been made up from the reserves held at home. The Official Historian states the case as being that at the beginning of 1917 the strength of British and Dominion fighting troops on the Western Front was 1,192,668 and that at the beginning of 1918 this had fallen to 1,097,906.[53] For the same dates the strengths of the Expeditionary Forces are given as 1,591,745 and 1,828,616 respectively, with the British component being 1,335,791 and 1,517,361.[54] Over and above these numbers there were also labour detachments, not organised as military units, totalling 2432 in January 1917 and 142,323 a year later. On the basis of these figures there can be little doubt that the total strength of the BEF rose during 1917 and, indeed, continued to rise in the first few months of 1918. On the other hand the total of British infantry in the army as a whole fell from 1,945,249 in January

1917 to 1,750,729 in January 1918 from which it would be reasonable to suppose that the Official Historian was correct in saying
that the fighting strength of the army in France fell across 1917.

On the question of reinforcements the Official Historian says
that there were 967,000 trained men in the United Kingdom on 1
January 1918 of whom 449,000 were ready for drafting. In his
memoirs the Prime Minister used the same figures.[55] Other figures
from official sources do not agree. For the same date 125,470 other
ranks are listed as available for general service with another 50,026
fit but under age. 279,473 are listed as unavailable but of these only
49,488 were trained, fit and over nineteen years old.[56] The total
strength of the army at home was just under one and a half millions
including the unfit, garrison forces, training cadres and establishments. Compared with this figure the Official Historian's estimate
of a million men being available appears improbable. Indeed, when
the crisis came in March nothing like this number could be
squeezed out of the army at home. Taken together, the 125,470
available general service men plus the 49,488 trained but unavailable represented a reasonable general reserve against emergencies
which could only have been used to make up establishments in
France at the price of dissipating that reserve. The balance of
evidence indicates that there was indeed a shortage of men in the
highest physical categories for the fighting formations.

The reduction in divisional establishments from twelve battalions
to nine was commenced on 23th January 1918 and it was eventually applied to all British divisions in all theatres. In France the process was barely completed by the commencement of the German
offensive in March. As can be seen from Figure 1.2 161 infantry
battalions were broken up in the first two months of 1918, those
dispersed being mainly 'second line' Territorial battalions or those
raised privately by individuals and local organisations. To add
to the organisational difficulties of the reduction itself, with the
tactical complexities introduced by the reduction of the number of
battalions in a brigade from four to three, the selection of battalions
for disbandment produced further disorganisation. The ultimate
objective was to improve the relationship between the number of
battalions in a regiment and the availability of reinforcements for
that regiment. The consequence was, however, that while in some
divisions a simple reduction of one battalion per brigade was possible, as in 11 (Northern) Division, in others a considerable cross-

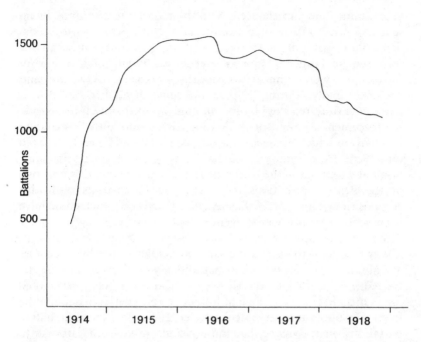

Figure 1.2. British Infantry Battalions: 1914–18. Sources: A. F. Becke, *Order of Battle of Divisions*, I–IV, H.M.S.O., 1935–46. E. A. James, *Historical Records of British Infantry Regiments*, Private, 1976.

posting of battalions from brigade to brigade or even from division to division took place. In 61 (2 South Midland) Division, a 'second line' Territorial formation, 183 Brigade's units were broken up and replaced by three units each from a different Brigade of 51 (Highland) Division. All this on the eve of a major enemy offensive.

At the same time as divisional establishments were being changed further economies were to be effected by 'Indianising' British formations in Egypt. The changes in the Yeomanry were referred to briefly on an earlier page but the largest savings were anticipated in the infantry. The original intention was to replace nineteen battalions in British divisions with Indian battalions from India, the British units being broken up to act as reinforcements for other British forces in the theatre. The implementation of this programme depended on the rate at which India could provide the relief battalions.[57] The German successes in March 1918 resulted in the programme being accelerated, with the relieved British units being sent to France rather than being retained in Egypt and in accordance with instructions received on 21st April fourteen battalions were sent to France in June. The relieving Indian units arrived in Egypt, or were improvised locally, between February and August. Finally, during July and August a further ten British battalions were replaced by Indian units and broken up to provide reinforcements. Four British divisions were 'Indianised' including 75 Division which had been improvised in the middle of 1917 from units sent from India. These had mostly been Territorial units originally sent out in the winter of 1914. After the changes only one of the British formations in the theatre retained its all-British composition. This was 54 (East Anglian) Division which could have been sent to France in the event of another emergency.

With the completion of the 'Indianisation' programme in Egypt it was proposed to extend the same principles to the British forces at Salonika. Thirty-six Indian battalions would eventually be deployed, twenty-four of the relieved British units being earmarked for France. In the event the first Indian battalion arrived at Salonika from Mesopotamia on 25th October 1918. It was with Indian battalions, in the main, that the divisions went from Salonika to Turkey and the Black Sea as an occupation force towards the end of the year.

vii *March 1918*

The German attacks starting on 21st March 1918 with the attendant loss of men, units and formations brought to a head the manpower crises which had occupied so much war Cabinet time across the winter. By the end of April 240,000 men had been lost. Calls for a levee-en-masse were made by Churchill and Wilson, the CIGS, but instead it was decided to prepare the second Military Service Bill of 1918.[58] The upper age limit for conscription was raised to fifty-one and the enlistment of eighteen-year-olds was, for the first time, placed on a rolling basis. Provision was made to raise the upper age limit to fifty-six and to extend the Act to Ireland by Orders in Council but these Orders were never made. The introduction of conscription to Ireland was still bound up with Home Rule issues which had little prospect of passing through Parliament. In June a call was made for 50,000 Irish volunteers but few responded and the Irish conscription issue was hotly debated inside and outside the Cabinet until the Armistice.

As one of the consequences of the German offensives nine British divisions were to all intents and purposes destroyed as fighting formations with a further five containing brigades in like case. One of the successes of the offensives was thus to strike a significant blow at the organisational structure of the BEF in France, at that time consisting of forty-seven divisions plus a further ten from the Dominions. As an immediate response four divisions were summoned from outer theatres, two from Italy and two from Egypt, but the reconstruction of the army was to prove a more difficult task occupying much of summer. Three divisions were re-formed in France in June and July and a further three were returned to England in cadre form, re-crossing to France in July and September. Brigades to complete the five incomplete divisions were re-formed between June and September. Sources from which the men and units were found to reconstitute the battered formations were various. In the first instance there were the regular drafts available, consisting of recruits and of men returning after periods at home, the number being increased by reducing the age for overseas service to 18½. These sources provided perhaps 170,000 men.[59] In the second instance there were the men and units being transferred from the outer theatres as a result of the economy measures instituted early in the year. For example 30 Division received five units formerly part of 60 Division in Egypt, while 50 Division received five battalions from divisions in Macedonia and another from 10 Division in Egypt. A new 94 Brigade for 31 Division was made up from three battalions taken from 74 Division, newly arrived in France. A third source of men was the pool thrown up by the disbandment of battalions in February. All in all it must be accounted a happy accident that the reduction in establishments together with the 'Indianisation' measures took place when they did, since it was these measures which provided ready at hand the means of rebuilding the shattered formations. A fourth and last source was found from the high rate of enlistment which followed the implementation of the 1918 Military Service Acts. This provided the source from which the divisions sent back to England were reconstituted.

It was not found possible to rebuild all of the divisions in their previous form and two were reconstructed as 'Garrison Divisions' with men of lower physical categories. The intention was that they would be used to hold quiet parts of the line. The men for these were found from the Garrison Battalions already employed on the lines of communication and by drafting such men out from home. One division was not re-formed and was employed as a training cadre.

viii   *The British Army in India*

The return of a considerable proportion of the British Regular units from India and their replacement by three Territorial Divisions was referred to earlier in this chapter. The normal composition of an Indian Army brigade was one British and three Indian battalions and the TF formations were therefore broken up and distributed across the sub-continent. By February 1915 only eight Regular battalions remained in the country. This situation did not persist for long. The demands of the war in Mesopotamia brought about the first transfer of Territorial units to that theatre in December and it became a function of those units to act as a reserve for the expansion of the Indian Army.

To maintain the strength of the British Army in India Garrison Battalions, composed of men unfit for more active duties, were sent out to replace the Territorials as they took up more active duties. A Territorial reinforcement was received in February 1916 with the arrival of four cyclist battalions, converted to infantry, and originally intended to serve as a brigade in East Africa. The reserve function of the Territorial units received further confirmation in 1917 when more units were transferred to Egypt to form 75 Division, again being replaced by Garrison Battalions.

The reserve role of TF units posted to colonial garrisons was repeated in the Mediterranean, incidentally, when the Territorial battalions which arrived in Malta and Gibraltar in 1914 were relieved by 'second line' units in February 1915. These were in their turn replaced by Garrison Battalions in the September.

Eight Territorial battalions remained in India to fight in the Third Afghan War in May 1919 and a further eighteen Special Service Battalions were improvised, mainly from Territorial soldiers awaiting embarkation. The last Territorials did not return home until 1920.

ix   *The Changing Army 1914–19*

From Figure 1.1 it will be seen that the numerical strength of the British Army increased month by month, apart from December 1915 and January 1918, from the outbreak of war to a maximum in March 1918. The fall in number then may be almost entirely attributed to the transfer of above 144,000 men to form the Royal Air Force. Thereafter strength drifted upwards to another maximum in September before tailing off. Even the severe casualties of the campaigns in France and Flanders in each year of the war were insufficient to halt the steady growth in numerical strength. At the very least recruitment exceeded wastage from all causes with something like a balance being approached towards the end of 1917. When dealing with grand totals, as these figures are, the effect of casualties tends to be diminished since, although the dead are deducted when reported, wounded and injured are retained until finally discharged so that wastage from this cause tends to be distributed over a long period. Submerged within the totals is a number of men, perhaps large, who are unfit for service. In contrast Figure 1.2 indicates that the maximum number of units organised as infantry battalions was reached in July 1916. The post-maximum fall is quite steady and was still taking place at the end of the war, which implies that the number of formations available in November 1918 could not have been maintained for long. Indeed the Adjutant-General was anticipating that the number of divisions in France would have to be reduced to about thirty-six.[60] It is clear that many more battalions were formed than could be maintained and from an organisational point of view the army probably reached its greatest fighting strength in 1917. Interestingly this is said to be the period Kitchener anticipated when embarking on the expansion of the army in 1914.

When considering the growth of the army as a whole it is worth considering the growth of each arm of the service as indicated in Table 1.1. From this it will be seen that the supporting arms tended to grow to a much greater extent than the fighting arms. The demands of 'siege operations in the field' were such that supply and maintenance services had to be expanded to a vast extent to support operations.

Of the Corps which did not exist at the beginning of the war, the Machine-gun Corps was formed in October 1915 and from early

Table 1.1   Strength of the Army by arm of service

	August 1914	November 1918	Ratio 1914 : 1918
Cavalry	46,496	75,342	1.6
Artillery	86,031	529,068	6.1
Royal Engineers	24,035	357,389	14.9
Infantry	306,654	1,648,039	5.5
Cyclist Corps	–	15,094	–
Machine-gun Corps	–	130,265	–
Tank Corps	–	28,299	–
Labour Corps	–	389,895	–
RASC	14,491	326,388	22.5
RAMC	17,840	138,017	7.8
RAOC	2,505	40,446	16.2
RAVC	508	27,471	54.1
Army Pay Corps	575	14,549	25.3
Non-combatant Corps	–	3,209	–
Royal Flying Corps	1,200	(144,078)*	(120.1)

* Strength transferred to the RAF in March 1918.
Source: *Statstics of the Military Effort of the British Empire*, H.M.S.O., 1922,
     pp. 228, 231.

1916 Machine-gun Companies were formed for each brigade. In
March 1918 these were amalgamated as Divisional Machine-gun
Battalions. If the Generals in France and the War Office appear to
have been obsessed by the shortage of infantry, it is after all the
infantry who must occupy and hold the ground, Lloyd George had
a valid point when he reminded them how much the fire power of
the army had been increased by automatic weapons.[61]

The Tank Corps was formed in May 1916 as a Section of the
Machine-gun Corps and was constituted as a Corps in its own right
in July 1917. From this modest beginning the first two tank
brigades were formed in February 1917 and by the Armistice thirty-
six battalions organised in seven brigades were formed or forming.
For the campaigns of 1919 these would have operated as three
'tank groups', each of twelve battalions. The end of the war thus
came before the new Corps had a full chance to demonstrate its
capabilities.

It was noticed earlier that Labour Battalions were formed in the
line regiments from 1915 and that these were absorbed into a new

Labour Corps in February 1917. 1914–18 warfare demanded vast amounts of crude labour and, indeed, from 1916 strenuous efforts were made to recruit labourers in all parts of the world for one or other of the theatres. Apart from the military labour corps, by the end of the war over half a million men were employed under some form of long-term engagement, with many others hired locally on a short-term basis.

From 1914 to 1918 the army as a whole expanded by a factor of 7·5. Of the pre-war corps, the infantry expanded by 5·5 and whilst the growth of the Engineers by 14·9 is not unexpected, bearing in mind the nature of the war, that of the Artillery seems quite modest when one considers the growth of heavy artillery. The increase in the RASC by a factor 22·5 indicates the importance of supply while the expansion of the Veterinary Corps is a reminder of the importance of animals as a means of conveyance.

The employment of women with the army at home and overseas officially commenced from August 1915 under authority given to the recently formed Women's Legion. Employment was at first on cooking and related jobs but later drivers were recruited. The Women's Army Auxiliary Corps was formed in March 1917 and this was shortly followed by the departure of the first contingent for service overseas. Minimum age for enlistment was eighteen and, at least for service in Britain, members were permitted to enrol on a 'mobile' or 'immobile', living at home, basis. The range of employment was now extended to include general administrative work and by November 1918 the strength of the Corps was 40,850 of whom about 10,000 were serving abroad.[62]

Returning to August 1914 and the problems then facing the Government and the Country, the fundamental question was how the war should be waged. Was the Country committed to a continental strategy or could a war of limited liability be conducted? Implicitly, through the development of policy over previous years, commitment was to a continental strategy, although the fact that the Government was not convinced of this is indicated by the need to summon a Council of War on 5th and 6th August. With a commitment to a continental strategy a large, continental, army was needed. With little appreciation of the issues involved the Government chose to delegate the day-by-day running of the war to the War Office and Admiralty, who proceeded to run the war in their own respective ways. Once Kitchener's decision to expand the army had been taken the next question was how should this be achieved. Here the anomalous position of the Territorial Force was a critical factor. Whether or not the Secretary of State for War was prejudiced against it is irrelevant. The Force was a limited service one and would have to be canvassed to find out if its members, one by one, were prepared to proceed on active service, and that before carrying out any effective expansion at all. Although this was done eventually, the decision to make the main avenue of expansion through the New Armies was logical and inevitable if the BEF was to be reinforced in reasonable time. One result of this decision was that since, in the event, expansion was taking place on four lines simultaneously, Regulars, Territorials, New Armies and private enterprise, there was great dispersion of effort which probably retarded the time needed to prepare some of these new forces for war. The New Army Divisions were ready to proceed to an active war theatre in 9·4 months on average. The Territorial Divisions were ready in an average of 8·7 months instead of the six months which was the estimate made in 1907 although, to be fair, the higher priority accorded the New Armies for equipment and instructors retarded the TF's progress. Many individual units were in action much more rapidly. Of the 'second line' TF Divisions which went to war these averaged nearly twenty-seven months before being ready.

With a commitment to building up a large army, a corresponding expansion in arms production became a requisite and the unrestricted army recruitment inhibited industrial development through the recruitment of skilled and semi-skilled men. Control of enlistment was therefore necessary, becoming merged with the question of conscription both for essential industries and for the armed forces. The implementation of direction and conscription of labour in 1914 might or might not have been politically feasible but it was certainly impracticable from an administrative point of view. Even so it would appear that the Cabinet was slow to recognise that some sort of action was necessary and that the sooner it was instituted the better. The effective delegation of the conduct of all aspects of the land war to Kitchener probably compounded the delay and for this the act of delegation itself must be primarily responsible.

The expansion of the army during the Great War was undertaken against a background of lack of pre-war preparation and planning. Almost to the last war was unexpected and its form unforeseen.

There is, however, evidence of unease about the adequacy or otherwise of the army, which makes the lack of even outline contingency planning for a continental army even more remarkable. In the lack of plans a New Army had to be improvised. Once the expansion had started it would appear that no-one, nowhere, sat down and said, 'We have a population of x millions, including y millions of young men. How many divisions can we create?' Instead men were formed up into units and formations as they came forward and were marched off to war in the hope that they wouldn't be seen again until victory was won. The realisation that an army is something more than merely the sum of its infantry battalions was slow to come and in the meantime the structure of the army had been expanded to a level it was impossible to sustain. The manpower problems of 1917 and 1918 stemmed directly from the lack of clear thought in 1914.

Notes

1 W. L. S. Churchill, *The World Crisis*, Macmillan, London, Single-volume edn., 1931, pp. 24–7.
  J. K. Dunlop, *The Development of the British Army*, Methuen, London, 1938, pp. 236 ff.
  J. Gooch, *The Plans of War*, Routledge and Kegan Paul, London, 1974, Ch. 9.
  P. M. Kennedy (Ed.), *War Plans of the Great Powers*, Allen and Unwin, London, 1979, pp. 106–12.
2 Gooch, *Plans of War*, p. 106.
  R. B. Haldane, *Autobiography*, Hodder and Stoughton, London, 1929, p. 187.
  M. Howard, *The Continental Commitment*, Temple Smith, London, 1972, pp. 18–20.
  E. M. Spiers, *Haldane: An Army Reformer*, Edinburgh U. P., 1980, Ch. 4.
  PRO/Cab/2/2.
3 Dunlop, *Development of the British Army*, pp. 42–52.
  Volunteer Act, 1863, 26 and 27 Vict., c. 65, s. 17.
4 *Territorial and Reserve Forces Act*, 1907, 7 Edw. VII, c. 9.
5 Cmd. 3297 of February 1907.
  Dunlop, *Development of the British Army*, p. 278.
6 Spiers, *Haldane*, Ch. 8.
7 *Parliamentary Debates* (*Commons*), LI, cols. 1517–94.
  D. W. French, 'Some Aspects of Social and Economic Planning for War', unpub. Ph.D., London, 1979, pp. 26–7.
8 PRO/Cab/2/2.

9   I. F. W. Beckett and K. Simpson (Eds.), *A Nation in Arms*, Manchester
     U.P., 1985, Ch. 5.
     The War Office, *Statistics of the Military Effort of the British Empire*,
     H.M.S.O., London, 1922, p. 30.
10 This appointment had apparently been anticipated by Kitchener as far
     back as 1909. Sir Frederick Maurice, *Life of General Lord Rawlinson*,
     Cassell, London, 1928, pp. 93–4.
11 R. Blake (Ed.), *The Private Papers of Douglas Haig*, Eyre and
     Spottiswoode, London, 1952, p. 69.
     J. Terraine, *Douglas Haig: The Educated Soldier*, Hutchinson,
     London, 1965, pp. 73–4.
     PRO/Cab/42/1/2.
12 Sir Philip Magnus, *Kitchener: Portrait of an Imperialist*, John Murray,
     London, 1958, pp. 283–4.
     Churchill, *The World Crisis*, p. 149.
     Viscount Grey, *Twenty-five Years*, II, Hodder and Stoughton,
     London, 1925, p. 68.
13 *Parliamentary Debates (Lords)*, XVII, col. 503.
14 Ibid., col. 736.
15 *Parliamentary Debates (Lords)*, XVIII, col. 248.
16 Sir C. E. Callwell, *Field Marshal Sir Henry Wilson: His Life and
     Diaries*, I, Cassell, London, 1927, p. 178.
17 G. H. Cassar, *Kitchener: Architect of Victory*, William Kimber,
     London, 1977, p. 197.
     Maurice, *Rawlinson*, pp. 122–3.
18 Army Orders 324, 382, 388, 434 and 510 of 1914.
     E. A. James, *Historical Records of British Infantry Regiments*, Private,
     1976.
19 Beckett and Simpson, *Nation in Arms*, pp. 68–74 and 100–10.
     James, *Historical Records*, p. 207.
20 *Parliamentary Debates (Lords)*, XVII, col. 738.
21 Beckett and Simpson, *Nation in Arms*, Ch. 5.
22 Army Order 399/1914.
23 Army Order 389 and Army Council Instructions 76 of October 1914
     and 96 of April 1915.
24 Army Council Instructions 397/September 1914, 28/December 1914
     and 172/January 1915.
25 Churchill, *The World Crisis*, pp. 149–50.
     Haldane, *Autobiography*, pp. 278–9.
     Howard, *Continental Commitment*, pp. 96–7.
26 M. J. Allison, 'The National Service Issue', unpub. Ph.D., London,
     1975, especially Chs. 1–4.
27 Haldane, *Autobiography*, pp. 196–7.
     Sir William Robertson, *Soldiers and Statesmen*, I, Cassell, London,
     1926, pp. 36 ff.
     N. W. Summerton, 'Development of British Military Planning,'
     unpub, Ph.D., London 1970, pp. 483–5.
28 *National Registration Act*, 1915, 5 and 6 Geo. V, c. 60, and 1918, 7

and 8 Geo. V, c. 60.
29 Cassar, *Kitchener*, Ch. 21.
    S. W. Roskill, *Hankey: Man of Secrets*, I, Collins, London, 1970, pp. 217–20 and 227–8.
    Blake, *Douglas Haig*, pp. 101–39.
30 PRO/Cab/37/132/21–133/10.
31 PRO/Cab/37/135/15.
32 *Military Service Act*, 1916, 5 and 6 Geo. V, c. 104.
33 PRO/Cab/37/142/11 and 145/35–6. PRO/Cab/27/3.
34 *Military Service (2) Act*, 1916, 6 and 7 Geo. V, c. 16.
35 War Office, *Statistics*, pp. 83–4. Robertson, *Soldiers and Statesmen*, p. 297, gives 5000.
36 D. Sutherland, *Tried and Valiant*, Leo Cooper, London, 1972, p. 132.
37 F. Loraine Petre, *History of the Norfolk Regiment*, II, Jarrold, London, 1924, p. 117.
    Beckett and Simpson, *Nation in Arms*, pp. 146–8.
38 Sir James E. Edmonds, *France and Belgium, 1914*, II, Macmillan, London, 1925, p. 467 and f. n.
39 Army Orders 142/1910 and 240/1911.
40 C. E. Fayle, *Seaborne Trade*, II, John Murray, London, 1923, pp. 284–90 and III, 1924, pp. 8, 166–67 and 337.
41 *Volunteer Act*, 1916, 6 and 7 Geo. V, c. 62.
    Army Order 206/1916.
42 PRO/Cab/37/153/12 and 160/24. PRO/Cab/42/21/1 and 26/3.
    Roskill, *Hankey*, p. 322.
    P. E. Dewey, 'Military recruiting and the British labour force', *Historical J.*, XXVII, 1, 1984, pp. 213–16.
43 D. Lloyd George, *War Memoirs*, I, Odhams, London, Two-volume edn., 1938, pp. 804–12.
44 PRO/Cab/23/1.
    Miltary Service (Review of Exceptions) Act, 1917, 7 and 8 Geo. V, c. 12.
45 Callwell, *Wilson*, II, p. 18.
46 War Office, *Statistics*, p. 368.
47 *Military Service Act*, 1918, 7 and 8 Geo. V, c. 66.
48 PRO/Cab/27/14.
49 Roskill, *Hankey*, pp. 390 and 401.
50 Callwell, *Wilson*, II, p. 50.
51 Churchill, *World Crisis*, p. 853.
52 Lloyd George, *War Memoirs*, II, pp. 1584–5.
53 Sir James E. Edmonds, *Short History of World War 1*, Oxford U.P., 1951, p. 275.
54 War Office, *Statistics*, table facing p. 64 and pp. 230–1.
55 Edmonds, *Short History*, p. 276.
    Lloyd George, *War Memoirs*, II, pp. 1584–5.
56 War Office, *Statistics*, p. 115.
    D. R. Woodward, 'Did Lloyd George starve the British Army of men', *Historical J.*, XXVII, 1, 1984, pp. 241–52.

57 C. Falls, *Egypt and Palestine* II, H.M.S.O., London, 1930, pp. 350, 411–12 and 417.
58 *Military Service (2) Act*, 1918, 8 and 9 Geo. V, c. 5.
   Roskill, *Hankey*, p. 512.
59 Callwell, *Wilson*, II, pp. 74 and 82.
60 Blake, *Douglas Haig*, pp. 320 and 334.
61 Lloyd George, *War Memoirs*, II, pp. 1572–3.
62 War Office, *Statistics*, pp. 205–6.

Chapter 2
The British Army 1919–45

i *Between the wars*

With the end of the Great War the army set about the task of reducing to peace-time establishments. The demands of widespread commitments around the world led to this being a protracted business. The campaign in North Russia did not end until the autumn of 1919, while British troops were in southern Russia for another year. In other theatres, war-formed units were in India and the Black Sea region until 1920. Indeed the demand for troops was so great that to provide the Rhineland occupation force it was necessary to use training battalions for that purpose.

It was not until the early 1920s that it became practicable to attempt any reorganisation of the army in the light of its experiences of the previous years. 1922 saw the disbandment of twenty-two Regular battalions, including the departure of the five Irish regiments, and the reduction of the cavalry from thirty-one regiments to twenty-two. The disbandment of the Irish regiments was due to Irish independence but the overall reductions owed much more to economic pressure than to any reduction in overseas commitments and as early as August 1919 the Cabinet established the principle that no expeditionary force would be required in the next ten years.[1]

In 1921 the Territorial Force was reconstituted as the Territorial Army under the Territorial Army and Militia Act.[2] Perhaps surprisingly the 1907 Act remained in force and in law the TA remained a home service body. However on enlistment individuals were required to take the general service obligation and the precise position of the TA was defined before the Commons by Sir Thomas Inskip, Minister for the Co-ordination of Defence, in 1936.[3] The TA was the second line of the land forces, a means of supporting and expanding the Regular Army and, if the House agreed, available for dispatch overseas. As re-formed the Territorial infantry divisions remained much as before but the Yeomanry was much altered with only fifteen regiments remaining mounted. Of the remainder, eight regiments became Armoured Car Companies, the first cavalry units of the army to be mechanised, while most of the others became artillery.

With the demobilisation of the Special Reserve units in 1919 the Special Reserve, as such, came to an end. Although statutory provision was retained no recruiting was undertaken and that sector of the Reserve became moribund.

Although economy may have been the inspiration of the 'Ten-year Rule' optimism about the future of world peace also had a part. By the Treaty of Versailles the German Army was strictly limited and a general system of collective security was hoped for under the League of Nations, coupled with general disarmament. In 1927 the 'Ten-year Rule' was redefined. No war was to be expected in Europe for ten years and the army should prepare for extra-European warfare only. A year later the 'Rule' was placed on a rolling basis permanently extensible into the future.[4]

In retrospect the transition from the optimistic 1920s to the pessimistic 1930s now seems quite abrupt. The transition was presaged by the collapse of the New York Stock Exchange in October 1929 which heralded increasing economic difficulties for countries throughout the world. These difficulties had their political counterparts in Germany and in the Far East, rising to a head with the departure of Japan from the League of Nations and Hitler's rise to power in 1933. For the time being the greatest apprehension was for the situation in the Far East where the defences for Hong Kong, Singapore and the Indian Ocean were totally inadequate. Although there were some last hopes in the success of the Disarmament Conference, by the end of the year the period of the 'Ten-year Rule' was over.[5]

The principal criticisms of the 'Ten-year Rule' are directed towards its contribution to the unprepared state of Britain in 1939. For the period throughout which the Rule operated the army was, certainly, directed to turn its attention to extra-European warfare. In this sense the fourteen years during which the Rule held were years in which few resources were available for war in a European setting and, increasingly, this was seen by some to mean mechanised and armoured warfare. Progress towards the development of British armoured forces was therefore slow. The protagonists for the development of armoured, mobile forces were articulate and skilful and did much to keep alive interest in this form of development, much stress being laid on the contribution mechanisation could make towards efficiency and economy.[6] The successes of German armoured formations in later campaigns in Western and Eastern Europe and in the desert have added much point to British limitations in this field but at this time, too, development in Germany was limited and it was not until 1935 that the first permanent armoured formations were created. It is difficult to sustain an argument that the years of the 'Ten-year Rule' seriously affected the development of the British Army in any direct sense. Major campaigns of the Second World War were fought in the mountains of Italy and the jungles of Burma under conditions where it could be alleged that 'extra-European' conditions prevailed. What is more significant is that the years were a period of severe economic restriction which lasted long enough to become a habit of mind.[7] They were also years in which it was easy to believe that war would not come for many years ahead and that preparations for such an event were not, and never would be, urgent. War industries were allowed to run down through lack of orders in the tacit assumption that time would be available to re-create them in case of need.

A Defence Requirements Sub-committee of the CID was set up in November 1933 to recommend measures to fill the accumulated deficiencies in defence preparations and to reconcile the competing claims of the three Services. Although the Cabinet laid down priorities, headed by defence against Japan, the Sub-committee took the view that already Germany should be considered the long-term enemy. For planning purposes a period of five years was envisaged and one of the objectives should be the preparation of an expeditionary force of four divisions, a cavalry division and other formations for the defence of the Low Countries. In addition the army would be responsible for air defence at home.[8] Decisions to implement this programme were confused by the Government's commitment to international disarmament, public unwillingness to rearm and by what was seen to be the more urgent need to expand the Royal Air Force. Fundamentally, too, there remained the recurrent question of what Britain's long-term strategical objectives were in the event of war and whether a continental or a maritime strategy should be adopted. Eventually economic considerations prevailed and although the Sub-committee's proposals were accepted the army's programme would have to be extended over a longer period than five years.

The dispute between Italy and Abyssinia which led to war between them in October 1935 introduced a fresh factor. Britain's support of the League reduced the possibility of obtaining Italian assistance in curbing a rearming Germany and, indeed, raised the possibility of incurring the enmity of Italy herself. This was recognised in the third Defence Requirements report of November 1935 which proposed the reinforcement of the expeditionary force by four Territorial divisions after four months and eight more in the next four months.[9] Since little could be done to modernise the TA within the planning period no decisions were made on the reinforcement recommendations. The matter was re-opened a year later by Duff Cooper, then War Secretary, who in effect re-opened the whole question of the role of the army. The question was referred back to the Chiefs of Staff who considered that if a continental army was required it should be limited to the existing expeditionary force supported by the TA. Further, and harking back to the experiences of 1914, it was desirable that the TA should be equipped with the same weapons as the Regular Army and trained in their use. These proposals implied a very large increase in the resources allocated to the army and led to considerable discussion. Increasingly, defence against air attack was seen as the supreme priority whilst there was a growing belief that, in the event of attack, France expected only limited assistance on land. A new series of priorities was assigned to the army from December 1937. The primary role would be the defence of Imperial commitments, including home air defence, with a secondary role in the maintenance of internal security at home. The expeditionary force would consist of three divisions with two to follow and a further two after four months. The force would be prepared for a destination outside Europe, probably Egypt. A policy of limited liability now held the field. This was a policy which had been advocated for some years by, amongst others, Chamberlain, the Chancellor of the Exchequer.[10]

The third Defence Requirements Report referred to a total of twelve Territorial divisions and this is, perhaps, a convenient point at which to return to the organisation of the army during the early 1930s.

Anti-aircraft defence was assigned to the TA as a major commitment from 1922 with particular emphasis on the defence of the South and South-east. The emergence of Germany as a potential enemy extended the areas under threat to include the Midlands and North.[11] Even had the resources been available the Territorial Army, 35,000 men under an establishment of 165,000, could not have met the new requirement by expansion. Instead, two of the existing infantry divisions were converted into anti-aircraft formations. Later, when more anti-aircraft units were needed, three new anti-aircraft divisions were formed in January 1938. These in some cases used units converted from other arms and other conversions took place when anti-tank units were formed. Three Territorial divisions were reorganised as Motor divisions with a reduced establishment of two infantry brigades.

In the Regular Army the development of mobile forces was taken a stage further in 1935 when a new style of division, the Mobile Division, was announced. This would consist of a tank brigade and a mechanised cavalry brigade and in 1936 eight cavalry regiments were selected for mechanisation, five as motorised cavalry and three as light tank regiments. This really marked the end of a long-running debate on the role of the cavalry in a modern army.[12] Changes in the organisation of the Mobile Division became almost annual events but during 1938 the mechanisation of the cavalry became widespread and by the outbreak of war only the Household Cavalry, two Regular and eight Yeomanry regiments retained their horses. Further expansion in the same period included the formation of two new battalions of the Royal Tank Corps, the conversion of six Territorial infantry battalions into tank units and the enlargement of the eight Yeomanry Armoured Car Companies into regiments. Early in 1939 all of the armoured units were grouped into a new Royal Armoured Corps.[13]

The Mobile Division, long proposed, was finally formed in October 1937 with two light armoured brigades and a tank brigade. In 1938 the formation became 1 Armoured Division, with a light and a heavy armoured brigade, and a similar formation was created in Egypt. These were, in fact, the two armoured divisions with which Britain entered the war. 2 Armoured Division was forming in the United Kingdom in September 1939 using, in part, brigades released when 1 Armoured Division's establishment was reduced.

For the army the late 1930s were a period not only of rearmament, taking place slowly against a background of economic stringency, but also a period of modernisation to take account of new weapons and means of transportation. The methods by which the new weapons and vehicles would be used were still not clearly seen and ideas were untried. The systems to maintain this new weaponry in the field had still to be worked out. Thus the period became one of successive reorganisation with, often, fresh reorganisation being imposed before the first was effective. At the same time production of many of the new items of equipment was not fully under way. In the fighting units the new equipment had often not been received and, if received at all, had only been received in sufficient quantity for demonstration. These shortages fell heavily on units converting to armour and, for example, in 3 Hussars by September 1938 only one squadron had tanks, the remaining two having trucks. In these units the training demands were particularly heavy for the care of horses provides a poor introduction to the care and maintenance of vehicles.

Before the limited liability policy had been in force a year the Munich crisis of September 1938 eventually led to a fundamental change in views about the role of the army in a future war. This change stemmed from a variety of pressures. In the first place there was increasing realisation that in the days of air power the defence of Britain rested in part on the defence of the Low Countries. In the second place there was pressure from France which, under threat of a German war, would have to face the German Army alone. Under existing commitments Britain had promised to send the first elements of the expeditionary force, equipped for extra-European warfare. In the French view this was not enough to redress a balance now heavily in favour of Germany and this view continued to be pressed at several levels of government contact across the winter of 1938/39. Within the British Cabinet, too, discussion continued with increasing realisation that, at the present scale of preparation, in the first year of a war the country would only be able to field four infantry and one armoured divisions, equipped for colonial warfare. But events were now moving rapidly and, although it does not appear that the limited liability role was ever formally abandoned, on 22nd February the Cabinet agreed to allocate funds to raise four Regular and four Territorial divisions to full continental standards.[14] Public opinion was also moving in favour of strengthening the armed forces and a national campaign to promote volunteering was announced in December 1938.[15]

Anglo-French Staff talks were resumed in March 1939, shortly after the German occupation of Czechoslovakia. At the talks it was said that Britain could send two Regular divisions twenty-one days after the outbreak of war with two more after four months. The Regular armoured division would be ready about the middle of 1940 with another one later. The twelve Territorial divisions with an armoured division, about to be formed, should be ready in a year.[16] Even while the talks were going on decisions were being taken to double the size of the TA. The decisions did not result from any discussions within the War Office, to which they came as a total surprise, but emanated from Hore-Belisha, the Secretary of State for War. The Prime Minister announced in the Commons on 29th March that the establishment of the TA was to be increased to 170,000 and then doubled to 340,000.[17] Contingency planning was taking place within the War Office regarding the introduction of conscription and when the Staff talks were resumed in April the programme of assistance for the French had become four Regular divisions in the first six weeks, ten Territorial divisions in four to six months and the remaining sixteen between the ninth and twelfth months.[18] This, indeed, remained the British commitment to the outbreak of war.

The manpower demands of the revised programme of assistance for the French, together with apprehension about the state of readiness of the country's anti-aircraft defences, caused a great deal of heart-searching within the Cabinet. The defences could not be manned without mobilising the Territorial Army and this could not be done without declaring a state of emergency, requiring the sanction of Parliament. The Cabinet's decision was to introduce to Parliament on 26th April two unprecedented measures. One would allow the calling out of personnel concerned with anti-aircraft defence,[19] the other introduced conscription.

Under the Military Training Act men reaching the age of twenty would be called up for six months' training and then be liable for service as militiamen under the 1907 Act.[20] Of the quarter of a million men likely to be called up about 80,000 were required for anti-aircraft duties with the intention that, in the event of a protracted emergency short of war, the Territorial units could be called out until relieved by trained militiamen. The remaining men would be available to complete establishments in the army in general.[21] The first militiamen were called up for training in July, mainly using existing Corps training centres. Although by now a Schedule of Reserved Occupations was in existence, specifying jobs which were considered to be of national importance and from which men would not normally be taken in the event of war, the provisions of this were disregarded on enlistment. Nor was there yet a National Register. It was apparently intended that the provisions of the Schedule would be applied after completion of the initial training period when Scheduled men would only be available for corresponding trades in the army or, perhaps, not available at all.[22] The early start of the war prevented this being applied.

The duplication of the Territorial Army was intended to be completed in six months and one unit, the Fife and Forfar Yeomanry, achieved this in a fortnight. Although Cabinet Minutes show that duplication would be achieved by over-recruiting to form a cadre from which the new unit would be formed, no precise instructions were issued and each unit went its own way. Some units, such as 4 Suffolk Regiment, divided themselves geographically, others, such as 4 KOSB, retained for themselves all men recruited before a more or less arbitrary date and formed a new battalion from those recruited later, others, such as 5 Royal West Kent Regiment, recruited to double strength and then split.[23] The principle consequence of this lack of guidance was reflected in the uneven state of readiness of the TA in the September, by which time some of the duplicate divisions had still to be formed. Individuality was reflected in the styles and titles adopted by the duplicate units and formations. Some repeated numbers used by the 'second line' in the previous war, others used former New Army titles, some revived units disbanded or converted in recent years while others simply continued the regiment's numerical series. On the outbreak of war a considerable amount of cross-posting was necessary from brigade to brigade or even division to division in order to adjust strengths. However valuable as a political gesture, the duplication of the Territorial Army left a great deal to do in the provision of administrative, corps and army troops before the whole could be an effective reinforcement.[24] As in the case of the militiamen, men in Scheduled occupations were sometimes recruited to help make up the number of men needed and, for the same reason, the minimum age of enlistment was reduced to 17½. All of this added to the sorting-out needed in the first winter of the war.

In the winter of 1938/39 the War Secretary raised the possibility of forming two additional divisions for colonial policing duties. Indeed the proposal had been suggested in the War Office in February 1938 and the two divisions actually existed in the shape of 7 and 8 Divisions on internal security duties in Palestine. Both had been formed using units borrowed from the expeditionary force to combat unrest in the Middle East. In April 1939 the formal proposal was revived and approved in principle by the Cabinet but since current plans were already to form and equip 32 divisions no specific allocations were made. As tensions in Palestine eased a little some of 7 and 8 Divisions' units returned home during the summer.[25]

The six months from March to September 1939 saw, at least on paper, a significant increase in the strength of the army. On the eve of war there were existing or in sight four Regular divisions and another forming, 24 Territorial divisions and two Regular and two Territorial armoured divisions. Conscription had apparently provided the manpower for these formations. What had not been provided was the equipment.

ii *The Phoney War*

In 1939 ten out of thirty Regular cavalry and tank regiments and seventy-nine out of 140 infantry battalions were abroad. Although the British component of the garrison of India was very much reduced between the wars the recent disturbances in Palestine had necessitated reinforcement and upset the Cardwell balance. Recruitment was for twelve years, the time being divided between service with the colours and in the reserve. The length of colour service varied from corps to corps but was seven years in the infantry and six years in the cavalry, artillery and engineers. Including militiamen the Regular Army totalled 258,800.

In the Territorial Army there were twenty-nine Yeomanry regiments of which eight were still horsed. There were also twelve tank and 232 infantry battalions. Even in its duplicated state the number of TA battalions was little more than the number in the TF in August 1914. Affiliated to the TA was the National Defence Corps formed in 1936 from men aged 45–55 with previous service. NDC companies would provide guard detachments for vulnerable points.

In addition to the Regular Reserve of men who had completed their colour service a Supplementary Reserve had been formed in 1924. This Reserve was to complete the requirements of some arms for men with specialist skills. According to category, training was for a maximum of two weeks per year. In 1936 an infantry section was added, 17,000 strong, with service conditions very similar to those of the old Special Reserve. It will be recalled that the TA did not exist in Northern Ireland and the only non-Regular unit raised there was an armoured car regiment, the North Irish Horse, which formed in the Supplementary Reserve in 1938.

The total number of Territorials and Reservists mobilised in September 1939 was 546,200.[26]

The Auxiliary Territorial Service formed in September 1938. It was open to women aged eighteen and upwards who could enlist either for General or Local Service. The training obligation was similar to that of the TA.[27]

On 21st August certain Territorial units were called out to man anti-aircraft and coastal defences and this was followed on 23rd by the mobilisation of certain reservists to complete establishments. On 25th and 26th National Defence Companies were called out and on 31st the Army and Supplementary Reserves were mobilised. When Germany invaded Poland on 1st September the embodiment of the TA was ordered. The declaration of war on 3rd September, in accordance with assurances given to Poland by Britain and France in March, was simply the final step in the progression of the previous days.

In Parliament the beginning of the war was marked by the passage of a mass of legislation deriving from the experience of the earlier war. Four Acts need particular notice; Armed Forces (Conditions of Service), National Service, Military and Air Forces and National Registration Acts.[28]

Under the Armed Forces (Conditions of Service) Act any Territorial became liable for overseas service, whilst in the related Military and Air Forces Act terms of service of all personnel were extended to the conclusion of the present emergency. By these measures the anomalous position of the TA with regard to the differences between the legal obligations of the force and the contractual obligations of individual members were resolved. One matter, the precise obligations of members of the National Defence Corps, remained obscure and to be dealt with later. The extension of service provision, coupled with authority to move men from corps to corps, gave the army unfettered use of the men under its command and cleared right from the start obstacles which in the Great War hampered the army until 1916.

The National Registration Act established an on-going register of all persons in the United Kingdom and following from this the National Service Act applied conscription for the armed forces on all males aged 18–41. Early in 1941 this was extended to include call-up for civil defence. Again a measure which had caused a great deal of heart-searching in the earlier war was rapidly taken through its Parliamentary stages. By the device of Proclamation men could be called for as required. No attempt was yet made to apply industrial conscription. That was a step which would have to wait for the greater emergency of 1940. As in the earlier war conscription was not applied to Northern Ireland.

Britain was committed to sending thirty-two divisions to France in the first year of the war and as early as 6th September the Minister of Supply informed the Cabinet that the output of equipment would only permit the departure of sixteen. Any expansion of industrial production could interfere with the programmes of the other Services and accordingly a Land Forces Committee was set up under the Chairmanship of Sir Samuel Hoare. The Committee moved quickly and made it first report on 8th September. As a target for production, and assuming that the war would last for three years, twenty divisions should be equipped in the first twelve months and fifty-five by the end of the second year. Britain would have thirty-two divisions, fourteen would come from the Dominions, four from India and an allowance was made for five to represent assistance to Allies. This was accepted by the Cabinet on 22nd September. For the moment there was no consideration of the size of the army after the first two years, indeed across that period no expansion in the number of British formations was contemplated. As yet there had been no consultation with the Dominions or India but it was apparently assumed that their contribution would be similar to that of 1914/18. Although the 55-division target originated as a target for the production of equipment it gradually came to be accepted as a target size for the army itself. The thirty-two British divisions contrasted sharply with Kitchener's seventy but as early as 15th November supply forecasts indicated that it would only be possible to equip fifteen divisions by September 1940. The matter was discussed at length in the Military Co-ordination Committee, argument revolving largely around equipment scales and wastage rates for both the army and the RAF. Indeed by some estimates it might only be possible to equip thirty-six divisions by September 1941. However on 13th February 1940 the Cabinet adhered to the 55-division target as being one to be met by the earliest possible date.[29]

Since the experiences of the Great War had indicated that the army would soon have need of labour in large quantities, the Auxiliary Military Pioneer Corps was formed in October 1939, becoming the Pioneer Corps in November 1940. This was composed of volunteers below call-up age and those between thirty-five and fifty. It was estimated that some 60,000 pioneers would be needed in France by June 1940.[30]

On mobilisation in September 1939 battalions in Britain were in their usual state with regard to strength. 2 Essex Regiment was 250 under a war establishment of 799 all ranks and 2 Hampshire Regiment needed a draft of 300 reservists, for instance.[31] Some Territorial battalions were also severely under strength, not having been able to duplicate in the time available. 7 Worcestershire Regiment could muster only 380 men at the end of the month, for example. Some Territorial units, using the precedent of the First World War, transferred men under age for overseas service from parent to duplicate unit, treating the latter as a 'second line'. No instructions for this seem to have come from any central authority and practices varied from regiment to regiment, some using 19 and some 20 as the age limit.[32] It was under these circumstances that the availability of the first militiamen to complete their training was invaluable and these men continued to provide the main army intake until 21st October.

In November 1939 the Companies of the National Defence Corps were grouped into battalions. The men of these units had originally been recruited under limited service conditions in the expectation that they would live at home even after mobilisation. Instructions were now issued that the men should be canvassed to obtain their agreement to general service terms, any not consenting to be discharged. Under the Armed Forces (Conditions of Service) Act it might have appeared that the men could in any case have been liable for general service but the Corps was formed of men above the age for National Service and they could not have been compelled.

The training function of the home units of the Regular Army ceased with their mobilisation and a replacement and training organisation had to be set up to deal with recruits and to provide drafts and reinforcements. In the infantry the existing Regimental Depots became Infantry Training Centres, providing a course of about four months. By January 1940 the main deficiencies in man-power establishments had been filled and Holding Battalions were formed to receive men from the ITCs and give sub-unit training. For armoured units seven Training Regiments were formed in September 1939, absorbing the former cavalry and Royal Tank Regiment depots. Further Training Regiments were formed later. The events of mid-1940 considerably disrupted the training organi-sation until the end of that year and further reorganisations were made in 1941.

iii *The crisis of 1940*

Following defeat in France, the evacuation of the BEF from Dunkirk and the western ports and under what appeared to be imminent threat of invasion, what became the principal expansion of the army commenced in June. In the emergency recourse was made to the more primitive methods of the Great War and about 140 battalions were formed on cadres of fifteen officers and 150 men drawn from the ITCs and Holding Battalions, then being filled up with 800 recruits. The Holding Battalions, having provided cadres, were themselves filled up with recruits and reorganised as infantry battalions.[33] No great attempt was made to preserve Regi-mental integrity and cadres were drafted from the ITCs according to availability. The historian of the Durham Light Infantry records, perhaps rather sadly, that 17 DLI formed on a cadre drawn from nine different regiments.[34] Equipment, too, was scarce and 7 Leicestershire Regiment formed with only a hundred Ross rifles.[35] Designated originally for coast defence, the new battalions were at first grouped into Infantry Training Groups which became Brigades in October 1940. Later they were gathered into 'County' Divisions, still with a local defence role. From 1941, as Figure 2.1 indicates, the battalions were often converted to other arms, particularly

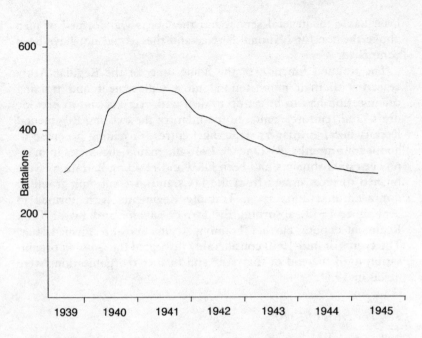

Figure 2.1. British Infantry Battalions: 1939–45. Sources: H. F. Joslen, *Orders of Battle*, H.M.S.O., 1960. PRO/WO/165–179 and 212. Unit histories.

artillery and armour, to restore the balance of the army as a whole. Concurrently with the increase in the number of battalions, work went ahead to reconstruct the formations depleted in France. In the course of this four of the duplicate Territorial Divisions were broken up but the five surviving Motor Divisions were reconstituted as standard infantry divisions. At the same time the Regular Army component was increased by the return of eight battalions from India.

From the end of May young soldiers who had voluntarily enlisted before being called up for National Service were posted to the former NDC battalions now employed on airfield defence. Since these units were widely dispersed to provide guard detachments there was little opportunity for unit training or the cultivation of group identity and many of these units seem to have been an unhappy mixture of the too young and the too old. From the end of 1940 the young soldiers were detached into Young Soldier Battalions but still with an airfield defence role and still split up into guard detachments. Airfield defence ceased to be an army responsibility in 1943 when that role was taken over by the RAF Regiment. The Young Soldier Battalions were then broken up.

Brief mention must be made of the Home Guard which formed as the Local Defence Volunteers following an appeal by the War Secretary on 14th May 1940. Originally formed in Companies, these were grouped into Battalions in July with a higher level of organisation known as the Zone. Administration was the responsibility of the TA Associations. From March 1941 the Zones were subdivided into Groups of approximately brigade strength and at about the same time units acquired anti-aircraft and coastal defence responsibilities. Legislation in January 1942 allowed the direction of men to join the Home Guard of which, in all, about 1100 battalions were formed.[36]

On 1st August 1940 the Cabinet returned to the question of the 55-division programme, with the emphasis turned from the provision of equipment for fifty-five divisions to the formation of the divisions themselves. Formed or in sight were 55⅓ divisions including three each from Australia and Canada, nine from India, three from Africa, one from New Zealand, a South African Brigade and the equivalent of a division from the Allies. Orders had been given for a tank programme to equip seven armoured divisions by mid-1941. A few days later the Prime Minister was pressing for a total of ten armoured divisions to be reached by August 1941.[37] The position of the Dominions provided an effect which could not be exactly calculated since it rested individually with each Dominion to decide what forces it would raise and place in the field. By 29th January 1941 the number of divisions had risen to fifty-eight with the South African decision to raise two divisions, one more each from Australia and the African colonies and with the Indian contribution reduced to eight. A degree of finality was reached on 6th March when, in a directive on army scales, the Minister of Defence referred to fifty-seven divisions of which thirty-six would be British. By 26th March adjustments brought this to 59⅓ 'equivalent divisions' including twelve armoured divisions and nine tank brigades.[38]

Although the provision of manpower for the army, the other Services and for industry continued to be a Cabinet pre-occupation it would appear that this was the last occasion on which the Cabinet addressed the specific problem of how many divisions could be raised and supported. No more was heard of the fifty-seven-division plan. The immediate problem became the completion and maintenance of the formations already created.

One of the problems with which the Minister of Defence and the Cabinet was struggling in the spring of 1941 was an attempt to find a yardstick by which the size of the army could be measured. A conventional yardstick is the division but the output in divisions from an input of a given number of men is not easy to determine. The Prime Minister minuted the Secretary of State for War on 9th December 1940 about his failure to understand why divisions, with an establishment of 15,500, seemed to need an extra 35,000 men to support them when the divisions were supposed to be self-contained. When it came to comparing the strength of one country with another even further confusion resulted.[39] It is surprising that the size of the British divisional 'slice' was found to be unexpectedly high for the experience of the previous war was available. As an example, in November 1918 the British Army contained 3·8 million men when there were sixty-two infantry divisions, including an allowance for independent brigades, three cavalry divisions, a cyclist division and smaller formations. Estimating all these as perhaps sixty-six 'equivalent divisions' this would have indicated a divisional 'slice' over the army as a whole of some 60,000 men. Refinement of the method is unnecessary since it is sufficient to note that from previous experience an army of a little over thirty divisions would require about two million men. Although in the new war there was no need for the large number of men who had been employed on labouring tasks in France from 1914 to 1918 the decisions to expand the armoured portion of the army had increased the need for maintenance services able to operate in unfavourable environments.[40]

The new British Army would contain a much greater proportion of armoured troops than before and it was accepted that a significant reduction in the number of infantry divisions would have to take place to allow for the change in philosophy. The question was not only one of providing armoured vehicles but also of determining the best relationship between armour and infantry and several changes in organisation resulted as experience accumulated. A pre-war armoured division comprised a Light and a Heavy Armoured

Brigade with a Support Group containing artillery and infantry. During 1940 the Armoured Brigades became homogeneous and each acquired a motor battalion. By 1942 experience had indicated that divisional organisations had become extremely ponderous and they were reduced to one Armoured Brigade and an Infantry Brigade each. Redundant armoured brigades were in the main retained as independent formations. Included in the armoured expansion were Army Tank Brigades intended to be employed on close infantry support. Tank brigades were basically independent formations but in June 1942 six infantry divisions were converted into Mixed Divisions, each with two infantry brigades and a tank brigade. These divisions reverted to standard infantry composition during 1943. It is a matter of interest that in Italy from 1943 armoured divisions were considered to have too few infantry and those in that theatre were each given an additional infantry brigade. Thus the Mixed Division establishment was returned to from the opposite direction, so to speak.

The units available to form the new armoured formations were the regiments of the cavalry, Yeomanry and Royal Tank Regiment. In the winter of 1940/41 six new regiments were formed on cadres provided by the cavalry but the main enlargement came a year later when thirty-three infantry battalions were converted (Figure 2.2). With so many of the former cavalry and armoured units committed to the armoured divisions and brigades there were no units left for divisional reconnaissance and a new Reconnaissance Corps was formed in 1941. The new Corps absorbed a further ten infantry battalions.[41]

To equip this vastly expanded armoured force proved a lengthy task. In addition to tank production in Britain and the Dominions assistance was available from the United States and for a time numerical strengths grew quite rapidly. The differing origins of the tanks were, however, reflected in the differing types available and unit equipments tended to vary considerably. Qualitative problems also had their effect and constant design changes reacted adversely on production. In consequence unit organisations and reorganisations varied with equipment availability and were often retarded. Once Russia entered the war the commitments undertaken to supply her with tanks introduced further conflicts in the priorities between the different theatres. The problem was one that did not even approach resolution until American tank production was in

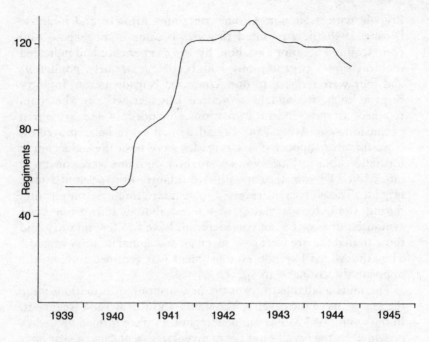

Figure 2.2. British Armoured Units: 1939–45. Sources: Joslen, *Orders of Battle*. PRO/WO/165–179 and 212. Unit histories.

full swing in 1943.

With much of Europe under German occupation, as early as June 1940 the Prime Minister was pressing for the development of raiding forces to harass the enemy coasts.[42] The Commandos grew out of ten Independent Companies which had been formed in the spring of 1940 and by 1943 all were grouped into four Commando Brigades, incorporating Royal Marine units which also dated from 1940. By then the Commandos had had considerable raiding and assault landing experience, the latter often extending into ordinary infantry experience after initial operations. Indeed one of the interesting features of Commando organisation is how, over the period of the war, it became more akin to that of the infantry battalion as the original amphibious role diminished. Parachute and Air-landing forces were originally part of the Commando organisation but achieved separate status in November 1940 and eventually grew to two Airborne Divisions. One of the features of the Second World War is the very large number of units and sub-units formed for raiding purposes of one kind and another. Certainly a considerable amount of effort was expended in developing such forces and in the eyes of some military authorities they did not give a worthwhile return for the resources they absorbed.[43]

iv *Manpower planning*

Manpower planning for the next war commenced as early as 1922 when a Sub-Committee of the CID was set up to examine National Service in a Future War. The Sub-Committee's report was presented in July 1922 when essential pre-requisites for any plan were held to be the completion of a National Register and the compilation of a schedule of industries and occupations of national importance. The Sub-Committee distinguished between the requirements of a major war and a minor war. In the latter case, where not more than 750,000 recruits would be needed, voluntary methods would suffice although even here the schedule of essential work should be applied. In the event of a major war conscription should be introduced as soon as practicable, with call-up by age classes and with protection for men in scheduled occupations. The protection should be by deferring the call-up of men in essential work rather than blocking it completely, preserving the principle of universal obligation to perform military service. These were, in fact, the principles upon which the Second World War scheme was built.[44]

A standing sub-committee of the CID continued to examine the problem over subsequent years. Since the National Register would not be available on the outbreak of war, and since the Schedule of Reserved Occupations was believed to depend on the Register, it was proposed that no men in the highest medical category under the age of twenty-five should be reserved. Further, in the first six months of war recruiting should be confined to men under twenty-five and in the second half-year to men under thirty. The yield from this procedure was expected to be 1½ millions in the first half-year and half a million in the second. In 1927 the Sub-Committee affirmed the principle that compulsory national service applied not only to military service but also to employment of national importance.

Events of 1937 were such as to confuse the contingency planning taking place. The 'limited liability' role for the army approximated to the requirements for a minor war but by now the Air Raid Precautions Department of the Home Office was claiming a million recruits for civil defence. At the same time the first stages of the rearmament programme were under way which could easily be impeded by volunteering for ARP work or for the TA. In January 1939, to improve public information on the subject, a booklet was distributed outlining the needs of the Services and civil defence and of the principles of the scheduling of occupations.

After the outbreak of war it was assumed that the pool of a million unemployed would be the source from which the munitions industries could receive workers to replace those who had been called for National Service. However, the slow development of the 55-division programme resulted in the first attempt to assess manpower needs. It was conducted by Humbert Wolfe of the Ministry of Labour and in January 1940 indicated that upwards of two million men would be needed by the engineering industries alone. Quite an optimistic view of the situation was taken by a Committee on Recruitment on 26th April. Expansion had gone more rapidly than had been expected and the army could expect to receive 60,000 men per month plus tradesmen and volunteers.[45] A Ministry of Labour memorandum attempted to assess the number of men who could be released from industry, concluding that 650,000 aged 20–25 and 1,230,000 aged 26–40 were available for general posting. Another 235,000 and 120,000 respectively were available as tradesmen. The document is interesting as being the first and last occasion on which an attempt was made to look forwards towards the total number of men which the Services could receive given the demographic limitations of Britian.

Under the emergency of mid-1940 the Government took powers under the Emergency Powers (Defence) Act to acquire control over the services of all over the age of sixteen.[46] Under this Act and its delegated legislation full industrial conscription was assumed. A Production Council was set up as a Cabinet Committee and in August 1940 this body established a Manpower Requirements Committee to survey the whole manpower scene. The immediate task of the MRC was to consider estimated manpower needs of the Services for the next two years. For the army a total of 357,000 was needed by March 1941 with 100,000 per month subsequently. The Committee submitted its final report in December 1940. The army's estimated requirement came to 1,203,000 men and 25,000 women out of a total for all Services and civil defence of 1¾ million men and 84,000 women. These needs could only be met by the withdrawal of half a million men from industry and their replacement by men transferred from less essential to more essential work and by increasing the number of women in employment.[47] In October the Cabinet had been advised that the existing sources from which the army received its men were drying up and in consequence a Minister of Defence's Directive dated 6th March 1941 placed a manpower ceiling on the size of the army.[48] The limit was 2,195,000, increased in September to 2,374,800 covering the period to June 1942. A change in manpower planning took place when the Production Council was replaced by the Production Executive, its Manpower Requirements Committee being replaced by the Manpower Committee of the Executive. One of the first tasks of the new Committee was to carry out a survey ordered by the Cabinet in July 1941. The Ministry of Labour carried out the survey for the Committee in October. An outline of the needs of the Services and civil defence to June 1942 showed that against demands for 829,000 men only 468,000 were available. To meet the shortfall the age for conscription was lowered from the ruling 19 to 18½ whilst the National Service 2 act of 1941 raised the upper age limit for National Service to fifty-one and extended the provisions of all of the National Service Acts to women.[49] As in the previous war the National Service Acts did not apply to Ireland and the practicability of doing so was considered at several Cabinet meetings. Opinion from the Northern Ireland Government and several prominent figures in the province was that generally the voluntary system in use was likely to be more effective than measures of conscription. A committee was appointed to prepare a draft Bill but the Cabinet deferred making a decision on the subject. The deferment proved to be indefinite.[50]

While the discussions were going on which led to the second National Service Act of 1941 a fresh examination was going on regarding the army's commitments. Hitherto discussion had focussed on the provision of a field army; in this review the world-wide responsibilities of the army were looked at for the first time as a whole. In a Directive on Army Strength on 9th October the total army strength including Dominions, colonial forces and garrisons around the world was given as ninety-nine divisions or their

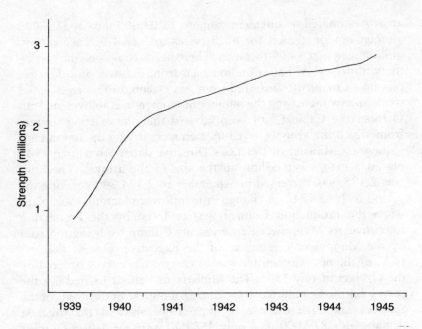

Figure 2.3. British Army Strength: 1939–45. Source: Central Statistical Office, *Statistical Digest of the War*, H.M.S.O., London 1951, p. 9.

equivalent.[51]

In the early part of 1942 the Production Executive was disbanded and its functions vis-a-vis manpower were taken over by a Labour Co-ordinating Committee which called for an interim report on the manpower position. The report was presented in April, by which time heavy losses had taken place in the Far East, the position in the Middle East was far from secure and there was every prospect of the opening of a new front in northern Iran and Iraq. Although the army ceiling still applied there was a considerable case for expansion, a figure of 100,000 being mentioned plus an addition to cover losses and wastage. These figures could be met, in part, by reducing call-up age to eighteen.[52] While this was going on a further review of the army was under way and this appeared on 1st November. Covering only British and British-controlled forces in Europe, the Middle East and South-east Asia, and excluding Commonwealth forces in the Pacific area, 100 divisions or their equivalent would be needed. This was, indeed, the last survey of the army to be undertaken. When the autumn manpower survey of the Ministry of Labour came before the Cabinet on 20th November the total requirements for the three Services came to 1·3 million men and 303,000 women plus another million men and women needed for essential industry. The maximum likely to be available to meet these needs came to 950,000 men and 650,000 women. For the future demands for additional men and women would have to be adapted and reduced to meet the supply. Service programmes would have to be cut.[53]

The manpower budget prepared in the autumn of 1943 marked the peak of Britain's mobilisation. As seen the demands for the Services and industry totalled 1,190,000 men and women. The Minister of Labour advised that total intake from all sources would not even balance wastage. Two broad alternatives were proposed. In the first it could be assumed that the maximum effort would be made in 1944 and that Germany would be defeated before the end of that year. In that case cut-backs could be made in manufacturing, training and, indeed, in any enterprise which would not deliver until 1945 or later. The second alternative was to assume a longer duration for the war which demanded an immediate scaling-down of effort. At a special meeting of Ministers and the Chiefs of Staff on 5th November it was decided to adopt the first alternative.[54] A large proportion of the men and women joining the Services in 1944 would have to come, directly or indirectly, from the munitions industries.

With an assumed date for the end of the European war it became necessary to prepare an outline manpower plan for the next stage, when Japan would be the only enemy. Progress on this fluctuated with the ups and downs of the war in North-west Europe and original assumptions that the Japanese war would go on for another three years were reduced to two years by the Cabinet in April 1944. Estimates of manpower needs showed a deficit of 1¾ million men and women but present urgencies prevented deeper consideration. In July the Cabinet approved recommendations that the army intakes in July and August should be 50,000 of which about 12,000 would be by transfer from the Royal Navy and RAF.[55]

The final manpower budget of the war was presented to the Cabinet in December 1944. In it the Minister of Labour thought that 120,000 men and 10,000 women might be found for the armed forces. The army were allocated the 120,000 men plus 20,000 transferred from each of the other Services but even at this stage all was not to run smoothly for on 12th February it was reported that the intakes could not be met in full.[56]

It will have been seen that across the years manpower planning evolved into a budgetary system with the Ministry of Labour responsible for the preparation of estimates which, collated with Service and industrial requirements, came before the Cabinet for decision. The Ministry of Labour had the primary task since it had the best information based on the mid-year exchange of industrial insurance cards. It was thus able to obtain a picture of the number and distribution of civilian labour on the given date. The committee system through which the Cabinet at first received reports now seems to have been cumbersome and ineffective and by the end of 1943 it had largely been eliminated. The methods used for allocations in 1944 and 1945 seem to have been hand to mouth but in the stringent shortages then prevailing this was, perhaps, inevitable. Three budgets were of real significance to the army as marking phase changes in the framework within which it was operating. The first was the imposition of a manpower ceiling in March 1941. The second came in December 1942 from which time plans had to be cast within the limitations of available manpower. The last dated from November 1943 from which time all allocations depended on an assumed date for the end of the war and within which the army was reinforced at the expense of the other two Services.

The manpower budgets were, in the figures presented in their reports, apparently a precise instrument for the allocation of men and women. In fact, although the basic information for the insurance card day was precise, the movements of people from one industrial group to another and from industry into the Services could only be the sum of movements of individuals moving under varying degrees of compulsion and pressure, official or unofficial, and self-motivation. In sum, therefore, the budgets were an imprecise and inexact instrument for obtaining the transfers needed. However, the system did in the end look at and take account of the total manpower position of the country. Even if that was the only criterion, which it was not, it represented a considerable improvement on the methods used between 1914 and 1918. In the end, on average, the system was seen to be fair. To the end, however, it remained an empirical system moving on from one planning period to the next without defined objectives in terms of what forces the country could, or should, place in the field.

v   *The army in Britain*

The early months of 1941 found the army in Britain in a state of disarray. The very high intakes of men in the second half of 1941 and the organisation of the greater part of them into infantry had provided a very great increase in one arm but the pressures to increase the armoured component and build up raiding and special forces were considerable. This, too, had to be accomplished within the framework of the manpower ceiling set in March. The possibility of invasion had still to be considered and although this consideration was, in practice, removed by the German invasion of Russia on 22nd June this could not be known at the time. The relative ease with which Germany could have transferred forces to the west if Russia collapsed kept this issue alive well into 1942.

The effect of reorganisations to the army within manpower limits implied a significant reduction in infantry and the first steps towards this took place in the autumn of 1941 when proposals were made to reduce the establishments of some divisions and to disband others. The Prime Minister protested vigorously at the reductions but the last two months of 1941 were the time for a major conversion of infantry to armour (Figures 2.1 and 2.2) and at the same time the Cabinet was facing problems of reducing the age of call-up and applying conscription to women. The army had been over-expanded and had to be reduced.[57]

Between October 1941 and January 1942 the nine County Divisions were broken up and seven of the field divisions were placed on reduced establishments, fitting them only for an immobile role in home defence. Two of the County Divisions were re-formed on the lower scale. The reduced infantry intakes had their effect on training organisation and in August 1941 the number of Infantry Training Centres was reduced to twenty-five.

If it was difficult enough to supply the army with the number of men needed it was even more difficult to provide men with special skills. Early in 1941 there was widespread belief that the Services in general, and the army in particular, were not making the best use of such men and a committee under Sir William Beveridge was set up to investigate the matter. The report of the committee in November supported the allegations quoting nearly 10,000 examples of misuse.[58] The intake of men with mechanical and engineering skills was then banned, the ban not being lifted until August 1942. Although the War Office, in its own investigations, considered that only 1300 of the cases were proved, the episode inspired a critical re-examination of how the army classified and allocated its men.

Although legislation had been passed to allow the transfer of men from corps to corps enlistment was still for a particular corps and machinery to effect transfer virtually non-existent. Once a man found himself in a particular corps, whether fitted for it or not, he was likely to stay there. This was of particular importance in the enlistment of those called up for National Service since in a brief interview it was almost impossible for a recruiting officer to sum up a man accurately.[59] Accordingly from July 1942 men recruited into the army were posted to a General Service Corps and sent to Primary Training Centres where they were given basic training and put through a selection process to identify skills and aptitudes. After primary training a man was posted to a corps training centre for a period which varied from corps to corps. On completion of training it was usual to post men to one or other of the home service formations until reaching the age of twenty and becoming eligible for overseas service. Some attempt was made to preserve regimental loyalties and affiliations until 1943 when shortage of infantry compelled posting to any unit in need.[60]

The training role of the home service divisions was formalised in the winter of 1942/43 when three of the lower establishment divisions, plus another newly formed, took over that function as Reserve Divisions. One of these became a Holding Division in December 1943 charged with the training and retraining of men who, for example, were returning to duty after long periods of illness or injury, after long periods overseas or who were changing their corps.

Brief mention must be made of the problem of officer selection and training. In general officer candidates were selected from men with six months' service and from July 1942 these were appointed to a pre-OCTU training unit. There the period of training was variable according to the experience and qualities of the candidate and could range from one to nine weeks. Final selection was made in the pre-OCTU after which men would go to an appropriate

Officer Cadet Training Unit where the length of course depended
on the corps for which the Cadet was intended. The infantry course
of seventeen weeks was the shortest, that of thirty weeks for the
Royal Engineers the longest.[61] A shortage of officers was manifest
throughout the war, to a great extent due to the priorities given to
the recruitment of aircrew for the RAF. This drew away many
thousands of young men with the education and ability to be
subalterns and was an unforeseen consequence of the decision to
expand the RAF in general and Bomber Command in particular to
the extent they were. The shortage became particularly acute in
fighting units in Italy and North-west Europe in 1944 and some
hundreds of young officers were seconded from the armies of
Canada and South Africa.

The report of the Manpower Requirements Committee towards
the end of 1940, with the imposition of the manpower ceiling in
March 1941, provided an inspiration for the expansion of the
Auxiliary Territorial Service. At the same time it provoked a re-
examination of the tasks women could undertake in the army. Progressively the role of the ATS was extended from the provision
of clerical, transport and domestic services to a wide range of
technical and maintenance duties. In April 1941 decisions were
taken to employ women on anti-aircraft gun-sites and the first
Mixed Battery was ready for duty in the August. Ultimately some
74,000 women were employed in Anti-aircraft Command. In April,
too, the women's Services became part of the Armed Forces of the
Crown. The reasons for this included the need to regularise the
position of women who might be employed on duties directly
related to combat and also to apply a more direct control on intake
and outflow from the women's Services as a whole. Under the
contractual type of engagement in use women were free to leave the
Services with little hindrance which wasted training and went a
long way towards reducing the value of the intakes. In the first sixteen months of the war nearly 32,000 women entered the ATS but
in the same period 13,212 left the Service. The first ATS drafts to be
posted overseas left for the Middle East in December 1941 and
subsequent parties went to all the major theatres of war.

The second National Service Act of 1941 applied conscription to
women but when registering they were asked to choose between
service in industry, civil defence or one of the women's Services.
Only those who made the latter choice were enlisted. From the

middle of 1943 precedence was given to recruitment for industry
and volunteering was also discontinued. The greatest strength of
the ATS, 212,500, was therefore reached in September 1943.
Volunteering was re-opened in January 1944 but was then
restricted to girls aged 17½–19 to ensure the minimum disruption
to industry.

vi   *The dispersion of the army*

The world-wide nature of the Second World War placed demands
on the army quite different from those experienced between 1914
and 1918. In the earlier war the colonial commitments of Britain,
together with the little threat the colonies faced, allowed a concentration in the main theatres and provided a valuable reserve from
which five British divisions were formed. In the later war there was
a need to supply garrisons for overseas and armies to fight major
campaigns in the Mediterranean and Far East, enforcing a continuing dispersion. Although the garrisons in North China were
withdrawn in 1940, the units involved had to remain to reinforce
those of Hong Kong and Malaya. A division had to be sent to
Iceland in June 1940 and a brigade to West Africa a few months
later. The garrison of Gibraltar had to be built up to a strength of
two brigades and that of Malta to four by the end of 1942. In the
West Indies it was not possible to relieve the British garrison until
February 1942. The Falkland Islands were garrisoned from 1942 to
1944.

The central problems were, however, those of the Mediterranean
and the Far East.

Before the outbreak of war the Middle East had become the
centre for the concentration of a considerable proportion of the
British Army's strength to maintain internal security and to guard
against the possible hostility of Italy. Not only were Egypt and
Palestine well situated for the creation of a central reserve but they
were also at the focus of the main supply route to India and the Far
East. With the closure of the Mediterranean the main sources for
reinforcement of the theatre became the Commonwealth countries
east of the Suez Canal and the major part of the fighting forces
came to be found from India, Australia, New Zealand and South
Africa. Indeed reinforcement from India commenced before the
outbreak of war. The problems of establishing a base for what

might grow to a force of twenty-three divisions in an under-developed area caused considerable manpower demands which were exacerbated by the need to maintain internal security, duties for which the forces from the Dominions were not available. To assist in these duties 1 Cavalry Division, still horsed, was sent out at the beginning of 1940 and to increase the size of the British component 2 Armoured Division arrived in October 1940 and 50 Division in April 1941. Attempts to build up British strength were long frustrated. 2 Armoured Division was destroyed in April 1941 and attempts to convert the Cavalry Division to armour were hampered by lack of equipment. It finally became 10 Armoured Division in August 1941. Attempts to build up British strength in the firing line are epitomised in the story of the Regular troops in the theatre. In 1939 these were in the rudimentary 7 and 8 Divisions, both of which were broken up by February 1940. In November 1939 6 Division was formed from such troops as were available but this was broken up in June 1940. The Division was re-formed in February 1941 and it was at first intended to include Commandos, which had been sent out from Britain, as its third brigade. After diversions caused by the campaigns in Syria and Crete the Division finally assembled as 70 Division in October. The outbreak of war in the Far East had considerable repercussions futher west and 70 Division was sent to India only to be broken up in 1943 as part of Special Force.

By the end of 1942 British forces in the Middle East had reached their greatest strength of four infantry and four armoured divisions but with local victory, the declining chances of a new theatre opening up in the north, and in face of increasing difficulties in maintaining strength, 8 Armoured and 44 Infantry Divisions were broken up. With the movement of the war on to Sicily and Italy the Middle East became a rear area, used as a rest area for divisions from Italy and with internal security in the hands of a variety of units and formations. Of forty-one unbrigaded cavalry and infantry units in November 1944 only one was British. Formations included Arab Legion, Jewish, Belgian Congo and South African Brigades. 10 Armoured Division, which had remained as a reserve formation for Italy, was broken up in June 1944.

Up to 1943 it might be said that manpower problems in the Middle East were essentially problems of distribution and allocation, compounded by the long sea haul from the United Kingdom.

From the opening of the Italian campaign the problem became one of absolute shortage. As usual, the problem was one which fell mainly on the infantry. From September 1943 to March 1944 the British Army in Italy suffered 46,000 battle casualties, 26,500 of them infantry, plus 20,000 casualties from illness. Reinforcements came to 23,500 but even this number was found by calling upon divisions in North Africa.[62] In March 1944, as a temporary expedient, battalion establishments were reduced from 844 to 726 all ranks and in September the number of companies in a battalion had to be reduced from four to three. In the winter of 1944/45 1 Armoured Division was broken up as were units, such as anti-aircraft artillery, for which there was a decreasing role.[63] Further losses to the army in Italy were caused by the diversion of divisions to police the civil war in Greece and the transfer of 5 Division to North-west Europe in March 1945.

For the army in India, in 1939 these comprised three cavalry regiments and thirty-nine battalions of which one regiment and eight battalions returned to Britain in 1940. Apart from these movements there was no reinforcement of the United Kingdom such as took place in 1914 but the Indian Army commenced an expansion programme ultimately directed towards the reinforcement of the Middle East. As in the previous war a British unit was an integral part of each Indian brigade and the battalions in India were thus drawn into the expansion. The movement of 4 Indian Division to the Middle East in 1939 and 1940, and that of 9 and 11 Indian Divisions to Malaya in 1941, took a number of British units with them.

The first transfer of British units to India took place in August 1941 when three infantry battalions embarked, earmarked for conversion to form a Heavy Armoured Brigade (later 50 Indian Tank Brigade). Following the entry of Japan into the war twelve battalions followed them in 1942, together with three RAC Regiments to form a second tank brigade. The RAC Regiments were reconverted to infantry in 1943 when a further two battalions were transferred from Britain. In addition to this piecemeal reinforcement, 70 Division arrived from the Middle East in March 1942, being followed by 5 Division in May and 2 Division in June. 36 Indian Division was improvised, with British personnel, to train for amphibious operations in the theatre. 5 Division remained in India only for a brief period before moving to the Persian Gulf and then still further west. The only other divisional movement was that of 18 Division which, diverted to Malaya, was lost there in February 1942.

The biggest organisational disruption which the British Army in India suffered was caused by the formation of a special force to operate behind enemy lines. This force owed its inception to the ideas of Wingate who arrived in India in January 1942 and who was allowed to form 77 Indian Brigade to test theories as to the effect of long range penetration dependent on air supply.[64] Following the partial success of his first operation in 1943, a success enhanced by comparison with concurrent operations in Arakan, the special force was considerably expanded. Decisions for this were taken at the Quebec conference in August 1943 where Wingate made a very favourable impression on the Allied leaders.[65] The force envisaged totalled some 19,000 British officers and men and 7500 Gurkhas or Africans. A modest expansion of Long Range Penetration forces had already been commenced with the formation of 111 Indian Brigade but the new force would considerably erode any British units earmarked for conversion to the new role since the process included weeding out all who did not fulfil stringent fitness criteria, a process which removed some forty per cent of the original personnel. On 25th August instructions were issued to break up 70 Division to form the nucleus of the new force which was to be styled 3 Indian Division or Special Force. To complete manpower requirements it was necessary to transfer another two infantry battalions and to break up two armoured regiments.[66] Following the very heavy wastage suffered by the force during 1944 and in view of the lack of British reinforcements it was broken up in February 1945. It is difficult to avoid the conclusion that the results achieved by the force did not represent an adequate return for the resources invested. Essentially a guerilla force, it was too lightly equipped either to capture strongly defended points or to hold them. Arguably it inflicted more damage and disruption on the British Army than it ever did on the Japanese.[67]

Because of transport problems the finding of drafts to make up the British units was a constant problem and by 1944 this theatre, too, was beginning to feel the effects of Britain's overall manpower shortage. In June 1944 the British infantry allocated to 14 Army were 3500 men under strength, with a further 3100 needed for Special Force, and by November it was estimated that the deficiency would have grown to 11,300 and 7300. Reinforcements in sight totalled 7100 to which could be added perhaps 3500 found by disbanding anti-aircraft units.[68] It thus became necessary to replace British units in Indian formations by Indian battalions.

The British manpower problems in the Far East were compounded by the relative remoteness of the theatre and by the question of just how long men should be expected to remain overseas. In the Regular Army long periods of overseas duty were common, often extending to five or six years in the pre-war period, but the needs of a largely conscript army were somewhat different. In the Mediterranean theatre it had been practicable to do something to alleviate the situation by the return of three of the longest serving divisions to the United Kingdom for the 1944 invasion, although even this was seen to be an inadequate measure made too late.[69] Over-long service also played a part in the problems suffered by the army in Italy in the winter of 1944/45. Formal recognition of the problem dated from January 1943 when a leave scheme, the 'Python' scheme, was introduced. Men with over six years' service were then returned to the United Kingdom and ruling periods of four years were established for India and four years nine months for other areas.[70] In fact in South-east Asia many had served for longer periods. The position was modified when the War Office decided in September 1944 that from the end of the year the qualifying period would be reduced to three years and eight months. As a consequence in October Mountbatten, the Supreme Commander, reported to the Chiefs of Staff that his overall shortage of men was about 30,000. On 6th June 1945 the War Secretary advised that the qualifying period for Python was to be reduced to three years and four months and that men in this range of service would be sent home as shipping offered without waiting for replacements.[71] Although 'operational necessity' clauses could be invoked the revision considerably affected planning for the forthcoming invasion of Malaya. Already, because of probable transportation difficulties after the operation was launched, men who would qualify for Python under the previous limits by December 1945 had been withdrawn from their units. In fact available transport to the United Kingdom could not cope with the additional 33,000 men who would be eligible for leave by the end of September over and above the 50,000 already due. The announcement was made in the Commons on 8th June and the effect was to remove 36 Division from the forces available for the invasion of Malaya, joining 2 Division which had already been withdrawn from operations. On 8th August the Supreme Commander announced that all men qualifying under revised Python before the end of the year would be withdrawn from their formations although 'operational necessity' might be applied to some cases. At the same time he cautioned that transport limitations might prevent those withdrawn from leaving India before the end of the year. The overall effect was to seriously weaken the forces available for what might have been a major operation of war.[72]

Planning for British participation in the final stages of the war against Japan stemmed from the Cairo conference of 1943. At first a British contribution of four divisions was contemplated but in May 1944 the Australian Defence Committee was advised that, subject to the European war ending later that year, two divisions might arrive from India in January and March 1945 and three from Europe by April. By August 1944 it was thought that six British divisions could be made available. The delay in the defeat of Germany, manpower problems and the uncertain attitude of the United States towards British participation all hindered planning. In January 1945 the Chiefs of Staff estimated that twelve months after the end of the war in Europe the British Army would need a strength of 1½ million men. By June 1945 the Commonwealth force for the assault on Honshu in 1946 was seen as a division each from Britain, India, Australia, Canada and New Zealand. The composition of the force varied as discussion developed, availability of shipping being one of the variables, and it was later reduced to a division each from Britain, Australia and Canada with possibly another from New Zealand. However, 'much debate must have lain ahead before British troops could have waded ashore onto the beaches of Honshu'.[73]

vii   *The end of the war in Europe*

The British Army for the invasion of France was formed in July 1943 as 21 Army Group, comprising ten infantry and five armoured divisions. The overt optimism implied by this event concealed a deep pessimism about the manpower situation. The autumn budget of 1942 had indicated that in manpower terms Britain was living beyond her means and that cuts would have to be made. It was useless to maintain what the CIGS referred to as 'emaciated' formations.[74] Indeed by the beginning of 1944 the army was preparing to return to the Continent in the knowledge that all of Britain's manpower was deployed and dependent on an assumed date for the end of the war. In face of these limitations two more armoured divisions were removed from the order of battle to further deplete the forces available for the final stages. With the development of the campaign and lack of reinforcements 59 Division was broken up in October 1944 and before the end of the year 50 Division had to be reduced to Reserve status. Although casualties were lighter than had been anticipated they were still heavy and it had been expected that it would become necessary to disband some of the divisions landed in France. Improvised methods were used to provide additional formations including two brigades of Marines and seven brigades formed from former anti-aircraft and other artillery units, of which three arrived in Europe before the surrender. A number of unbrigaded units were used much earlier in, for example, the blockade of Dunkirk. In an attempt to strengthen the forces in the major theatre a Canadian Corps was transferred from Italy and this was to have been accompanied by three British divisions of which, in the end, only one was transferred.[75]

viii Aftermath

In 1945 the strength of the British Army was just under 3 millions at which time nineteen infantry divisions, including airborne, and five armoured divisions were being supported. There were, however, forty independent brigades, including fifteen armoured, so that the number of 'equivalent divisions' in service was about forty-two. Over the army as a whole the 'divisional slice' was about 65,000, contrasting with the 60,000 obtained in the earlier war. In operational theatres the 'divisional slice' was, of course, much smaller. In Italy the ruling figure was 40,000 while in North-west Europe the planned figure of 41,000 had stretched to about 49,000 by the close of the campaign.[76] The big difference between the number of formed divisions and the number of 'equivalent divisions' is another contrast with 1918 and, perhaps, points to a move towards a smaller tactical formation than the division. If so, the move appears to have been implicit rather than explicit since at least one successful Commander was very much an exponent of the

Table 2.1   Strengths of the Armed Forces

	November 1918	June 1945
Army	3,759,000	2,920,000
Royal Navy	407,000	783,000
Royal Air Force	291,000	950,000*
TOTALS	4,457,000	4,653,000

* Maximum, 1,002,000 in June 1944.

philosophy that divisions should be fought as such.[77]

The overall size of the army was significantly smaller in the Second World War than in the First. One of the reasons for this is, of course, the greater demand for industrial support in the later war but the comparative sizes of the three Services are worth noting (Table 2.1). In spite of the greater industrial demands, larger numbers of men served in one or other of the Services in the Second World War than in the First. The country's population grew between the Wars, which accounts for part of the increase in total enlistment. The effect of the considerable American assistance over the entire range of munitions production cannot be properly assessed but it certainly added greatly to the number of people Britain was able to place in uniform. One thing the Table does indicate is how much the smaller growth of the army in the Second World War was due to the greater growth of the other Services.

The extent to which the army's resources were devoted to the development of armoured forces was commented on earlier. Using numbers of divisions is by no means a precise instrument for comparison but Table 2.2 illustrates how untypical that development was. The reasons behind Britain's development of a blitzkrieg army are unclear. If, at the time, the case was ever argued in those terms the documents have not survived. The Prime Minister was clearly the instigator but he was certainly not opposed, and was indeed supported, by the Chiefs of Staff. The success of the German Army in applying tactics which had been advocated by British writers between the wars was outstanding and the reasons for attempting to emulate them were considerable. One of the results of the policy was, though, to add to the chronic shortage of infantry experienced in operations in the Far East, in Italy and finally in the

Table 2.2   Divisions in service

	Armour	Infantry
United Kingdom, 1945	5	19
United States, 1945	16	79*
Germany, 1940	10	149
Germany, 1944	33	298
Italy, 1941	4	76
Japan, 1945	4	160

* Includes six Marine Divisions.

campaign in North-west Europe. One of the reasons was, perhaps, subconscious. There was an ingrained British aversion to returning to the immobile warfare of 1914–18. Brooke, the CIGS for the second part of the war, in his private writings returns again and again to the shortage of leaders due to losses in the Great War. General Alexander, Commanding in Italy, also referred in his papers to attitudes attributable to First World War experience.[78] Armoured, mobile warfare, seen against the British manpower shortage and desire to avoid casualties, promised to be inexpensive. On the enemy side Guderian could write that tanks were a life-saving weapon.[79] If this was one of the objectives of British armoured development it was one sadly frustrated by the qualitative inferiority of British tanks which persisted into the final campaign.

The duration of the war, almost six years, with until nearly the end the prospect of another two or three years to finish the war with Japan, began to raise questions which did not appear in any degree in the Great War. The questions related to just how long could a nation, an army and individual men be expected to remain at war. In the 1914–18 War although one or two units were kept overseas, particularly in the Far East, for five years much of the campaigning was near to home where leave was possible. In the later war much longer separations became usual. The development of the Python Scheme owed a great deal to the visualisation of an end to the war and to political events at home but, in its effects on operations, it would have placed considerable impediments on the effective continuation of the war. Had the war continued, under circumstances where there was no immediate threat to the soil of the United Kingdom, the maintenance of an army to fight distant causes would have become a matter of great difficulty. Indeed the distribution of formations and manpower in mid-1945 suggests that Britain was well on the way towards withdrawing altogether from the land war in the Pacific.

The very great dispersion forced upon the British Army by undertaking campaigns in widely separated regions, supported by forming an excessively wide variety of special-service organisations, considerably reduced the contribution the army was able to make to the final, and vital, campaign in Europe. The campaigns in the Middle East and South-east Asia were based in under-developed regions where the army had to create for itself large elements of the infrastructure of transportation, supply and support systems found in more developed regions. These needs demanded a much greater devotion of the army's scarce manpower to 'tail' services and in these circumstances when, too, the growth of technical demands in the army are considered, it is remarkable that such a small proportion of the army's manpower was absorbed per fighting formation. Yet the dispersion itself, forcing the army to live and fight in unhealthy and relatively remote regions, both increased manpower wastage and forced the break-up of fighting formations due to lack of adequate replacements. The use of second-line soldiers to provide garrisons in back areas was noted in connection with the Middle East in 1944, and such economies were useful, but they were only able to ameliorate a fundamentally wasteful situation. All in all the British Army had the strength to make a major contribution to one campaign. Of necessity it had to fight three.

Notes

1 PRO/Cab/23/15.
  N. H. Gibbs, *Grand Strategy*, I, H.M.S.O., London, 1976, pp. 3–6.
2 *Territorial and Militia Act*, 1921, 11 and 12 Geo. V, c. 37.
3 *Parliamentary Debates (Commons)*, CCCXVII, col. 733.
  Cmd. 5107.
4 Gibbs, *Grand Strategy*, p. 55.
  B. J. Bond, *British Military Policy Between the Two World Wars*, Oxford U. P., 1980, Ch. 3.
5 Gibbs, *Grand Strategy*, p. 86.
  PRO/Cab/23/58 and 70.

6   B. H. Liddell Hart, *Memoirs*, I, Cassell, London, 1965, pp. 95–6, 132–3, 174–7.
    G. P. Armstrong, 'The Controversy over Tanks in the British Army', unpub. Ph.D., London, 1976, pp. 47–52.
7   Lord Ismay, *Memoirs*, Heinemann, London, 1960, p. 80.
8   Gibbs, *Grand Strategy*, pp. 96–7.
    PRO/Cab/24/247.
    B. J. Bond (Ed.), *Chief of Staff: The Diaries of Lt. Gen. Sir Henry Pownall*, I, Leo Cooper, London, 1972, pp. 24–5.
    Bond, *Military Policy*, Ch. 7.
9   Gibbs, *Grand Strategy*, pp. 262, 442–3.
    PRO/Cab/24/259.
10 PRO/Cab/24/265 and 267 and 23/90.
    Gibbs, *Grand Strategy*, pp. 455–60, 465–72.
    Bond, *Chief of Staff*, p. 42.
    M. Howard, *The Continental Commitment*, Temple Smith, London, 1972, pp. 113–6.
    Bond, *Military Policy*, Ch. 8.
11 Gibbs, *Grand Strategy*, pp. 460–1.
    B. Collier, *Defence of the United Kingdom*, H.M.S.O., London, 1957, Chs. 1 and 2.
12 Armstrong, 'The Controversy over Tanks', pp. 200–3.
13 Army Order 58/1939.
14 Gibbs, *Grand Strategy*, pp. 502–14.
    Bond, *Military Policy*, pp. 299–300.
    PRO/Cab/23/97.
15 *Parliamentary Debates (Commons)*, CCCXLII, cols. 597 ff.
    P. Dennis, *Decision by Default*, Routledge and Kegan Paul, London, 1972, pp. 145–50, 163–5.
16 PRO/Cab/16/209.
17 *Parliamentary Debates (Commons)*, CCCXLV, col. 2048.
    Dennis, *Decision by Default*, pp. 196–8.
18 Bond, *Chief of Staff*, pp. 189, 196–7.
19 *Reserve and Auxiliary Forces Act*, 1939, 2 and 3 Geo. VI, c. 24.
    Bond, *Military Policy*, pp. 308–10.
    Dennis, *Decision by Default*, pp. 211–33.
    PRO/Cab/23/98 and 99.
20 *Military Training Act*, 1939, 2 and 3 Geo. VI, c. 25.
21 Gibbs, *Grand Strategy*, p. 521.
    Bond, *Chief of Staff*, pp. 200–1.
    Howard, *Continental Commitment*, pp. 129–30.
    PRO/Cab/24/285.
22 H. M. D. Parker, *Manpower*, H.M.S.O., London, 1957, p. 55.
23 PRO/Cab/23/98.
    W. N. Nicholson, *Suffolk Regiment, 1928–46*, E. Anglian Magazine, Ipswich 1948, pp. 190–1.
    H. Gunning, *Borderers in Battle*, Martin's Printing Works, Berwick, 1948, p. 26.

H. D. Chaplin, *Q.O. Royal West Kent Rgt., 1920–50*, Michael Joseph, London, 1954, pp. 115, 122.

24 J. R. M. Butler, *Grand Strategy*, II, H.M.S.O., London, 1957, p. 28.
F. de Guinand, *Operation Victory*, Hodder and Stoughton, London, 1947, p. 26, takes a more positive view.

25 Gibbs, *Grand Strategy*, pp. 503–11, 522–4.
Bond, *Chief of Staff*, I, p. 136.

26 Derived from Central Statistical Office, *Statistical Digest of the War*, H.M.S.O., London, 1951, p. 11.

27 Army Order 199/1938.

28 *Armed Forces (Conditions of Service) Act*, 1939, 2 and 3 Geo. VI, c. 68.
Military and Air Forces Act, 1939, 2 and 3 Geo. VI, c. 90.
National Registration Act, 1939, 2 and 3 Geo. VI, c. 91.
National Service (Armed Forces) Act, 1939, 2 and 3 Geo. VI, c. 81.

29 PRO/Cab/66/1. WP(39) 14, 15, 37, 41, 48.
PRO/Cab/65/1 and 2.
P. Cosgrave, *Churchill at War*, I, Collins, London, 1974, pp. 44–8.
Parker, *Manpower*, pp. 62–4.
de Guinand, *Operation Victory*, pp. 26–8.

30 Army Orders 200/1939 and 200/1940.
Army Council Instructions 741/1939.
PRO/Cab/92/116.

31 T. A. Martin, *Essex Regiment, 1929–50*, Essex Rgt. Assn., Brentwood, 1952, p. 130.
D. S. Daniell, *R. Hampshire Regimental History*, III, Gale and Polden, Aldershot, 1955, p. 59.

32 Lord Birdwood, *Worcestershire Regiment*, Gale and Polden, Aldershot, 1952, p. 158.
R. C. G. Foster, *History of the Queen's Regiment*, VIII, Gale and Polden, Aldershot, 1953, p. 68.
D. S. Daniell, *History of the East Surrey Regiment*, IV, Benn, London, 1957, pp. 76 and 86.

33 No detailed instructions appear to have survived. A W. O. circular letter is quoted verbatim in Chaplin, *West Kent Regiment*, p. 165.

34 S. G. P. Ward, *Faithful: The Story of the D.L.I.*, Nelson, London, 1963, p. 462.

35 W.. E. Underhill, *Royal Leicestershire Regiment, 1928–56*, The Regiment, Leicester, 1958, p. 167.

36 Bond, *Chief of Staff*, II, p. 5.

37 PRO/Cab/65/14.
W. L. S. Churchill, *The Second World War*, II, Cassell, London, 1949, pp. 218–9, 405, 701–4.

38 PRO/Cab/66/15. Annex to WP(41) 69.

39 Churchill, *Second World War*, II, p. 620 and V, Cassell, London, 1952, pp. 589, 594.

40 Bond, *Chief of Staff*, II, p. 46.

41 Army Council Instruction 360/1941.

42   Churchill, *Second World War*, II, pp. 217–8, 412–4.
43   Field Marshal Viscount Slim, *Defeat into Victory*, Cassell, London, 1956, pp. 535–6.
     A. Bryant, *The Turn of the Tide*, Collins, London, 1957, p. 210 (f.n.).
44   PRO/Cab/21/683.
     Parker, *Manpower*, pp. 40–2.
45   Ibid. pp. 62–4.
     PRO/Cab/92/116.
46   *Emergency Powers (Defence) Act*, 1940, 3 and 4 Geo. VI, c. 20 and c. 45.
47   Parker, *Manpower*, pp. 101–5.
     PRO/Cab/92/102.
48   PRO/Cab/66/15. Annex to WP(41) 69.
49   PRO/Cab/66/19. WP(41)247, 257, 258.
     National Service (2) Act, 1941, 5 and 6 Geo. VI, c. 4.
50   PRO/Cab/66/16. WP(41) 104–12.
51   Churchill, *Second World War*, III, pp. 452–3.
52   Parker, *Manpower*, pp. 172–3.
53   PRO/Cab/66/30. WP(42) 504.
     PRO/Cab/66/31. WP(42) 534, 539.
54   PRO/Cab/66/42. WP(43) 472, 490.
     PRO/Cab/78/18.
55   PRO/Cab/66/52. WP(44) 375.
     PRO/Cab/78/21.
     PRO/Cab/66/54. WP(44) 487.
     Parker, *Manpower*, pp. 233–6.
56   PRO/Cab/66/59–61. WP(44) 718, 751. WP(45) 87.
57   Churchill, *Second World War*, III, pp. 373–4, 446, 750.
58   Cmd. 6339.
59   Parker, *Manpower*, p. 153.
     B. Ungerson, *Personnel Selection*, War Office, London, 1953, pp. 3–4.
60   C. J. C. Molony, *Mediterranean and Middle East*, V, H.M.S.O., London, 1973, pp. 422–3, comments on reinforcement difficulties in Italy caused by regimental loyalties.
61   Ungerson, *Personnel Selection*, Ch. 10.
     J. H. A. Sparrow, *Morale*, War Office, London, 1949, pp. 21–2.
     I. Hay, *Arms and the Men*, H.M.S.O., London, 1950. Ch. 12 gives a short summary.
62   Molony, *Mediterranean and Middle East*, p. 423, and VI, 1, H.M.S.O., London, 1984, pp. 447–50.
     E. Linklater, *The Campaign in Italy*, H.M.S.O., London, 1951, p. 368.
63   A. Bryant, *Triumph in the West*, Collins, London, 1959, p. 324.
64   S. W. Kirby, *The War Against Japan*, II, H.M.S.O., London, 1958, pp. 243–4.
65   Churchill, *Second World War*, V, pp. 73, 78–9.
     Kirby, *War Against Japan*, II, pp. 309–404.
66   Kirby, *War Against Japan*, III, pp. 5, 37, 445.
     J. Connell, *Auchinleck*, Cassell, London 1959, pp. 745–6.

67 Kirby, *War Against Japan*, IV, pp. 27–30.
68 Ibid. p. 26.
    Slim, *Defeat into Victory*, pp. 370, 469.
69 I. S. O. Playfair and C. J. C. Molony, *Mediterranean and Middle East*,
    IV, H.M.S.O., London, 1966, p. 462.
    Linklater, *Italy*, p. 418.
    Sparrow, *Morale*, p. 12.
70 PRO/Cab/66/59. WP(44) 705.
    Sparrow, *Morale*, pp. 8–9.
71 Kirby, *War Against Japan*, IV, p. 27, and V, pp. 83, 85.
72 Slim, *Defeat into Victory*, pp. 509–10.
    Kirby, *War Against Japan*, V, pp. 90–1.
73 J. Ehrman, *Grand Strategy*, V, H.M.S.O., London, 1956, pp. 421–4,
    and VI, pp. 239, 265–71.
    G. Long, *The Final Campaigns*, Australian War Memorial, Canberra,
    1963, pp. 12–3.
    PRO/Cab/79/36 and 80.
74 Bryant, *Turn of the Tide*, p. 539.
75 L. F. Ellis, *Victory in the West*, I, H.M.S.O., London, 1962, pp. 307,
    453 (f.n.), 493.
    Bryant, *Triumph in the West*, p. 229 (f.n.).
76 Ellis, *Victory in the West*, p. 536.
    Molony, *Mediterranean and Middle East*, VI, 1, p. 437 (f.n.).
77 Field Marshal Montgomery, *El Alamein to the Sangro*, Hutchinson,
    London, 1948, p. 19.
    Connell, *Auchinleck*, pp. 507, 549–50.
78 Bryant, *Turn of the Tide*, pp. 132, 198.
    J. North (Ed.), *Alexander Memoirs*, Cassell, London, 1962, pp. 27,
    156.
79 H. Guderian, *Panzer Leader*, Michael Jospeh, London, 1952, p. 73.

Chapter 3
The Indian Army

i *The approach to 1914*

The intimate relationship between the British Army and India was referred to in passing in the previous chapters. In peace-time many British Army units spent years on garrison duties in Indian towns or in the defence of its frontiers and from many points of view the whole organisation of the British Army was governed by the needs of India. The Army in India comprised the Indian Army and the British Army in India under the administrative and operational control of the Commander-in-Chief of the Indian Army. The Indian Army consisted of units raised in India and, at least in the early part of the century, it was composed of Indian other ranks with British and Indian officers. British officers held the King's, or Queen's, Commission. Indian officers came almost exclusively from the ranks and held the Viceroy's Commission.

The Indian Army grew out of the armed guards raised by the East India Company and, for reasons based in the manner in which the Company was formed and grew, was to all intents and purposes three armies in the mid years of the nineteenth century. The three armies were those of the Presidencies of Bengal, Bombay and Madras and in addition there were several quasi-independent forces such as the Punjab Frontier Force and the Hyderabad Contingent. The Presidency armies were combined in 1895 but a complete reorganisation was delayed until after Kitchener was appointed C-in-C on the conclusion of the Boer War.

The principal strategic threat to India was long seen to lie on the North-west Frontier where a weak Afghanistan formed a buffer against the encroachment of Russia. The re-activation of this threat in 1900 was extensively examined in London and Calcutta, the two headquarters taking differing views on the location of possible attack as well as the most effective means of countering it. Associated issues involved both the size of reinforcement Britain could provide and the time it would take to arrive.[1] In 1907 the signing of a Convention between Britain and Russia settled most outstanding differences, for the time being, but the threat had meanwhile provided a background for an Indian Army reorganisation.

The objective of the reorganisation was to form a force of nine field divisions in place of an army which, in Kitchener's view, was intended to hold India against the Indians.[2] The basis of the reorganisation was the formation of two Armies, Northern and Southern, divided into divisional districts which had a peace-time training and internal security role and which, on mobilisation, would divide to produce a field division which would leave behind the internal security units. Each of the divisional areas included a cavalry brigade or units to form one. In addition to the nine divisions there was also a Burma Division providing the garrison of that country, at present administered from India. Economic considerations imposed themselves on the scheme in that by 1913 only six divisions and six cavalry brigades were fully equipped for war.[3] It was proposed that the British troops should be brigaded separately since this would simplify supply arrangements but the idea was rejected and a British unit remained included in each brigade.

As a part of the reorganisations the Indian units were re-numbered in one line from 1903. At the same time a number of units were disbanded, particularly in Madras, and re-formed with what were considered more martial classes of men.

The concept of martial castes and classes is a complex one which has long been inherent in Hinduism. In British experience the concept was reinforced by the Mutiny after which classes and groups, such as the Sikhs and Gurkhas, who had fought for the British were favoured and others not. In post-Mutiny reorganisations units were formed or re-formed on a class-company basis partly to provide a counter-weight of one group against another. In the context of the Indian Army the martial class concept was reinforced and refined by the recruiting systems in use. Although the classes for a battalion or regiment were officially specified, recruiting was in the hands of the unit itself which would send out recruiting parties made up of NCOs and other ranks who would inevitably seek recruits from their own villages and clans, thus narrowing still further the range from which recruits were drawn. The process was one with great merits in a peace-time army, contributing at its best to the maintenance of a good spirit within a unit and providing an intrinsic discipline.[4] The implication of the class system was that each unit had its own individual composition. 25 Cavalry, for example, had a squadron each of Sikhs, Dogras and Punjabi Mussalmans and half-squadrons of Hindustani Mussalmans and Pathans. 9 Bhopal Infantry had two companies each of Rajputs, Sikhs, Brahmans and Mussalmans. On mobilisation each unit formed its own small depot to train and draft recruits but the re-placement of wastage in a long campaign was likely to be difficult since not only had numbers to be replaced but also they had to be of appropriate classes and ranks. The creation of reserves was also difficult in that enlistment was for twenty-one years with the option of serving another four to qualify for a pension.

The cavalry had its own replacement problems in that, except in Madrassi regiments, enlistment was under the 'sillidari' system under which each man provided his own horse and equipment or, more usually, purchased them from the regiment. Although recruiting for the cavalry was popular, and demanded men of some substance to make the initial investment, it was not a system likely to ensure efficient replacement of men or horses during an arduous campaign. Most cavalry regiments of the period possessed exten-sive commercial interests such as stud and forage farms to satisfy their domestic needs.[5]

The possibility of Indian troops reinforcing the Expeditionary Force in France was mentioned to the Committee of Imperial Defence in 1911 but it does not appear that any planning was undertaken to effect that. In the following year an Army in India Committee was set up under Field Marshal Nicholson to consider whether measures to reduce military expenditure were compatible with the army's possible obligations in the next few years. In a Majority Report the roles of the Indian Army were defined as being internal security, frontier defence against the tribes and adjoining states and defence against an attack from a major power, such as Russia, until reinforcement could arrive from Britain. For these purposes a field force of seven divisions and five cavalry brigades would be sufficient. It was not the duty of the Government of India to maintain forces out of Indian revenues to serve overseas in excess of those needed for self defence. It was, however, conceded that in some great Imperial emergency risks might have to be run in local defence in order to support the forces operating in the decisive theatre. The Minority Report was more pessimistic about defence of the frontiers, recommending that a further two divisions would be needed. The Majority Report was accepted as a basis for discussion but the fundamental assumptions on the role of the Indian Army remained that it should be organised and equipped solely for frontier warfare.[6]

In July 1913 the Army Council enquired as to what assistance India could provide in the event of war in Europe. The Government of India replied on 30th July 1914 that two divisions and a cavalry brigade could be sent and that this could be increased by another division at some risk to India. The reply was not received until after the war had started.[7]

In August 1914 the Indian Army consisted of thirty-nine cavalry regiments and 118 infantry battalions plus twenty battalions of Gurkha Rifles. Eight battalions were on garrison duties outside India. The Army was complete with supporting arms, except that the artillery was confined to twelve Mountain Batteries. All other artillery was British. Battalion establishments were significantly smaller than their British counterparts, comprising thirteen British and seventeen Indian officers with 723 other ranks. The strength of the Indian Army was just over 240,000, including reserves (see Table 3.1).[8]

The auxiliary forces in India were quite considerable although only a proportion could be made available for service overseas. There were, for example, eleven regiments of volunteer horse and forty-two volunteer infantry units, 40,000 men in all. These were mainly composed of men in supervisory positions in civil life who. could ill be spared but they were available for internal security duties in emergency. Other forces, also unavailable, were the 34,000 men of the frontier militias and military police.

The largest useful section of the auxiliary forces was that found from the Indian States. These were the armies of the independent or quasi-independent States of India. In the past their rulers had often offered their private armies for Government service and the system was regularised in the Imperial Service Troops scheme of 1888. Under this, specific units were earmarked for Imperial purposes and organised to Indian Army establishments. In 1914 the strength of

Table 3.1   Strength of the Indian Army, 1914

British Officers	2,333
Reserve of Officers	40
Indian all ranks – serving	159,134
reservists	34,767
non-combatants	45,660
TOTAL	241,934

Source: *India's Contribution to the Great War*, Govt. of India, Calcutta, 1923, pp. 79–80.
Statistics of the Military Effort of the British Empire, H.M.S.O., 1922, p. 777.

the Imperial Service troops was 22,613 and twenty mounted regiments and thirteen battalions were ultimately offered for service.[9]

ii   *Two years of war*

At the extraordinary Council of War in London on 5th and 6th August it had been decided that the Indian Government would be asked to provide two divisions for Egypt and on the 8th 3 and 7 Divisions were ordered to mobilise together with a cavalry brigade. The strength was, thus, that envisaged in the Indian Government's letter of 30th July. The Divisions mobilised to the standard Indian establishment, that is to say each comprised three brigades of four battalions. Divisional troops included a cavalry regiment – a British division had a squadron – and a pioneer battalion, a type of unit which was not added to British divisions until 1915. The strength of a division was about 13,000 and, due to smaller infantry establishments and a weaker artillery, was significantly smaller than a comparable British division.

Even before the Expeditionary Force embarked its destination had been changed to Marseilles and further calls were being made on the Indian Government for units to relieve colonial garrisons, another brigade for service in Egypt, enlargement of the force sent to Europe and preparation of a force to attack Tanga in East Africa. Increasing tension with Turkey was also causing anxiety and on 25th August the Admiralty recommended the preparation of an expedition at Karachi to defend oil installations at Abadan.[10] India was being called upon to provide forces for a multitude of purposes far exceeding those for which the Indian Army was said to be maintained. In fact at this stage of the war the Indian Army was being used as an Imperial Reserve to meet contingencies as they arose.

Taking the force in Europe first, this arrived in France in September and October and it is a commentary on the equipment state of the Expeditionary Force that it had to be re-equipped with up-to-date patterns of rifle and to improvise a transport service before being able to proceed to the Front.[11]

To follow these formations 6 Division and 1 Cavalry Division were ordered to mobilise on 6th September and when 6 Division was diverted to Mesopotamia it was replaced by cavalry brigades to complete 2 Cavalry Division. The two cavalry divisions arrived in France before the end of 1914.

Two infantry brigades and other units mobilised for service in East Africa and took part in the abortive attack on Tanga on 3rd November. Thereafter the Indian troops in East Africa were kept up to about divisional strength, suffering badly from disease and a waste on India's resources, until the end of 1917.

In view of the continuing deterioration of relations with Turkey, on 26th September it was decided that 6 Division would be retained in India for the time being to "demonstrate at the head of the Persian Gulf".[12] The leading brigade left Bombay on 16th October and, war with Turkey having commenced in the meantime, the rest of the Division followed in November. Thus another major campaign commenced.

The decisions to send the IEF on to Europe and relieve the British garrison in Egypt by 42 Territorial Division and an Indian brigade represented but an intermediate stage in the demands being made upon India for troops. By the middle of October forces earmarked for Egypt included two brigades of Indian State Forces troops, the Bikaner Camel Corps, three improvised Indian brigades and eight battalions.[13] These troops arrived in Egypt in mid-November when they were formed into 10 and 11 Indian Divisions. With the repulse of the Turkish attack on the Suez Canal, the growth of Australian and New Zealand forces in Egypt and the decision to open the Gallipoli campaign the Indian Army concentration in Egypt was not maintained for long. In March 1915 a brigade was sent to Mesopotamia, the next month another went to Gallipoli and then a third went to Aden before going on to Mesopotamia, as did many other units.

The months of August and September 1914 were marked by a succession of demands upon India to send troops to, almost, all quarters of the globe. One more call remains to be recorded. On 17th September the War Secretary asked that thirty-nine of the fourty-two British battalions then remaining in India should be exchanged for Territorial units from home.[14] The Government of India, however, felt that they must retain the nine battalions required for the divisions on the North-west Frontier and these wishes were respected. One of the battalions went to Mesopotamia early in 1915 to leave eight in India for the remainder of the War.

In contrast to the British Army of 1914 the Indian was not required to provide major colonial garrisons and battalions in India were nominally at full strength. The Indian Army Reserve was known to have short-comings but should not have been needed at the mobilisation stage. Battalions mobilised at a strength of 753 all ranks and were to embark with ten per cent reinforcements. The need to mobilise some 830 all ranks proved difficult for many units and complements could only be filled by drawing on related units. For example 57 Wilde's Rifles, mobilising for 3 Division, received three Indian Officers and 169 other ranks from 55 Coke's Rifles. 9 Bhopal Infantry, also for 3 Division, needed 52 men from 17 Infantry and 111 from 89 Punjabis. Even units as popular as the Gurkhas were under strength and 2/8 Gurkha Rifles, mobilising for 7 Division, needed 3 Gurkha Officers and 120 other ranks from 1/3 Gurkhas.[15] It would appear that even to mount the various expeditionary forces provided a major task, which did not augur well for the future.

Once the Indian Corps had arrived in France and taken its place in the front line the continuous drain of casualties commenced, adding to the drain of sickness induced by fighting a winter campaign. By the beginning of January 1915 5250 reinforcements had been received by the Corps and not only was this number inadequate but, even more alarming, 876 of them had been found to be unfit for service. Out of a sample of 331 of the unfit, 85% were unfit due to old age, poor physique or on medical grounds, all of them causes which could easily had been established in India before the reinforcements were sent.[16] Even at this early stage the Indian Army's reserve system had broken down and for the future

only hand-to-mouth expedients were left. To relieve heavily depleted battalions others were drawn from the Mediterranean and
from as far afield as Hong Kong and North China. Drafts were
found from the units left in India. For the battalions left in France
the result of these measures was to erode the internal structure of
the units. Once the class structure of the companies was damaged
by the introduction of men of differing classes and clans the morale
of a battalion was damaged and its fighting ability reduced. How
mixed a battalion could become is indicated by an example drawn
from 9 Bhopal Infantry which in May 1915 mustered three double-
companies as follows:

1 – Sikhs from the parent unit and from 21 Punjabis. Rajputs from
4 and 16 Rajputs.
2 – Mussalmans from the parent and from 17 and 18 Infantry and 19
Punjabis.
3 – Rajputs from 11 Rajputs. Brahmins from 1 Brahmins and
89 Punjabis. Others from 8 Rajputs, 89 Punjabis and 96 Infantry.[17]

From early in 1915 drafting from battalions in India was mainly
in the form of complete companies which reduced the worst effects
of class mixing. In the battalions which received them the mixture
of drafts and sub-units which had not trained together was not the
way to rebuild an effective fighting unit. How wide the net was cast
to find drafts is indicated by 39 Garhwal Rifles which received a
draft of two Indian Officers and ninety-six other ranks from the
Tehri Garhwal Field Company, an Indian States Forces engineer
unit, and 240 other ranks from the Burma Military Police.[18] It was
against this background that it was decided at the end of 1915 to
withdraw the Indian Corps from France. The destination of the
Corps was Egypt, where it was hoped that the formation would be
able to recuperate, but the crisis in Mesopotamia resulted in
transfer there where, apart from climate, similar conditions to those
in France obtained. The two Indian cavalry divisions, rarely
engaged and without the drafting problems of the infantry,
remained in France until March 1918 when they were transferred
to Egypt and reformed as 4 and 5 Cavalry Divisions for the final
campaign in Palestine.

To meet the demand for drafts for France and Mesopotamia the
battalions in India to all intents and purposes transformed themselves into a training organisation and three divisions (5, 8 and 9)

were so reduced as to be only available for internal security. Fortunately, for the first eighteen months of the War the Frontier was quiet and no major expeditions were called for. Before the end of 1914 battalions in India began forming additional companies as and when recruits were available and during 1915 this procedure became widespread.[19] What drafting meant to a battalion in India may be illustrated by 82 Punjabis which sent off six British and thirteen Indian Officers and 667 other ranks before mobilising for Mesopotamia early in 1916.[20] It was not until a lull in the various campaigns in 1916 that the Indian Army was able to attempt any expansion at all. Although levels of recruiting remained high, with nearly 200,000 men entering in 1914/16, the energies of the Army in India were directed solely to maintaining the forces already placed in the field and that at the low unit establishments already referred to.

The problems of finding troops in India were highlighted towards the end of 1915 by the need to find a relieving force for 6 Division, then beseiged at Kut. To form an additional division for the relieving force twelve garrison battalions were sent out from Britain to free other troops for the division. Thus a process of relieving Territorial troops in India was commenced, freeing them for service in more active theatres.[21]

The entry of Turkey into the War provided problems more than the simple addition of one to the list of enemies. The Sultan of Turkey had been the Khalif of Islam, the successor to the Prophet. Operations against the Turkish Empire could well bring war to the vicinity of Muslim holy places. On 14th November 1914 the Sultan proclaimed a Jihad, or Holy War, on all making war on Turkey and her allies. All of this created disquiet in India and it was difficult to foresee what would be the response of the Indian Army with its significant proportion of Mohammedan troops. Fears in India were compounded by the possibility that a Jihad would combine the Frontier tribes and Afghanistan with a rising within India itself.[22] This fear was to be a continuing one, accompanied by desertions of soldiers from trans-Frontier tribes, until the Afghanistan War of 1919. So far as the Indian Army overseas was concerned some desertions occurred on the Suez Canal but the general effect of the proclamation was small. The most serious events took place in areas far from the war zones. A mutiny of a company of 130 Baluchis took place in Rangoon in December 1914 and a much more serious affair took place in Singapore two months later, when four companies of 5 Light Infantry were involved. Although Muslim soldiers took part in these events and the war with Turkey was a factor, in both battalions domestic mismanagement was also an issue and the reasons for the outbreaks were complex. Some desertions took place in France, the largest probably being that of an Indian Officer and fourteen men from 58 Rifles. Here of course the factors included all of the features of trench warfare, together with the breakdown of the class structure of the units. In sum the events were small but they were sufficient to cause uncertainty about the reliability of some units of the Indian Army. The Commander in Gallipoli decided that it was unsafe to employ two battalions of his Indian brigade so near to Constantinople, since they included Muslims, and they were transferred to France, being replaced by Gurkha battalions.

iii   *The period of expansion*

1916 opened unfavourably with 6 Division shut up in Kut and with the remainder of the British and Indian troops in Mesopotamia, including 3 and 7 Divisions, attempting to relieve it. In April the garrison surrendered and active operations ceased in that theatre for some months. Wastage was therefore considerably reduced and a breathing space given to restore an organisation which was breaking down. In 3 and 7 Divisions few battalions had more than 400 men, some much less than that.[23]

On mobilisation each unit departing for the front had left behind a small depot to train recruits but in practice, in 1914 and 1915, the depots had been unable to meet the demand and the main source of drafts had become related battalions and regiments. No formal training schemes were apparently issued but training must have been rudimentary if one considers the example of 82 Punjabis, already quoted, which in a little over a year sent off drafts equal to its original strength and then itself went to war. From 1916 the depots were able to take over more of their proper function, assisted by ad hoc groupings of the depots of related regiments. From the end of 1916 it became possible to replace the units lost at Kut and to undertake a modest expansion. General Monro, newly appointed Commander-in-Chief, India, ordered the formation of sixteen new battalions shortly after taking up his appointment in

November 1916. New units were formed by creating duplicates of existing ones, based on cadres provided either by the parent or by the regimental depot. Indeed at a later stage of the expansion the cadres were provided by any unit or units of similar composition. Thereafter the unit would complete with recruits, training being a unit responsibility. Before new Gurkha battalions could be formed permission had to be obtained from Nepal since recruiting there was governed by treaty. This was not the only assistance given by Nepal. Ten battalions of the Nepalese Army were provided for internal security duties in India from January 1916, the last of which did not return to Nepal until March 1920.

It was not until the end of 1916 that positive steps to stimulate recruiting were taken by improving service conditions and rates of pay. Service conditions changes included the rationing of troops, who had hitherto provided for themselves when not on active service. The civil authorities were brought into the recruiting system through the creation of a joint Central Recruiting Board which, with subordinate provincial boards, was to coordinate recruiting taking account of the requirements of industry. About 11,750 combatants and 8250 non-combatants were required each month simply to replace wastage and the Board was to devise schemes and to distribute quotas to meet present and future needs.[24]

One of the bigger difficulties in the expansion of the Indian Army, and indeed simply in the replacement of wastage, was in the provision of officers. At the outbreak of war the establishment of officers was 2586 and those who were in the United Kingdom in 1914 were taken for the New Armies. Attempts were made in 1915 and 1916 to secure the return of as many as possible but the requirements far exceeded the number who might be returned. Steps had to be taken locally to recruit and train in India officers who, in addition to their military duties, had to speak the languages of their men and have some knowledge of their social usages. Some of the shortage was made up through secondment from the British forces in India, including the Territorial Force, and by commissioning other ranks but about two-thirds of the 9493 Indian Army commissions granted during the war went to members of the British community in India.[25]

On 2nd February 1917 a Registration Ordinance required the registration of all British males in India between the ages of sixteen and fifty and on 21st February an Indian Defence Force Bill was introduced. This made all British males aged 16–18 liable for military training, while those aged 18–41 were deemed to have been enrolled for general service in India with those 41–50 enrolled for local military service. The volunteer forces were reorganised as the Indian Defence Force with an internal security role to free a greater proportion of the British garrison in India for overseas service. A further enactment in the autumn of 1918 would have made men under forty-one liable for overseas service or for direction to industrial employment, a stricter requirement than that applied in Britain, but the Act was not enforced.[26]

On 28th March 1917 the Secretary of State for India telegraphed the Viceroy enquiring what additional effort India could make towards the campaigns of 1918 and speaking of the relief of British troops in India, Egypt and Mesopotamia and the possible employment of Indian troops in France. In a reply on 11th April the Viceroy said that India would raise twenty-three new battalions, modifying this on 8th May to the raising of two new divisions.[27] This exchange of signals heralded a considerable increase in the size of the Indian Army as can be seen in Figure 3.1. Considerably enhanced recruitment was needed and it is apparent that there was a considerable revision of attitudes as to what were or what were not 'martial classes'. The traditional 'martial classes' were already heavily recruited and by the middle of 1917 63,000 Punjabi Mussalmans had been recruited out of an estimated 145,000 who were fit for service and 43,500 out of 112,000 Sikhs.[28] Newly formed units included a number fresh to the Indian establishment such as 49 Bengalis, 111 Mahars and 71 Punjab Christian Battalion. Recruiting was also commenced in Burma. Formation of such new units was particularly difficult because of the lack of NCOs and Indian Officers of the right classes. Much of the expansion, though, was through the formation of second battalions of existing units although it was frequently not found possible to duplicate in the second the structure of the parent. 9 Bhopal Infantry with a company each of Sikhs, Brahmans, Rajputs and Mussalmans had a second battalion with Ahirs, Gujars, Hindustani Mussalmans and Jats and third and fourth battalions with different compositions again. Nor was it always possible for existing regiments to retain their original composition when this was heavily dependent on the more popular classes. 36 Sikhs had, for

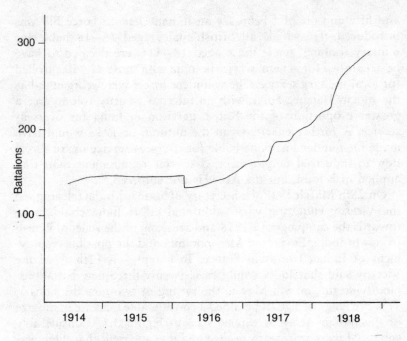

Figure 3.1. Indian Infantry Battalions: 1914–18. Sources: IO/L/MIL/17/5/ 851–913. Indian unit histories.

example, to change one of its Sikh companies for one of Jats.[29] The complexities of Indian recruiting are illustrated by the official record which is divided into forty different classes plus 38,000 recruits who are merely referred to as 'other Hindus' and 4000 'other Mussalmans'.

Concurrently with the 1917 expansions a belated increase was made in battalion establishments which became 992 all ranks. Embarkation strengths, including first reinforcements, were usually about 1030.

In spite of all difficulties the overall response by recruits was favourable and by July 1917 the Government of India was able to propose raising a further twenty-one battalions as a reserve against future demands. The two new divisions proposed in May began to assemble in Mesopotamia from August and by December a third new division was being contemplated.[30] These events were overtaken by the increasing British manpower crisis and on 4th December the transfer of an Indian division from Mesopotamia to Egypt was ordered to permit the release of a British formation. The same day the CIGS telegraphed to India for Indian units to replace British in the formations in Egypt. Fundamental issues concerning priorities in the war against Turkey were also being considered at this time with the eventual decision going in favour of concentrating effort in Palestine. As a consequence of this decision orders were issued to transfer a second Indian division from Mesopotamia to Egypt.[31]

The German successes of March 1918 induced a need to accelerate the 'Indianisation' process foreshadowed in December. The units available for this process were the twenty-one forming as a result of the decisions in July but these were, in the main, not yet ready. To provide the necessary number of units recourse was had to expedients. Twenty-two battalions were formed by taking a company or half-company from Indian units in Egypt and Mesopotamia, the donors being completed with drafts from India. Thus, 1/150 Infantry was formed with a company each from 2, 4, 8 and 13 Rajputs, and so on. A similar process was used to form six additional cavalry regiments required for service in India. Here the drain on the resources of units in active theatres of war was not so severe since the extra squadrons needed could often be found from the depots. When at a later stage it was proposed to 'Indianise' the British divisions in Salonika the units needed were found by reducing divisions in Mesopotamia from twelve to nine battalions. This step was taken in September 1918 and the unis were just arriving in their new theatre at the end of the war. This was to be but an intermediate stage for in India there were proposals to raise another sixty-seven battalions to complete the Salonika 'Indianisation' and to reform the single British division in Mesopotamia.[32]

Between the beginning of 1917 and the end of the war the Indian Army just about doubled in size, a very large expansion considering the social and economic background against which the expansion was taking place. Indeed the quality of the Army was now giving grounds for concern, not on account of its inherent qualities but on grounds of lack of training and experience. This was especially apparent in Egypt but the force was relatively well fed, well supplied and in good health and opposed by an exhausted, poorly supplied and discouraged enemy.

If the British Army in France had a great need for labour, the

Indian Army in the Middle East and Mesopotamia had even greater needs. For Mesopotamia, on 19th October 1918 the ration strength was over 414,000 but of these only 217,000 were in combatant and administrative units. Of the remainder, 71,000 were in the Labour Corps and 42,000 in the Inland Water Transport. The majority of the followers were Indian but, in addition to local recruits, there were men from China, Mauritius and the West Indies. The Order of Battle for that date shows such unmilitary units as Grass and Dairy Farms and a Detachment, Madras Gardeners. In Egypt and Palestine the ration strength of 458,000 on 1st November included 152,000 followers.

The principal Indian non-combatant units were in Labour, Porter and Syce Corps. Individuals were recruited for these Corps for six, nine or twelve months at a time so there was a considerable turnover of personnel. Total recruitment was 445,600 to the end of the War and there were 391,033 embarkations for overseas.

No overall figures for the strength of the Indian Army appear to have survived. 826,855 combatants were recruited by the Armistice, whilst 552,311 all ranks embarked for service overseas. Table 3.2 gives establishments for 1914 and 1918. In November 1918 the infantry strength, in anticipation of expansion, was 520,000 out of a total strength of 573,484. In addition there were 48,806 Imperial Service troops of whom 26,099 were overseas.[33]

iv Retrospect: 1914–18

The role of the Indian Army from 1914 to 1918 was to form an Imperial strategic reserve, a role for which it was unfitted by equipment, state of preparedness and, above all, by attitude, believing itself only to exist for defence against local threat and for internal security.[34] In addition to the reserve role the Indian Government and Army for eighteen months conducted a major campaign in a minor theatre, Mesopotamia, a role for which it simply did not have the resources. The world-wide nature of the commitments which the Indian Army acquired is illustrated by the travels of 40 Pathans which began the war in Hong Kong, served in France in 1915, moved to East Africa and finished up on the North-west Frontier.[35]

What the war clearly indicated was that the Army did not have an effective reserve and training system. Virtually until the end of

Table 3.2   Indian Army establishments, combatant arms

	August 1914	November 1918
Artillery	10,457	52,410
Cavalry	25,727	33,650
Engineers	4,802	17,518
Signals	352	7,733
Infantry	151,915	437,000
TOTALS	193,253	548,311

Source: *India's Contribution to the Great War*, p. 278.

1916 the principal problem of the Army was one of survival and in attempting to keep in the field such forces as had been placed there it came very close to destroying itself. The ease with which, from a manpower point of view, the Army was able to expand once the opportunity arose gives a clue as to the expansion which might have been possible with a better basic organisation. At no time was the manpower capacity of India tapped, while the extension of recruiting to hitherto unconsidered classes was an illuminating experience that was only partly assimilated. In the post-war Army although the Garhwali was added to the list of 'martial classes' and Burmese were retained, in anticipation of separate status for Burma, recruiting of other war-time classes ceased.

The pattern of expansion of the Indian Army in no way repeated British experience. The Indian Army was still expanding at the end of the war and, indeed, the maximum expansion was not reached until 1919 when, with war against Afghanistan, it proved possible to form fourteen new brigades for the war in a week or two. The Indian Army was well placed to provide many of the post-war internal security and occupation forces and Indian units remained in Egypt and Turkey until 1922, in Palestine to 1923 and Mesopotamia until 1928, additional forces having to be found for the Iraq Rebellion of 1920.

What the war of 1914–18 did was to underline the ambiguous status of the Indian Army and, indeed, of India itself. Neither fully independent nor fully subordinate to London, India and the Army followed policies partly originating in India, partly in London, and with no clear responsibility or control of events. The climax of this divided policy control was witnessed in the events in and around Kut in 1916.

iv   *Between the wars*

For the Indian Army the Great War was a long time in finishing and substantial forces remained overseas well into the 1920s. In India, the Afghan War was followed by Frontier disturbances which lasted into 1921 but by December 1920 the situation was sufficiently stable to allow an internal reorganisation. The nine-division organisation was abandoned and replaced by a brigade system in which some had an internal security role only. Further reorganisations grouped the brigades into Districts, four of which had divisional status, but no field force as such was envisaged.

Major reforms in the fundamental structure and organisation of the Indian Army were reserved for the early 1920s and these broadly followed the recommendations of the Esher Committee in 1920. From 1922 infantry regiments were grouped into large regiments of half a dozen battalions, one of which was the regiment's training unit. An essential part of the organisation was that class composition had to be uniform within each of the regiment's battalions, that of 1 Punjab Regiment, for example, being a company each of Ranghars, Hindustani Mussalmans, Rajputs and Jats. As before, though, each regiment had its favourite recruiting grounds within the classes it was officially given.[36] Cavalry regiments were reduced from thirty-nine to twenty-one, loosely grouped in threes, but no training arm was really developed until 1937 when three regiments were given this role. The lateness of this reorganisation is an indicator of the strength of the belief that the cavalry still had a viable role.

Short-service enlistment was introduced from 1923 with recruits signing-on for from four to seven years depending on arm. Re-enlistment was permitted to complete fifteen years' service for a pension, with a Reserve for those not re-engaging. At the same time the cavalry's silladar system was done away with, when terms of service became the same as for other arms.

The Indian Territorial Force Act of 1920 announced the formation of a voluntary reserve to supplement the army. Territorials enlisted for six years with the possibility of extending for a further four. Initial training of one month with annual periods of one, later two, months were onerous conditions but the seventeen battalions seem to have had little trouble in reaching satisfactory strength. The TF was more popular in rural areas than urban and in 1928 a special effort was made to improve recruiting in the towns. Five battalions were formed but strengths remained weak and unstable. The Force was liable only for service in India.

As part of the reorganisations of the 1920s the former volunteer units which had become the Indian Defence Force were again reorganised into the Auxiliary Force (India). Liability was only for service within the province in which a unit was raised. At about the same time the forces of the Indian States were re-classified and an Indian States Forces scheme replaced the former Imperial Service Troops scheme. State forces were grouped into three classes of which Class A was equipped on the scale of the regular army.

On 20th August 1917 a statement was made in the House of Commons that the Government's policy was aimed at eventually granting responsible government to India. So far as the Indian Army was concerned this meant that, for at least some sectors of the Indian community, development should be in the direction of producing an army for an independent India and much of the debate of the 1920s and 1930s had this as a background. Initially much of this attention became focussed on the issue of granting Commissions to Indians. The first of these was granted in 1917 but, more importantly, from 1919 Indians were admitted to Sandhurst with ten places being reserved annually. Such officers would be commissioned into the British service and would be on the same footing as any other British officer.[37]

In March 1921 the Indian Legislative Assembly suggested that 25% of Indian Army Commissions should be offered to Indians, the percentage rising annually thereafter. However an Indianisation Committee set up in 1922 reported in favour of a scheme consisting of three stages each of fourteen years. In the first, twenty battalions and seven regiments of cavalry would be Indianised; in the second, forty battalions and seven regiments and in the last, the remainder. Commissions awarded would be for the Indian Army only and thus would be comparable with those awarded to officers in the land forces of the Dominions. The scheme was rejected but in February 1923 it was announced that two cavalry regiments and six battalions would be Indianised as a first step. Indians with the King's

Commission would be encouraged to transfer to these units and no more British officers would be posted. It is clear that the appointment of Indian officers caused considerable disquiet, mainly directed as to whether or not sufficient officers of the right qualities would come forward and also how they would be received by the men and by British-born officers who might not be prepared to serve under Indians. In the summer of 1921 Lord Rawlinson, the C-in-C, expressed the view that it would take thirty years to breed and train an officer class, later putting this as two or three generations.[38] Indeed many senior British officers looked upon the affair as a dubious experiment which was bound to fail.[39]

A Progress of Indianisation Committee of 1923 endorsed the concept of Sandhurst-trained officers but was concerned at the high wastage rates suffered by Indian cadets. The Skeen Committee of 1925 again looked at the supply of Indian officers and, pointing out that the number of Sandhurst places was in any case too low, recommended the establishment of an Indian Military Academy.[40] Following the publication of the report the number of Sandhurst places was increased to twenty with a further six at Woolwich. Many senior officers, including Lord Birdwood, the C-in-C, were opposed to the establishment of an Indian 'Sandhurst', believing that with an untried Indianisation experiment under way the foundation of such a college would be premature. However the proposal was revived during the meeting of the Indian Round Table Conference in 1930 and the Academy opened two years later. The original eight-units scheme was replaced by an enlarged version and the practice of granting Commissions in the British service to Indians ceased. In future Commissions awarded to Indians would be in His Majesty's Indian Land Forces only and these would amount to a third of the annual intake. The old Indian Officers, with Viceroy's Commissions, were henceforward known as Viceroy's Commissioned Officers.

Across the inter-war years there was a continuous debate as to what the proper role of the Indian Army was. The view of the Esher Committee was that the Army was part of the armed forces of the Empire as a whole but this was repudiated by the Indian Legislative Assembly which in March 1921 resolved that its role was one of defence against external aggression and the maintenance of internal security. These views were not incompatible but they were confused by debate as to where financial responsibility for the Army lay in its various roles and also by differences in view as to what the proper role of an army for a potentially independent country should be.[41] As in the pre-1907 period the greatest threat was seen to lie in a Russian advance through Afghanistan and a defence plan of 1927–28 envisaged a need for 250,000 reinforcements from Britain at an early stage. However by the early 1930s this threat was believed to have receded and attention turned again to India as a contributor to Imperial defence.

The first formal call on India to earmark forces for overseas in emergency came in September 1929 with a request for two brigades for the Iranian oilfields, with a third needed for other garrison duties in the Gulf. The case for India obtaining financial support for these, and other, duties was considered by the Garran Tribunal in 1933 when it was held that although the principal duty of the Indian Army revolved around India it had, in practice, an Imperial Reserve role and an annual grant was awarded in recognition of this. Indeed by 1936 external commitments had grown to a brigade each for Singapore, the Persian Gulf, the Red Sea and Burma. Later the same year a commitment to earmark two brigades for Egypt was accepted.[42]

The position of the Indian Army was again brought to the fore in February 1938 in a paper on the Organisation of the Army by the War Secretary, Hore-Belisha. In it, while noting that the largest part of the British Army overseas was located in India, he advocated that part of the Imperial strategic reserve should be east of the Mediterranean. Reorganisation of the Army in India was needed. A Committee was set up under Major-General Pownall to report on the defence problems of India and this, while recognising that India had a vital contribution to make to Imperial defence as a whole, acknowledged that India could not develop this contribution without assistance.[43]

A double-faceted movement was thus coming into view with a formalisation of the Indian Army's role in Imperial defence on the one hand and a modernisation of the Army on the other. A Modernisation Committee under Major-General Auchinleck reported in October 1938 and this body's conclusions were largely absorbed by those of the Chatfield Committee, reporting in June 1939. The Chatfield Report went into considerable detail in attempting to produce an economical modernisation programme. The traditional division of the Army in India was into a field army

for operations in Afghanistan, covering troops for tribal warfare on
the North-west Frontier and forces for internal security. In place of
this, troops were allocated for frontier defence, coast defence, internal security and external defence with a general reserve. The
Report included a detailed distribution of units and establishments
for the different types of unit. One of the features of the Pownall
Report was echoed in the support given for an Imperial Reserve
Division, although this was watered down by the reservation that
it need only be fit to operate in Asiatic theatres of war, charac-
terised as being theatres of great distances, poor communications
and with supply difficulties so that only small, mobile formations
were needed. Under the Chatfield distribution one British and three
Indian cavalry regiments and two British and fourteen Indian
battalions were surplus to requirements. These economies would,
across five years, allow for the modernisation of an Army which,
according to the Auchinleck Committee, was showing signs of
falling behind the forces of such states as Egypt, Iraq and
Afghanistan.[44]

The Chatfield Report was accepted by the Cabinet and published
on 5th September 1939. £34 millions would be allocated for the
modernisation programme. But the war had already begun.

v *The expansion programmes*

On 1st October 1939 the strength of the Indian Army was 194,373,
including 34,515 non-combatants, and comprised eighteen cavalry
regiments and 96 infantry battalions. Approximate strengths of the
other forces in India were:

Frontier Irregular Forces	15,000
Auxiliary Force (India)	22,000
Territorial Force	19,000
Indian States Forces	53,00C

Class A ISF units included four cavalry regiments and seven
infantry battalions. In addition to these forces there were four
battalions of Assam Rifles and two other Military Police battalions.

Shortly before the outbreak of war one brigade reinforced the
British garrison in Egypt and another went to Malaya, while in
October a second brigade was sent to Egypt where the two were
grouped as 4 Division. Reservists were recalled to duty on a regi-

mental and corps basis between September 1939 and June 1940. On the outbreak of war the seventeen Territorial battalions were embodied to relieve the troops of 4 Division which had gone overseas and these were supplemented by the arrival of the first ISF contingents in British India and, in March 1940, by the arrival of two Nepalese Brigades. With these additional forces in hand the Indian Government was able to offer two additional brigades for the Middle East with a divisional headquarters (5 Division), as well as to offer another brigade for Burma. As yet no expansion of the army was envisaged, in part due to the lack of equipment but also pending clarification of the complex financial liabilities of expansion. Settlement of the financial questions was completed in February 1940 but the equipment question was more difficult. With India's limited industrialisation Britain must be the principal supplier but there, too, equipment shortages were a limiting factor. So far as the mechanisation of the army was concerned India was dependent on the United States, for the main motor vehicle plants in the country were American-owned, but here the British shortage of dollars added its own limitations. Thus, although the period of the Chatfield reforms was reduced to two years this was likely to be more apparent than real.

In May 1940 a plan to support Afghanistan against Russian attack was submitted to the Secretary of State for India. This envisaged the formation of one armoured and five infantry divisions over the next twelve months. The plan was approved before the end of the month and at the same time the Government of India indicated that it would be prepared to allow these forces to go overseas if Britain would provide the necessary equipment and would finance replacement divisions for Indian defence. In the first instance four of the divisions were accepted, one for Malaya and three for Iraq, and India became committed to a second phase of expansion. 3 Motor Brigade of the armoured division was to be prepared for the Middle East but the remainder of the armoured division was not accepted because of equipment difficulties. The divisions were expected to be ready May–December 1941. The attitude of Japan was also causing concern and in the autumn of 1940 two brigades with an improvised divisional headquarters (11) were sent to Malaya.

The five infantry divisions formed in 1940 were numbered 6–10 and the units to form them were found by drawing on Regular battalions in India which were then replaced by Territorial or ISF troops or by forming new battalions. The units for 31 Armoured Division already existed, some of them still horsed, and in October outline planning commenced for a second armoured division although this might involve the creation of additional units or the use of State Forces troops.[45]

The method used to form the new units was to draw cadres of trained men from related units in the country which were then, with the new unit, completed with trained and partially trained men from that arm's training organisation. For example 8 Frontier Force Rifles was formed in August 1940 with two or three VCOs and 100–115 other ranks from each of the 1, 2, 4 and 5 Battalions of that Regiment plus 230 other ranks from 10 Battalion, the training unit.[46] War establishment was 773 all ranks. Although this procedure was one likely to produce effective new battalions in a relatively short time it was at the expense of reducing the effectiveness of the battalions drawn upon, particularly when more than one new battalion was formed at a time. The units drawn upon were said to have been 'milked'. The number of battalions grew rapidly (Figure 3.2) although recruiting had to be extended to hitherto unfavoured districts in the traditional recruiting areas.[47]

The ear-marking of four of the new divisions for service overseas and their replacement by new formations was accompanied by a revision of the Defence of India Plan in March 1941 which envisaged five divisions and a heavy armoured brigade for Frontier defence. The 1941 expansion plan thus encompassed five new infantry divisions (14, 17, 19, 20 and 34), an armoured division (32) and an armoured brigade (50). Of these formations 50 Armoured Brigade was formed from units sent out from the United Kingdom, as was mentioned in Chapter 2. In view of the later employment of these formations it is interesting to observe how that employment came almost as an after-thought. The reason for their formation was the defence of the North-west Frontier which continued to be a pre-occupation even after Germany's invasion of Russia. The prospective enemy to be faced on the Frontier had by then become Germany itself – if they ever got so far.[48]

Under the 1941 expansion plan some fifty new battalions were needed. In addition to the units for the five divisions there were increasing demands for battalions for lines of communication and garrison duties, the guarding of prisoners of war in India alone

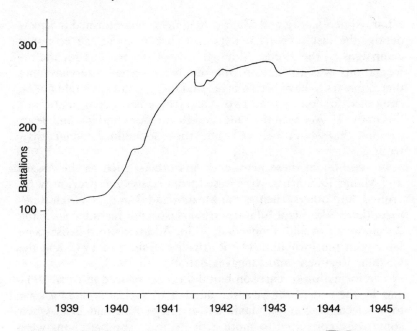

Figure 3.2. Indian Infantry Battalions: 1939–45. Sources: IO/L/MIL/17/5/ 1087–1111 and 1455–80. Indian unit histories.

requiring fourteen battalions. In general the same methods of expansion were used as in the 1940 programme, with the 1940 battalions themselves being called upon for contribution. Drafts tended to be smaller, though, being usually of thirty or forty men. On the donating units the effects were cumulative, however, and 2 Frontier Force Regiment posted away thirty-seven Officers and 385 other ranks between July 1940 and embarking for Malaya in March 1941. By December 1941 this battalion had only 121 other ranks with over a year of post-recruit service.

Towards the end of 1941 the Territorial battalions had been embodied for two years and the decision was taken to reform them, together with the duplicates which had been formed for some units, into general service units. All ranks were given the option of accepting regular liability, limited liability for service in India only, disembodiment or discharge. Response was very variable but in general over 50% of personnel agreed to stay on. Usually Territorial units re-formed as battalions of their parent regiments but the

Bihar, Ajmer, Coorg and Madras Regiments were formed independently, the last reviving a Regiment disbanded in the economy campaigns of the 1920s. Although one of the reasons for the reformations was to increase the number of general-service units there appears to have been a belief that the Territorials could not be embodied for longer than two years. There is no confirmation of this in the TF Act or in the Rules and Regulations and it could be an example that what is believed to be true is sometimes stronger than truth itself.

In addition to these new regiments others, such as the Assam and Mahar Regiments, were raised from classes not previously recruited, and others, such as the Mazhbi and Ramdassia Sikh Regiment (later Sikh Light Infantry) from classes not recruited since the disbandment of Sikh Pioneers in 1933. Additions to this list came later with the formation of the Afridi Battalion in 1942 and the Chamar Regiment and Lingayat Battalion in 1943.

The formation of garrison battalions commenced in April 1941 and by the end of the year the number of such units had grown to nineteen, reaching a maximum of forty-six in mid-1943 when some were converted to more active status. The battalions were formed individually to meet specific needs as these were seen at the time and some were formed for service in India only. Thus, if later required for overseas service, men had to be persuaded to extend their liability and cross-posting became necessary to complete establishments. Recruits were found from pensioners, other ex-soldiers, lower medical category men and those aged over twenty-six, too old for normal enlistment.

The conversion of cavalry regiments to complete 31 and 32 Armoured Divisions and the need to train regiments in the role of divisional cavalry demanded a re-casting of the training organisation and the three training regiments were converted into an Indian Armoured Corps Training Centre and an Armoured Car School. As was forecast in 1940, additional armoured units were required to complete establishments and in the first half of 1941 seven new regiments were formed by 'milking' the old cavalry regiments.

Equipment shortages continued to be a limiting factor throughout 1941. With the closing of the Mediterranean to through traffic an Eastern Group Supply Council was set up in March 1941 to co-ordinate purchases, allocate supplies and promote the manufacture of weapons in the Commonwealth countries around the Indian and Pacific Oceans. Some degree of specialisation was agreed between the various countries but development was likely to be slow and Britain remained the main source of supply. Allocations to what was then an inactive theatre held low priority and by October 1941 even to complete the 1940 programme India had received only 36% of her needs for field artillery, 19% for Bren-guns and 11% for mortars.[49] On 11st September Wavell drew the attention of the Cabinet to India's deficiencies, warning against the political consequences if Indian troops now abroad suffered disaster through lack of equipment.[50]

The formation of units in the technical arms was a particular difficulty in that India was fundamentally an agricultural country with an absolute lack of men with mechanical skills. The Indian Army reflected this in being an unmodernised force, lacking technical training facilities and adequate cadres from which an expansion could flow. If skilled men were in short supply, skilled instructors were even more so, particularly instructors who could teach in the language of the recruits. This was a problem which became acute when recruiting was extended to classes not previously considered. In the artillery, for example, pre-war recruiting was largely confined to Punjabi Mussalmans and Sikhs and the extension of recruiting to such classes as Madrassis, Rajputs and Mahrattas produced considerable problems of communication between trainers and trainees. In units formed from the new classes recruits lacked the experience necessary to become NCOs and Viceroy's Commissioned Officers and these places had to be filled by members of the old classes, causing a lot of ill feeling.

The 1941 expansion was not allowed to proceed without considerable interruption as the war situation developed. In the spring 9 Division had to be sent to Malaya. A brigade was sent to Burma in March, followed by another later in the year, while a crisis in Iraq caused the diversion of one of 9 Division's brigades to that country in April. The Iraqi commitment was compounded later in the year by the occupation of Persia and by September three infantry divisions and the first elements of 31 Armoured Division were in the Persian Gulf area. These widespread commitments were fulfilled by drawing on the larger part of the 1940-programme formations before they had completed their training and was accompanied by the disruption, in part, of the 1941 expansion plan. With the German advances into Russia and the possibility of a break-through to the Caucasus, Iraq and Persia became a major preoccupation. It was decided to create a base for ten divisions in Iraq as well as to develop a supply route to Russia through Persia. India suggested that the force should be reduced to six infantry divisions and an armoured division, forces which could be supplied from India by April 1942 if they could be equipped in time. Indeed anxieties about possible German successes in Russia persisted into early 1943 and repeated attempts were made to find reinforcements for the area.[51]

With the 1941-programme divisions earmarked for Iraq, India was committed to a further stage of expansion in 1942 when it was proposed to raise 23, 25, 28 and 36 Divisions and 43 Armoured Division. This programme was largely frustrated by the successes of Japan in the latter part of 1941 and 1942 and, in the event, 28 Division was not formed, the units intended for it going to reconstruct divisions shattered in the fighting. 36 Division was constructed from British brigades which had reached India. A division was improvised for the local defence of Calcutta and this became 26 Division in May 1942. In terms of formations the Indian expansion had reached its peak. In December 1941 the Viceroy telegraphed an outline plan for the formation in 1943 of an infantry and an airborne division, together with a second heavy armoured brigade, but in face of all the difficulties involved in reviving the 1942 programme this expansion was not undertaken. The airborne division was finally formed in 1944 although it was still incomplete at the end of the war.

vi *Disaster and recovery*

The outbreak of war against Japan found India without an effective reserve of troops. The divisions of the 1940 programme had all been dispersed to Malaya and the Gulf and the remaining division had lost two brigades to Burma. Of the 1941 programme, 17 Division was furthest advanced and this had lost two brigades to Malaya while the Headquarters and remaining brigade were sent to Burma. There was considerable dissatisfaction with the performance of the Indian troops in Malaya and Burma and local leaders attributed this to the cumulative effects of 'milking', shortage of leaders and training for Middle East rather than bush conditions.[52] On the basis of the evidence 'milking' would seem to be a hazardous procedure to use as a method of expansion. Certainly it would appear to be so when carried to the extremes it was in the Indian Army, where the number of battalions was more than doubled in a period of eighteen months. The effect of 'milking' is to spread the post-basic training load and thus to reduce the overall time needed to produce new units. On the basis of the Indian Army experience of 1918 when large numbers of new battalions were produced in a very short time the method was effective. It does, however, rely on the gamble that the army will not be required to face a first-class enemy during the period of expansion. In the Indian Army experience of the first few months of the Japanese war the gamble was lost.

With the completion of the initial Japanese campaigns the whole orientation of the Indian Army was altered. The dispersion of that Army to Burma, Malaya and detached garrisons in South-east Asia was reduced to the defence of India's North-east Frontier. The considerable part taken by Indian troops in the Middle East and Gulf remained but was accorded a lower priority in Indian thinking. There was much to think about. The immediate threats were to the Frontier but for a long time invasion through southern India was feared. To meet these threats there were the formations of the 1941 programme and the part of the 1942 programme that remained. All of these formations contained units depleted by the processes of the previous expansion and by the need to find reinforcements for Malaya and Burma. There were, too, the questions posed by the qualitative inferiority the Army had displayed. The British Army reinforcement of India for some time provided the backbone of Indian defence.

In the inquests following the withdrawal of the surviving formations from Burma it was decided that existing Indian formations were over-mechanised and road-bound. 17 Division and 39 Division, lately Burma Division, were reconstructed as Light Divisions with only two brigades, animal transport and remaining lorries of four-wheel-drive capability. Three other divisions had part of their mechanical transport replaced by mules. Divisional establishments came under review again in the autumn of 1943 when two battalions were added to divisional troops and yet again in May 1944 when divisional establishments were standardised at three brigades with three more battalions as divisional troops.

The domestic background to these attempts to reorganise the

Army, prepare for the defence of India and commence preparations for future offensive campaigns was unhappy. In May 1942 an outbreak of terrorism in Sind demanded the attention of units amounting to two brigades and this was followed in July by the need to collect three brigades to mount an expedition on the North-west Frontier. More serious was the failure of the Cripps Mission to progress India's moves towards independence, which resulted in a campaign of civil disobedience, degenerating into open riot. Communications with the front in Assam were cut for days at a time and the sum of these events was to disrupt the reorganisation programme. Using what was essentially an improvised formation, 14 Division, an offensive operation in Arakan was commenced in the autumn of 1942 but with a success reminiscent of the recent operations in Malaya and Burma.[53]

The failure of the Arakan operations led to a series of searching enquiries into the Indian Army and its capabilities and into the command structure for fighting the Japanese war. At the level of high command, following the Trident Conference the appointment of a Supreme Commander for South-east Asia was announced on 25th August 1943. The conduct of the war was to be separated from command in India, which henceforward became responsible only for internal security and administration of base services in support of operations. The criticisms of the Prime Minister on the operations recently concluded were harsh. On receipt of them the Deputy Commander-in-Chief, India, observed that the Indian Army had been grossly over-expanded to meet Imperial needs and had become a second-class army. The Secretary of State for India noted that the expansion had exhausted the manpower of the martial classes and classes with no military background had been recruited. The situation was not improved by the recruitment of officers with little knowledge of the social background or language of their men. Another factor lay in the deteriorating economic situation of India. Further expansion of the Army would be dangerous and future efforts should be directed towards improving quality.[54] The Prime Minister was in favour of reducing the size of the Army to improve its quality but on 20th May the Cabinet decided it should remain at its present size but that this should not be exceeded.

An Infantry Committee, India, was appointed to investigate the readiness for war of units in India and recommend improvements.

The Report of this Committee in July 1943 detailed recommendations on the organisation of Indian units and formations and made
proposals which may be summarised as follows:[55]

1 The infantry should be given first claim on cadet officers and educated
  recruits. The quality of officers and NCOs should be improved. Pay
  should be increased. 'Milking' should cease.
2 Basic training should be increased to nine months and should be
  followed by two months of jungle warfare training.
3 The reinforcement system should be improved and drafts should include
  an adequate proportion of experienced NCOs.
4 Brigades should include a British, Gurkha and an Indian battalion.

These proposals were accepted almost in their entirety and by the
end of 1943 India had developed a more comprehensive training
organisation than any other country at that time. The specific orientation of the organisation was towards jungle warfare and drafts
and units destined for the west were relatively neglected, although
able to benefit from some of the side effects of the revised structure.

Although in May 1943 the Cabinet decided that the Indian Army
should not be reduced the possibility of reduction was mooted
again later and in January 1944 the Prime Minister was still
minuting on the importance of reducing the 'mass of low-grade
troops' in India. A letter from the C-in-C to the CIGS in September
1943 reviewed the question. If the Army had been expanded to a
point such that it was unable to carry out its tasks in the Far East
then the experienced three divisions in the Mediterranean should be
returned to fight the Japanese. The point was unwelcome, as one of
the divisions was in the line in Italy with the other two destined to
follow it. The critical question, in the view of the C-in-C, was the
impossibility of finding sufficient officers of the right quality and it
was this which precluded further expansion of the Indian Army.
In June 1944 the C-in-C attempted to obtain 600 officers from
Australia and in the end 168 were seconded.[56]

The Indian training organisations had been developing steadily,
particularly across 1942 when schools and training centres were
established for the specialised arms and the demand placed on units
to train or provide post-basic training for their own men was much
reduced. In the infantry the training battalions were successively
enlarged into Training Centres and finally into Regimental Centres
by February 1943. One of the critical shortages was that of men
who could read and write and of those who had mechanical

experience and from February 1942 sixteen-year-old boys were recruited to be given a basic education course of eighteen months before commencing military training. Between July and October 1943 14 and 39 Divisions were converted into Training Divisions with a similar establishment to a conventional division but with the task of giving post-basic and jungle training to drafts destined for units fighting the Japanese. The course was two months long and considerable attempts were made to make the training as realistic as possible. The training needs of battalions coming to jungle warfare from other duties were taken care of by allocating 116 Brigade for that role. In this formation individual jungle training was given followed by unit and brigade training. A battalion spent from four to six months in the Brigade before replacing a tired unit in one of the fighting divisions. 150 Brigade joined 116 Brigade in May 1944 and both were used for occupation duties after the Japanese surrender. 155 Brigade was also formed in 1944 to give unit and brigade training to units bound for western theatres.

The greatest problem to be overcome was the problem of morale. In its experiences of 1941 to 1943 the Indian Army acquired the habit of defeat. It had come to believe that the enemy could not be defeated. Fortunately the Command was able to recognise and identify the problem and produce a solution. This was to develop an individual superiority through successful patrolling and to extend this into successful minor operations using only such methods as would ensure success. The time available to complete the spiritual rebuilding of the army was short. The Arakan operations closed down in May 1943 and the respite before opening operations in Arakan and Assam in February 1944 was but nine months. The Indian Army in February 1944 looked much as it had in May 1943 but qualitatively it was a very different force.[57]

The weak economic structure of India has already been referred to and it was obvious that the development of India as a base for offensive operations would be a lengthy task. By December 1942 agreement was reached that the base should be able to take thirty-four divisions including forces for the re-occupation of Burma, which was envisaged to be carried out by an amphibious operation through Rangoon. The forces listed included two British, twelve Indian, one West African and one East African divisions, plus the remnants of the Burmese Army, the Chinese Army in India and local forces. Such a body would require a considerable development of India's ports. A re-examination ordered in August 1943 was concerned with the deployment of an offensive force of twenty-five divisions, with three or four of the divisions for the offensive operation by-passing India, and with at least part of the operations, when launched, maintained from bases outside India. By April 1944 it was estimated that the base would be two-thirds complete by the end of the year but the decisive repulse of the Japanese offensive in Assam demanded that the plans for the offensive should be recast. Once decisions to defeat the Japanese overland had been taken, planning for the base was directed more towards operations in Malaya and the Dutch East Indies. In October 1944 the Chiefs of Staff directed that the base would have to maintain eighteen divisions early in 1945, with another nine to be redeployed after the defeat of Germany. The prolongation of the war soon made their tentative allocations unrealistic. In July 1945, before mounting the operation for the invasion of Malaya, divisions to be supported were reduced to 15⅔ with a further 7⅔ to be redeployed from Europe. Here again there were elements of fantasy, for the listed divisions included one from New Zealand when the New Zealand Government was far from sure what its future participation in the war would be. The war was, however, nearly over and further development of the base was unnecessary. In retrospect it would appear that the base was developed to handle far greater forces than were needed to beat the Japanese. Some of the developments, particularly those of ports, were of great value to India in the post-war world.[58]

The account of the development of India as a base, much of which was in military terms redundant, was paralleled by the development of the Indian armoured forces. An armoured division was included in each of the 1940, 1941 and 1942 plans. Originally 31 Division was intended, in view of the shortage of tanks, to be formed with one armoured and two motor brigades but towards the end of 1940 this was to be one motor and two armoured brigades and then, when the motor brigade was diverted to the Middle East, the British establishment of two armoured brigades and a support group was adopted. The crises of 1941 interrupted the armoured development and a brigade of 31 Division, without tanks, took part in the Persian operation, with the whole of the Division being complete there by the end of the year. Indeed shortage of tanks inhibited the growth of the armoured formations until well into 1942. A review was undertaken in June 1942, when it was decided to adopt the British standard of one armoured brigade per division and to form 43 Armoured Division of the 1942 programme to this establishment. The surplus armoured brigades would be independent formations. Two of the armoured brigades and the tank brigade were composed of British personnel, the Indian units originally intended for these having been used as divisional cavalry on the North-west Frontier. The changing needs of the war, together with the shortage of technical personnel, led to a further review in March 1943. 32 and 43 Divisions were amalgamated as 44 Division, surplus brigades being converted to infantry. In the September the demands of Special Force caused an extensive cross-posting of units and the disbandment of one of the brigades to free further British units for conversion, or re-conversion, to infantry. After another review of operational requirements in March 1944 the armoured forces were reduced to 31 Armoured Division, now in the Middle East, and three tank brigades.[59]

The Women's Auxiliary Corps (India) was first formed in May 1942 and grew out of the Women's Auxiliary Service (Burma) which provided the first platoon. The WAS(B) was originally formed to undertake cypher duties for the army in Burma in January 1942, being later evacuated to India and disbanded. WAC(I) formed with local terms of enlistment, at first, with recruitment open to those over the age of eighteen. Usual duties were of a clerical and domestic nature. General service enlistment was opened in December 1942 and at about the same time the minimum age was reduced to seventeen. In a society in which women had a limited role the growth of the Corps was slow but it performed useful services within its limits, reaching a strength of 11,500 by the end of the war.[60]

As in the First War the provision of officers for the Indian Army was a major difficulty. In the 'Indianised' regiments and battalions VCOs had ceased to be appointed, since platoons were commanded by newly-commissioned officers, and one of the early war-time acts was to appoint VCOs back to those units, bringing them back into line with other Indian Army units. Officers, whether British or Indian, were thereafter appointed to any unit in need. A source of British candidates for commissions was the British Army in India and by mid-1943 this was providing 200 per month but by 1944 this source was approaching exhaustion. Considerable attempts were made to increase the supply of Indian officers but wastage rates in the selection process were high; even so by mid-1943 the intake of candidates to the cadet schools was averaging 160 per month. The formation of pre-cadet schools and extensive publicity ensured a steady supply of Indian candidates but over half of the applicants were weeded out by Provincial Selection Boards and of the rest nearly 75% were rejected by the GHQ Selection Boards.[61] For the British community in India, registration for national service was undertaken in February 1940 and in the July conscription was applied to all males in the age range 18–50. At a later date the evacuation of British civilians from Hong Kong, Malaya and especially from Burma brought a supplementary source of British officers. The supply of officers scarcely met needs throughout the war and although in practice the way was open for full 'Indianisation' advantage was not taken of the opportunity. Even so the proportion of Indian officers rose throughout the War and the formation of the Armies of India and Pakistan would not have been possible had that not been so. The 3031 British and 697 Indian Officers serving in 1939 grew to 18,752 British and 13,947 Indian by the end of the War, to which must be added about 14,000 seconded from the British Army.[62]

As indicated in Figure 3.3, in terms of sheer numbers the size of the Indian Army grew throughout the War and there is little doubt that these numbers could have been increased had it been thought necessary or desirable. The concept of the martial classes has been referred to earlier in the Chapter and is in need of further discussion in the context of World War Two and of post-Independence India and Pakistan. The view one takes of the concept depends upon one's standpoint. From a British point of view the Indian Army was a means of policing a dependency or acting as an Imperial Reserve and the martial class concept was one of identifying the groups from which mercenaries could be obtained. Some writers, such as Churchill, preferred the term 'volunteer'[63] but what the British needed from the Indian Army was a force which would fight, if necessary, for causes that were British rather than Indian and the term mercenary seems to fit more accurately. The qualitative inferiority displayed by the Indian Army fighting the Japanese in 1942 and 1943 would suggest that the size of Indian Army the British could raise was limited by the size of the groups that

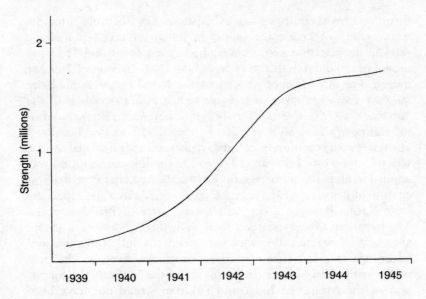

Figure 3.3 Indian Army Strength: 1939–45. Source: Sri Nandan Prasad, *Expansion of the Armed Forces and Defence Organisation*, Combined Historical Section, Delhi, 1956, Appendix 2.

exhibited the necessary mercenary, or martial, virtues. If that was so then by mid-1943 the Indian Army had reached and perhaps exceeded the size of Army it was desirable to raise.

The Indian point of view is conditioned by the desire to raise an Army that would fight for Indian causes and from this point of view the concept of martial classes was abhorrent. Recruitment from these classes was merely a 'subterfuge' which prevented the 'infection of patriotism', Indian patriotism that is, from reaching a more widely based Indian Army. A National Army, based on India's vast population, could undergo almost unlimited expansion. Yet Indian opinion on recruitment for the Army was neither unanimous nor consistent. As early as the Esher Report of 1919 opposing views were displayed by Indian members and the Indian Official Historian acknowledged that out of India's population of 390 millions only ten million men had the necessary intelligence, aptitude and mechanical sense.[64]

In general the Indian soldier came from the villages and

recruiting was influenced by rural conditions. When farming was prosperous recruiting tended to decline and vice versa. During the famine periods, which marked the years from 1943 onwards, recruiting improved markedly in the affected districts but this was counter-balanced by the fact that many ill-nourished would-be recruits were unable to meet the prescribed physical standards. In spite of these factors recruiting in the early years of the war was very good, many more offering themselves than could be accepted. A system of registration was adopted under which men not immediately required were given subsistence payments but this was regarded as being unsuccessful since too many changed their minds about enlistment during the waiting period. In 1941 recruit reception camps were opened to hold men against future requirements and to give elementary training. This expedient was more successful but desertion of recruits was a continuing problem, amounting to about 1% of the intake during the pre-enlistment period.[65]

Recruitment for the Army between the outbreak of war and the end of August 1945 came to a total of 2,499,909 of which 2,038,001 were classified as combatants. Punjabi Mussalmans made up the largest class, amounting to 15% of the total, with Madrassis providing almost as many. Compared with the Great War 3.4 times as many were enrolled but the old 'martial' classes were not able to show increases of this magnitude. Several changes were made in the composition of regiments to allow for the relative shortages. In the Sikh Regiment, for example, by 1945 Punjabi Mussalmans were recruited into all battalions and in the Frontier Force Rifles, Sikhs had to be mustered out of some units in 1944. Battalions of the Baluch, Sikh, Frontier Force, 14 Punjab and 16 Punjab Regiments and Frontier Force Rifles had to be disbanded due to shortage of men of the right classes. In the artillery, recruiting into Field and Anti-Aircraft Artillery was confined to Madrassi classes from 1942. Madrassis, Bengalis and Assamese were recruited into the Army Service Corps but that of the latter had to be discontinued because of the high rate of desertion.[66] The Indian States Forces provided significant numerical assistance with 41,463 in Indian Government service in 1945 out of a total strength of 99,367.

If the first two years of the war had seen a dispersion of the Indian Army comparable to that of the Bitish Army, the Japanese victories of 1942 secured the concentration of the Army in two

theatres, one eastern, one western. So far as the western theatre is
concerned, by mid-1942 there were two Indian divisions in the
Middle East with three and an armoured division in the Persian
Gulf area. 10 Division shortly moved from the Gulf to the Middle
East and with the decline in the possible German threat from the
north a movement from the Gulf was soon under way. 31
Armoured Division and 8 Division moved to the Middle East in
1943, when 5 Division returned to India. 4, 8 and 10 Divisions
took part in the campaign in Italy, with 4 Division being diverted to
Greece in December 1944. Indian forces in Italy included three
States Forces battalions and a number of these units were on
internal security duties in the Middle East, being used for
occupation duties in the Dodecanese after the German withdrawal.
General Alexander attempted to obtain 31 Armoured Division and
6 Division for Italy in July 1944 and although this was refused the
infantry brigade of 31 Armoured went went there the following
month. With the end of the war in Europe the return of the Indian
divisions was regarded as a matter of urgency and 8 Division
returned to India in July 1945, being shortly followed by the
others.

6 Division was left in the Persian Gulf area until November 1944
when it was broken up. This left three independent brigades there
of which two went to the Middle East in mid-1945. From the latter
part of 1943 the Gulf appears to have been regarded as a source
of reinforcements for the Indian divisions in Italy and by 1945 the
brigades in Iraq and Persia were largely made up of State Forces
personnel.

For the Indian Army in the Far East after the defeat of the
Japanese in Burma the main problem was the replacement of under-
strength British units in the Indian formations. This was done by
brigading Indian States Forces units and by the withdrawal of units
from the North-west Frontier and their replacement by State Forces
units or others, newly formed. In fact this process could be seen as
the last stage in a successive movement, observable throughout the
war, in which a newly formed unit moved from internal security
duties to the North-west Frontier and then on to Burma, being
relieved at each stage by units less ready than itself. After the
Japanese surrender Indian divisions were the first Allied formations
into Thailand and Indo China, as well as into the western islands of
the Dutch East Indies where they were drawn into the civil war

there until the end of 1946. An Indian brigade relieved Australian forces in Borneo in January 1946 and Indian units remained in South-east Asia until after Independence.

vii *Retrospect: 1939–45*

For the Indian Army the Second World War was the precursor to partition and Independence. The civil disturbances of 1942, the failure of the Cripps Mission and the formation of the Indian National Army by the Japanese should all have indicated a limitation to the part played by the Indian Army. Within India the indifference of the Indian population at large and the outright hostility of many Indian politicians to British rule all tended to undermine India's part in the War. Yet the Indian Army was largely uninfluenced by the Indian clamour, was expanded and fought much as it had always done once the difficulties of 1942 and 1943 were past. A squadron of the Central India Horse refused to embark for overseas service in 1940 and an outpost of 3 Gwalior Lancers, a State Forces unit, went over to the enemy in the Arakan in 1944 but these remain the only known examples of outright disaffection. In the Central India Horse case the mutiny bore a resemblance to the mutinies of 1914 and 1915 in that internal matters had some part to play in the incident. For the Indian National Army, although the post-war trials of its leaders caused outcry in India, during the war it had little impact. Its members showed a persistent tendency to surrender to the Allies whenever possible, not always with success, and orders had to be issued to give them a kinder welcome.[67]

At least until the outbreak of war with Japan, from which time the defence of India became a major priority, the role of the Indian Army was to continue to be an Imperial Reserve. Indeed throughout the first half of the century this was the Army's role, however much it was denied publicly, a role required by Britain's possession of a colonial empire and by Britain's inability or unwillingness to accept the role. Even after the start of the Japanese war the role continued, in that Indian formations were retained in the Gulf and Middle East to serve Imperial purposes even though they would have been invaluable for the defence of India's frontiers. The Indian divisions in Italy increased the size of British participation in that theatre by 50% and one of those divisions was overseas for more than six years. Without the Indian Army Britain would have been

quite unable to meet her many commitments in the Middle East and
Far East.

Notes

1 J. Gooch, *The Plans of War*, Routledge and Kegan Paul, London,
   1974, Ch. 7.
2 Sir Philip Magnus, *Kitchener: Portrait of an Imperialist*, John Murray,
   London, 1958, p. 198.
   Lord Birdwood, *Khaki and Gown*, Ward Lock, London, 1941,
   pp. 142–4.
3 F. J. Moberly, *The Campaign in Mesopotamia*, I, H.M.S.O., London,
   1923, p. 59.
4 P. Mason, *A Matter of Honour*, Peregrine Books, Harmondsworth,
   1976, Ch. 14, pp. 529–30.
5 W. A. Watson, *Central India Horse*, Blackwood, Edinburgh, 1930,
   pp. 93–106.
   Birdwood, *Khaki and Gown*, pp. 44, 48.
6 IO/L/MIL/17/5/1751, I and IA.
   Cd. 8610, p. 10.
7 Moberly, *Mesopotamia*, pp. 68–9.
8 Apart from Burma Division and Aden Brigade, eight battalions were
   on garrison duty outside India.
9 IWM file K33761.
10 Moberly, *Mesopotamia*, p. 79.
11 J. W. B. Merewether and Sir Frederick Smith, *The Indian Corps in
   France*, John Murray, London, 2nd Edn., 1919, p. 19.
12 Telegram to the Viceroy in Moberly, *Mesopotamia*, p. 89.
13 Sir George Macmunn, *Egypt and Palestine*, I, H.M.S.O., London
   1928, p. 15.
14 W. L. S. Churchill, *The World Crisis*, Macmillan, London, Single-vol.
   edn., 1931, p. 201 provides an illuminating insight into how this
   decision was made.
15 W. E. H. Condon, *Frontier Force Rifles*, Gale and Polden, Aldershot,
   1953, p. 28.
   J. P. Lawford and W. E. Catto, *Solah Punjab*, Gale and Polden,
   Aldershot, 1967, p. 39.
   H. J. Huxford, *History of 8 Gurkha Rifles*, Gale and Polden, Aldershot, 1952, p. 67.
16 Merewether and Smith, *Indian Corps*, pp. 464–5.
17 Lawford and Catto, *Solah Punjab*, p. 55.
18 J. Evatt, *Historical Records of 39 Garhwal Rifles*, Gale and Polden,
   Aldershot, 1922, p. 54.
19 Sir Charles Lucas (Ed.), *The Empire at War*, V, Oxford U.P., 1926,
   p. 184.
20 Md. Ibrahim Querishi, *The First Punjabis*, Gale and Polden, Aldershot, 1958, p. 226.

21   Moberly, *Mesopotamia*, II, 1924, p. 150.
     PRO/Cab/42/6.
22   Moberly, *Mesopotamia*, I, pp. 72, 82, 187.
23   Moberly, *Mesopotamia*, II, Appendices 27 and 28.
24   General Sir George Barrow, *The Life of General Monro*, Hutchinson,
     London, 1931, pp. 136–9.
25   *India's Contribution to the Great War*, Govt. of India, Calcutta,
     1923, pp. 81–2.
     Barrow, *General Monro*, pp. 162, 165–6.
26   *India's Contribution*, pp. 204 ff.
27   Moberly, *Mesopotamia*, III, 1925, p. 301.
     PRO/Cab/23/1.
     Barrow, *General Monro*, pp. 140–1.
28   *India's Contribution*, Appendix C, pp. 276 ff.
     War Office, *Statistics of the Military Effort of the British Empire*,
     H.M.S.O., London, 1922, p. 381.
29   Indian Army Lists, 1918.
30   Moberly, *Mesopotamia*, IV, 1927, p. 19.
31   Moberly, *Mesopotamia*, IV, pp. 113–15.
     C. Falls, *Egypt and Palestine*, II, H.M.S.O., London, 1930,
     pp. 297–8.
32   Moberly, *Mesopotamia*, IV, pp. 255–6.
33   *India's Contribution*, pp. 79, 97, 277, 278.
     IWM file K33761.
     Sir Frederick Maurice, *Life of General Lord Rawlinson*, Cassell,
     London, 1928, p. 275.
34   J. O. Rawson, 'The Role of India in Imperial Defence', unpub. D.
     Phil., Oxford, 1976, pp. 6–9.
35   R. S. Waters, *History of 5/14 Punjab Regiment*, Bain, London, 1936.
36   Cmd. 943.
37   *Parliamentary Debates (Commons)*, XCVII, cols. 1695–96.
     Barrow, *General Monro*, pp. 124–7.
     Rawson, 'India's Role,' pp. 11–12 and Ch. 3.
38   Maurice, *Rawlinson*, pp. 295–6.
39   J. Connell, *Auchinleck*, Cassell, London, 1959, Appendix 2.
     PRO/Cab/53/14.
40   IO/L/MIL/17/5/1779 and 1783.
     Barrow, *General Monro*, p. 127.
41   Sri Nandan Prasad, *Expansion of the Armed Forces and Defence
     Organisation*, Combined Historical Section, Delhi, 1956, pp. 8–9,
     170–6, 179–80.
     W. H. Jacobsen, 'The Modernisation of the Indian Army', unpub,
     Ph.D., California, Irvine, 1979, pp. 170–6.
     Bisheshwar Prasad, *Defence of India: Policy and Plans*, Combined
     Historical Section, Delhi, 1963, pp. 1–2.
42   Cmd. 4473.
     Jacobsen, 'Modernisation of the Indian Army', pp. 280–6.
     Sri Nandan Prasad, *Expansion of the Armed Forces*, pp. 10–11.

43 PRO/Cab/24/274.
Rawson, 'India's Role', pp. 287–97.
PRO/Cab/53/39. COS 737, Annex 2.
Jacobsen, 'Modernisation of the Indian Army', pp. 378–9.
44 IO/L/MIL/17/5/1801.
Jacobsen, 'Modernisation of the Indian Army', pp. 388–95, 397–409.
PRO/Cab/24/287.
45 IO/WS/4445.
Sri Nandan Prasad, *Expansion of the Armed Forces*, pp. 58–60.
46 Condon, *Frontier Force Rifles*, p. 337.
47 G. Betham and H. V. R. Geary, *The Golden Galley*, Oxford U.P., 1957, p. 317.
48 J. Connell, *Wavell: Supreme Commander*, Collins, London, 1969, p. 24.
49 S. W. Kirby, *The War Against Japan*, II, H.M.S.O., London, 1958, pp. 47–8.
50 Connell, *Wavell*, pp. 29–30.
51 Kirby, *Japan*, III, 1961, p. 425.
Connell, *Wavell*, p. 36.
52 Ibid., pp. 85–6, 122.
Kirby, *Japan*, II, pp. 440–1.
53 Ibid., pp. 246–8.
Connell, *Wavell*, pp. 230, 255.
Field Marshal Sir William Slim, *Defeat into Victory*, Cassell, London, 1956, pp. 135–7.
54 Kirby, *Japan*, II, p. 383.
PRO/Cab/66/36. WP(43) 197.
PRO/Cab/65/34.
55 IO/WS/33252.
Kirby, *Japan*, II, pp. 386–7, III, Appendix 6.
56 Connell, *Auchinleck*, pp. 755–8.
W. L. S. Churchill, *The Second World War*, V, Cassell, London, 1952, p. 600.
D. Dexter, *The New Guinea Offensives*, Australian War Memorial, Canberra, 1961, pp. 781–2.
57 Slim, *Defeat into Victory*, pp. 179–89.
58 Kirby, *Japan*, II, pp. 299–300, 489–91, III, pp. 17–19, 27, 313, IV, pp. 16–17, V, pp. 77–9.
PRO/Cab/79/35, 36, 65, 81, 82.
Sir Arthur Bryant, *The Triumph in the West*, Collins, London, 1959, p. 253.
59 Connell, *Wavell*, p. 44.
Kirby, *Japan*, II, pp. 243, 389, III, pp. 37, 317.
60 Sri Nandan Prasad, *Expansion of the Armed Forces*, pp. 106–8.
61 Ibid., p. 102.
62 Ibid., pp. 64, 181–3.
Connell, *Auchinleck*, p. 189.

63 Churchill, *Second World War*, IV, p. 187.
64 Bisheshwar Prasad in Sri Nandan Prasad, *Expansion of the Armed Forces*, pp. xx, xxviii–xxix and p. 78.
   Cmd. 943.
65 Sri Nandan Prasad, *Expansion of the Armed Forces*, pp. 51, 89–92.
66 Ibid., p. 85 and Appendices 13 and 16.
   Indian Army Lists.
67 Sri Nandan Prasad, *Expansion of the Armed Forces*, p. xxx.
   Mason, *A Matter of Honour*, pp. 513–14.
   Slim, *Defeat into Victory*, p. 323.

Chapter 4
Canada

i *Imperial co-operation*

From a constitutional point of view the position of the Dominions in 1914 was not, from some aspects, dissimilar to that of India. Although full internal self-government had been granted at various dates – Canada in 1867, Australia in 1901, New Zealand in 1907, South Africa in 1910 – the status of the Dominions fell short of independence in all respects. When Britain declared war in 1914 she did so on behalf of the Empire as a whole. The Dominions reserved for themselves, however, the nature of the contribution they would make in both kind and quantity. By 1939 the status of the Dominions had changed. Whilst in 1939 the line of authority in and over India led from the Viceroy to the Secretary of State for India and thence to the British Cabinet the Dominions were free to declare war, or not, as they chose. The development of the Dominions' Armies across the two World Wars was, thus, part of the Dominions' own development towards full nationhood, a factor more readily recognised in the Dominions themselves than in the Home country. What the Armies of the Dominions contributed to this development was to enhance the growth of a sense of national identity. If in 1914 the soldiers of the Dominions' Armies saw themselves as Britons from overseas, increasingly they began to see themselves as Canadians, Australians, New Zealanders.

The emergence of a distinctive Dominions, or Colonial, point of view of Imperial defence dates from the 1880s with, probably, the Colonial Conference of 1887 marking the commencement of a long wrangle about the degree of control to be exercised by Britain, who should pay for those forces and how much. The early disputes principally involved naval forces but there was no united front displayed by the Colonies since each had a different perception of the threats to be faced. For the land forces, although each possessed a defence force of some sort, it was not until after the Boer War that such forces really entered the discussion. The only one of the larger colonies facing a conceivable over-land threat was Canada and here it was soon recognised that in military terms no effective defence was possible. The 1902 Colonial Conference discussed the formation of a reserve of troops for Imperial purposes but this soon foundered on Colonial suspicions of being involved in a war which might be, or might become, unpopular. Indeed what was being witnessed was a transfer in the focus of Imperial defence from Britain's defence of the colonies to colonial assistance for Britain in some grave emergency. This attitude became more explicit in the Colonial Conference of 1907 where initial proposals to unify defence organisation received a cautious approval which fell short of full agreement.[1]

At this time the creation of an Imperial General Staff was being contemplated, complementing the Committee of Imperial Defence, responsible for defence planning and monitoring and controlling the activities of local Staffs. This was very sensitive since the issue of the internal independence of the Colonies was at stake. The Chief of each local General Staff would be responsible for advising his own government, would be head of his own General Staff, but would be supervised himself by the Chief of an Imperial General Staff. If common standards of military knowledge were to prevail graduation from the Staff Colleges at Camberley or Quetta would be necessary, since these establishments would be able to exert an 'educational stranglehold' unless and until the Colonies saw fit to establish similar places of their own.[2]

The Colonial Conference of 1909 was called in part to consider the implications of German naval expansion but on other military matters agreement was reached to standardise organisations and weapons on the practices of the British Army. A recommendation was also made that General Staff officers throughout the Empire should be members of an Imperial General Staff, remaining responsible to their own governments. This was not quite the Imperial General Staff foreseen two years earlier. With hindsight it is easy to see that the development of a true Imperial General Staff in its full sense was impracticable. The Dominions were prepared to co-operate on their own terms in an emergency but they were not prepared to take part in a military federation. Such a procedure would have been inconsistent with their development towards full independence. Through the circumstances of geography each Dominion was faced with differing threats, real or potential, and a close military combination could only benefit the mother country. The Imperial General Staff proposal was therefore bound to fail. Although the agreement to standardise weaponry and organisation was a substantial achievement, the failure of the attempts to secure a central control ensured that each Dominion would go its own way and it is to the developments in each Dominion that we must now turn.[3]

ii *Canada before the war*

Canada's army originated in the militia formed by the French in the seventeenth century, continued and supplemented by units formed in British Canada. The militia, volunteers and fencibles fought in the War of Independence and the War of 1812 but, although some units were mobilised to meet local emergencies, such as those of 1837, by the mid-nineteenth century the militia was moribund. A Volunteer Militia was authorised in 1855 and a regular force, the Permanent Militia, was established in 1883 to serve as an instructional corps and to man the fixed defences of the ports. The Canadian military tradition was continued in the Boer War when several contingents, numbering about 7400 in all, saw service in South Africa.

Canada's security was based on the shield provided by the Royal Navy although there were perennial fears of invasion from the United States. However by 1905 the CID had decided that effective defence against attack from this quarter was impracticable. In spite of this Canadian interest in defence remained at low level. Indeed at the Colonial Conference of 1902 Prime Minister Laurier's view was that Canada's main contribution to security would be the development of the Canadian Pacific Railway. In the following years Britain's increasing concentration on European dangers indicated that the maritime shield might be weakening and in May 1910 the Canadian Navy came into being but political support for its future remained uncertain until the 1920s.

Until 1904 the Canadian Militia was commanded by a British officer. From that date the administration of the force was conducted by a Minister of Militia, advised by a Militia Council and with a Chief of General Staff as the Government's principal military adviser. It was clearly Canada's intention to develop its own strategic planning organisation and after the 1909 Imperial Conference attempts to establish the Canadian Staff as a section of the Imperial General Staff were bound to founder.[4]

By 1914 the Canadian Militia comprised three elements, the Permanent Force, the Non-Permanent Active Militia and the Reserve Militia. The Permanent Force, with an establishment of 3110, was organised as an infantry battalion, two mounted regiments and supporting arms. The Reserve Militia, existing on paper only, consisted of all able-bodied men, with some exceptions, aged bewteen eighteen and sixty. The NPAM, with an establishment of 74,213 all ranks of whom 59,000 trained in 1914, was the real army of Canada. Organised as thirty-seven mounted regiments and 109 infantry battalions Active Militia members signed on for three years at a time and had training obligations of the same order as those of the Territorial Force in Britain. The NPAM was available for service anywhere in Canada, or overseas if necessary, in the defence of the country.

From 1911 plans were made to mobilise NPAM formations for home defence and also to prepare a division and a mounted brigade for service overseas. NPAM districts and areas were allotted quotas for the expeditionary force in which service would be voluntary, preference being given to men with previous military experience or training.[5]

iii The Canadian Army in the Great War

Although from a constitutional point of view Canada entered the war through the action of Britain, that action was by no means unpopular. On 1st August the Governor General cabled the Secretary of State for the Colonies with assurances of support, intimating that 'a considerable force' could be made available. No numbers were mentioned although it appears that a force of about 20,000 men was envisaged and on 10th August the Canadian Cabinet fixed the number at 25,000. On 4th August a telegram to the Canadian Government gave the discouraging reply that there seemed to be 'no immediate necessity' for a force but two days later the offer was accepted. The Permanent Force was mobilised to man the fortifications of the defended ports and details of the NPAM were called out to provide guard detachments. The NPAM retained its responsibilities for local defence until October 1917, using detachments of NPAM units supplemented by extemporised battalions. The Royal Canadian Regiment, a Permanent unit, sailed on 6th September for Bermuda to relieve 2 Lincolnshire Regiment and became the first Canadian unit to serve overseas in the war.

The formation of the Canadian Expeditionary Force was set in train on 6th August by the Minister of Militia who, setting aside pre-war plans, communicated directly with the commanders of Militia units, instructing them to prepare rolls of volunteers for return to Militia Headquarters. What the Minister had in mind, he later said, was a call to arms similar to the 'fiery cross' of old but on the 10th August the established Militia organisation was brought back into play and District and Area Headquarters were allocated units of the CEF for which they were responsible. The Expeditionary Force assembled at Valcartier, near Quebec, utilising a site which had been acquired for Militia use in 1912 and which had to be rapidly developed to meet the influx. Recruits arriving at the camp were assigned to battalions according to the Province from which they had come, although some were formed directly from volunteers from NPAM units. 7 Battalion, for instance, came from British Columbia's 6 Rifles and 8 Battalion from 90 Winnipeg Rifles.[6]

Volunteers had to be aged between eighteen and forty-five and, although previous military experience was specified as a prerequisite for recruitment, it would appear that the standards of recruits were very uneven. It is a matter of interest that under 30% gave their birthplace as Canada.

The structure of the Expeditionary Force was modified several times as assembly proceeded but it was eventually organised as a division (1 Canadian Division) of four brigades, with two spare battalions and with the two Permanent Force mounted regiments. There was little time before embarkation to carry out extensive training, which was a unit responsibility and which was much hampered by lack of equipment. Local sources of supply made energetic efforts to complete the major deficiencies but much had to be improvised and some re-equipping was necessary before the CEF moved to France.[7] There were several suggestions that units could be raised either by Provinces or through private channels but of these only two units survived. One was a battalion of ex-soldiers raised by a Captain Hamilton Gault who contributed $100,000 to its cost. Named Princess Patricia's Canadian Light Infantry it sailed in September to join the British 27 Division before the end of the year. The other was a Motor Machine-gun company.[8]

The selection of an officer to command the Expeditionary Force was a matter of crucial importance. No Canadian officer had enjoyed the experience of commanding a force of comparable size and Kitchener provided the Prime Minister with a list of three Canadian-born officers of the British Army as possible candidates. On 5th September Kitchener, following the advice he had received, appointed General Alderson to the Command. This provides an interesting illustration of the status of the CEF in 1914. The fact that the British War Secretary had the authority to appoint a Commander for the Force, even though this was done in consultation with the Canadian Government, indicates that it was a Canadian contingent loaned or seconded to the British Army. It was not at this time recognised that the CEF, or the Expeditionary Force of any other Dominion, represented a distinctive national force with distinctive national interests. The fact that a Commander of a Dominion Expeditionary Force had responsibilities not only within the British chain of command but also to the Government of his Dominion was only slowly recognised and the development of this recognition is part of the development of the Dominions' Armies during the Great War.[9]

1 Canadian Division arrived in the United Kingdom in October 1914 and was quartered in tented camps on Salisbury Plain, occupying sites previously used by the Territorial Force for summer training. Lack of accommodation was a factor which retarded the development of the New Armies and the Canadians were to suffer also. The building of hutments was overtaken by the arrival of an unusually wet autumn and living conditions were poor. Some units were billeted but one brigade saw the winter through in tents. The Canadian experience prompted the diversion of the Australian and New Zealand Expeditionary Forces to Egypt to complete their training. Thirteen weeks were available before the Division moved to France in February 1915, just six months from first formation and including the disruption caused by an Atlantic crossing. The division was in the main composed of men from the Militia and this invites comparison with how long British Terri-

torial Divisions took to prepare for war. These it will be recalled needed 8·7 months on average, although 46 Division crossed to France in the same month as the Canadians. Prescribed training for the Militia was a little less than that 'for the Territorials but this seems to have made little difference to the time needed to prepare for service. Shortly after the Division arrived in France the Canadian mounted units were joined in a Canadian Cavalry Brigade by 2 King Edward's Horse, a British Special Reserve unit. The latter was relieved a year later by the Canadian Fort Garry Horse.

On 6th October 1914 the Governor General telegraphed the Secretary of State for the Colonies offering a second Canadian contingent and, correctly anticipating a favourable response, the mobilisation of a second series of units was ordered. Units were formed by calling upon NPAM units to provide quotas and, in the Canadian winter, the new units trained locally. Although the expansion included fifteen infantry battalions it was at first intended to include the fourth brigade of the first contingent in the new formation but this was reconstructed as a training depot. It was not long before 1 Division began to need reinforcements and early in 1915 three battalions had to be sent over to Europe where they were broken up for drafts. As early as October 1914 it was decided to keep 30,000 men in Canada as a reserve for the forces overseas and in November this number was increased to 50,000. The expansion plans, together with the need for reserves, thus led to an ad hoc system of forming battalions and other units which trained in Canada as part of the reserve and then crossed the Atlantic either to join a new formation or to be broken up as reinforcements. In all 258 battalions were formed and used up in this way before the system was fundamentally altered in 1917.[10]

Figure 4.1 indicates the rate at which Expeditionary Force battalions were formed. So far as the majority of these units are concerned they may best be thought of as groups of men assembling and training in the NPAM areas and slowly building up to strength. Between April and December 1915 thirty-five of them were called upon for drafts of five officers and 250 men, some more than once. Often the process of growth was quite slow, as in the case of 110 (Perth) Battalion, CEF, which, sponsored by 28 Perth Regiment of the NPAM, began forming in October 1915, although not finally complete until a year later when it moved to Britain to be broken up

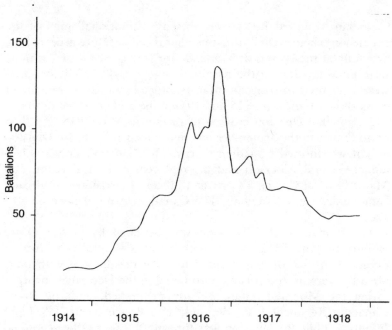

Figure 4.1. C.E.F. Infantry Battalions: 1914–18. Sources: *Canada in the Great War*, VI, United Publishers, Toronto, 1921, Appendix 1. Unit histories.

in January 1917. In general the embarkation strengths of battalions declined year by year, showing that the standard by which a unit could be declared to be 'formed' depended more on the need for men in France than on conformity with established standards. 258 (French Canadian) Battalion, CEF, embarked in October 1917 at a strength of 236 all ranks. As a means of obtaining recruits and providing basic training the system had merits. Men would probably be more eager to join a unit with local affiliations, where they could enjoy the companionship of friends and the privileges of belonging to a group with local connections, than to simply join an anonymous draft-finding organisation. The formation of 5th (later 4th) New Army units in Britain had used similar considerations. The system was, however, very cumbersome with many disadvantages.

During November and December 1914 thirteen battalions of

Canadian Mounted Rifles were raised as additional units of the expansion scheme. On 28th November the War Office accepted the first four of these units as a brigade for service in Egypt but none were fated to serve in the mounted role. 1 and 2 CMR Brigades were later used to form an infantry brigade, while the remainder crossed the Atlantic in 1915 and 1916 to be broken up for drafts.[11]

2 Canadian Division crossed to Britain in May 1915 and then on to France in the September where it joined 1 Canadian Division in a newly-formed Canadian Corps. The Commander was Lieutenant-General Alderson and his replacement in 1 Division was Major-General Currie, a Canadian officer. 2 Division was already commanded by a Canadian. The Canadian Army was coming of age.

The formation of 3 Division was heralded by a War Office enquiry in June 1915 as to whether Canada could raise further bodies of troops. It was decided to form the division with units already overseas and it came into being in the December incorporating the Mounted Rifles, already mentioned, and the Royal Canadian Regiment from Bermuda and Princess Patricia's Light Infantry. While the Division was forming the War Office enquired if further units could be found for Egypt. Canada's counter-proposal was that a fourth division should be formed for the Western Front and accordingly it came into being in April 1916.

During a visit to Britain in the summer of 1916 the Minister of Militia undertook to raise a fifth division and referred to the possibility of adding a sixth. No action was taken then and the heavy casualties of the Somme battles deferred consideration until the matter was raised again by the CIGS in October. Doubting its ability to support five divisions in the field the Canadian Government withheld approval until after a conference in January 1917, when 5 Division was formed as a home defence formation for the United Kingdom. This division was broken up a year later as an alternative to reducing the establishments of brigades in France from four to three battalions. Attempts were made in 1917 and 1918 to revive the proposal that Canada should place two more divisions in the field. A reduction to nine-battalion divisions would have permitted the increase but six divisions would be too many for a Corps and too few for an Army. By this time it would appear to have been unquestioned that Canadian formations should normally operate together under their own command. The success of the Canadian Corps at Vimy in 1917, with the appointment of Lieutenant-General Currie as Corps Commander, appears to mark the emergence of the Canadian Army as a separate entity. The retention of the four-battalion brigades in 1918 helped to confirm this status. With divisional establishments 5000 above the British 16,000, Canadian and British Divisions could not efficiently relieve each other in the line. The numerical superiority also ensured that Canadian Divisions, as divisions, enjoyed a qualitative superiority over British formations. During the German offensive of March 1918 when divisions were taken away from the Corps to plug gaps protests from all Canadian quarters descended upon Field Marshal Haig who was moved to remark that the Canadians regarded themselves more as Allies than as part of the Empire. That, indeed, is what they were becoming.[12]

The headquarters and training organisations which evolved in the United Kingdom to support the CEF in the field took a long time to develop. 1 Division arrived in Britain as, to all intents and purposes, a Canadian formation of the British Army. Its official channel of communication to the Canadian Government lay through the War Office. The unreality of this was soon realised and General Alderson was permitted to communicate directly with the Canadian authorities on Canadian matters. When 2 Division arrived in Britain the training depot for Canadian troops became Canadian Training Division, Shorncliffe and subsequently a Training Division, Bramshott was formed as a holding formation for CEF units arriving in Britain. Various ad hoc commands were created to control what was becoming quite a confused and complex scene and it was not until October 1916 that a Minister of Canadian Overseas Forces was appointed to represent the Canadian Government in Britain. Two months later Major-General Turner was appointed GOC, Overseas Military Forces, to complete the centralisation of control over the training and administrative services.[13] One of the earlier acts of the new Headquarters was to carry out a review of the training system in Britain where there were some seventy nominal CEF 'battalions' of strength varying from cadre upwards. A reconstruction of the system was not effective until January 1917 when both Training Divisions were reduced to contain a total of twenty-six battalions, each linked to a specific unit or units in France. During the summer the reorganisation was extended to Canada where one or more Depot Battalions were

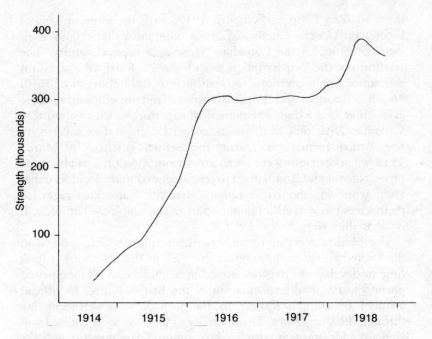

Figure 4.2. Strength of the C.E.F.: 1914–18. Source: G. W. L. Nicholson, *Canadian Expeditionary Force*, Queen's Printer, Ottawa, 1962, Appendix C, Table 2.

formed in each Province, each linked to one of the reserve units in Britain.

The greatest problem for the Canadian Army in the Great War, the problem of recruitment, was slow to develop. Enlistment continued at a high level into 1916 and the strength of the army showed a corresponding increase (Figure 4.2). To promote recruiting some standards were relaxed, such as reducing minimum height to five feet two inches, and the practice of recruiting for rank was introduced. The latter resulted in the accumulation in Britain of senior officers for whom there was no employment once their units had been broken up and in May 1917 officers senior to Lieutenant were required to revert to Lieutenant or be returned to Canada once they were unemployed.[14]

The steady growth of the army gave confidence in the ability of Canada to raise additional formations, and support them, and it was against this background that Sir Robert Borden, the Prime

Minister, announced in December 1915 that the authorised strength of the army would be doubled to 500,000. The announcement gave a great stimulus to recruitment and it was at this stage that the Minister of Militia referred to the possibility of raising 5 and 6 Divisions for France. The reasons behind Borden's announcement are unclear. It might be surmised that additional forces would strengthen his hand in negotiations with the British Government. Whatever the reasoning, after the rush in the early part of 1916 recruiting fell to low levels and the manner in which the CEF's strength abruptly plateaued at about 300,000 is striking. Competition with industry and agriculture was becoming acute and, although Recruiting Officers were instructed to prevent the enlistment of men in important work, some of the Provinces were calling for more formal schemes. A National Service Board was set up in August 1916 to oversee the distribution of labour and early in 1917 this body carried out a voluntary labour survey. Although some twenty per cent of the working population failed to respond, the cards of nearly 300,000 men not in essential work were passed to the recruiting authorities so that the men could be canvassed. In a final attempt to raise more men it was planned to mobilise 50,000 of the Militia on a voluntary basis to take over garrison duties in Canada and it was hoped that some would be prepared to go overseas but the proposal aroused little interest. Opposition to recruiting was particularly strong in Quebec where a nationalist movement was opposed to participation in the war although popular reaction could more accurately be described as one of apathy.[15] Although available statistics did not provide the data on which reliable figures for French-speaking enlistment could be based there was a widespread belief, particularly in English-speaking Canada, that it was poor. The scene was becoming set for the introduction of conscription.

In attempting to form a united front for the introduction of conscription Borden sought to form a coalition government but in this he was unsuccessful and the Military Service Bill became law as a party measure in August 1917. The intention was to obtain 100,000 men and a liability was placed on all aged 20–45, of which the first to be called up would be the unmarried or childless widowers aged 20–34, Tribunals were appointed to deal with claims for exemption and disputes. Although the Act passed through Parliament with little delay the Government majority was slender. In consequence Parliament was dissolved on 6th October, with a general election to be held on 17th December. Returns from overseas took a long time to collect and Parliament did not reassemble until 18th March 1918 when Borden resumed office, leading a coalition government with a large majority.

The first proclamation under the Military Service Act was made on 13th October 1917 and by the middle of November 20,000 men had reported for duty, with another 310,000 claiming exemption. Pleas had been made that the Act should not be enforced in Quebec but these were disregarded and at the end of March 1918 disorders broke out in Quebec City, lasting for a week, when a man who was not carrying an exemption certificate was arrested.

The implementation of the Act was therefore not followed by any great improvement in the flow of men into the army and by April the flow was so poor that the Prime Minister tabled an Order in Council to reduce enlistment age to nineteen and to cancel exemptions which had already been granted. The Order was challenged as being unconstitutional but it passed through Parliament only to be balked by a ruling of Alberta's Supreme Court that the Order did not have the force of law. The point caused delay until July. Thereafter the flow of reinforcements improved considerably. In all about 28,000 men either failed to register, failed to appear when called or deserted. About 5500 surrendered when an amnesty was announced in August but some 20,000 men were still at large at the Armistice. Pursuit of the defaulters, particularly of those who had not registered, was slow, difficult and expensive and in some cases hampered by not even knowing the names of culprits. Out of the 400,000 who registered over half were granted exemption on various grounds, 26,000 were awaiting summons for service in November and 121,000 joined the CEF.[16]

iv *1919–39*

With the end of the war the Canadian Expeditionary Force was rapidly disbanded and the Militia returned to its former position as Canada's principal military force. In 1919 a committee was set up under Major-General Otter, a former CGS, to report on the future of the NPAM. The conclusions of the Committee were largely taken as the basis for a reorganisation of the Militia undertaken in the early 1920s. Eleven infantry and four cavalry divisions were envisaged but these existed on paper only and basic organisation was founded on the Military Districts. The larger paper organisation was marked by some increase in the number of units and two former CEF units, Princess Patricia's Canadian Light Infantry and the Royal 22e Regiment, were re-formed and added to the Permanent Militia. The extent to which all of these units were little more than a skeleton is indicated by the strength figures for 1931, when the Permanent Force held 3688 men against an establishment of 6925 and the NPAM 51,287 against an establishment of 134,843.[17]

For Canada, as for most other countries, the 1920s and 1930s were years of depression and economy and although the 'Ten-year Rule' was not formally applied its provisions were tacitly accepted. However, the deteriorating international situation of the mid-1930s caused attention to again be directed towards defence and in 1935 a memorandum by Major-General McNaughton, Chief of General Staff, pointed to the major deficiencies. Lack of anti-aircraft weapons and obsolescence of coastal defences were the immediate shortages but more serious was the lack of industrial capacity to produce materials other than rifle ammunition and a limited output of shell.

In September 1936 an appreciation by the Joint Staff Committee, for the newly-formed Defence Committee, formally stated the roles of the armed forces, apparently for the first time. The direct defence of Canada held the first priority, followed by indirect defence in co-operation with other Empire forces in a war overseas. The latter, it was acknowledged, could well be the requirement demanding the greater effort. To meet these needs, what became a five-year programme was instituted in the financial year 1937–38. The order of priority was not formally stated to the Commons until April 1939 but it had been in operation for two or three years.[18]

a. Coastal defence, with the Pacific coast taking priority over the Atlantic.
b. The order of priority for the Services was air force, navy, army.

An extensive reorganisation of the Militia took place in 1936 to produce a smaller but better balanced force. The former 135 infantry battalions were reduced to eighty-eight, with six tank battalions, and the cavalry from thirty-five regiments to eighteen plus two armoured car units. Most of the redundant units were converted to artillery or other supporting functions and although, for the time being, the cavalry retained their horses only economic considerations impeded full mechanisation. There were, indeed, only sixteen tanks in Canada in September 1939.

Defence planning was expressed as a series of Schemes which were developed and refined across the inter-war years. Scheme No. 1 envisaged defence against the United States, which was seen to be a political rather than a military problem. Scheme No. 2 was concerned with the maintenance of Canadian neutrality in the event of war between the United States and Japan. Scheme No. 3, last revised in 1937, envisaged a major war in which direct threat to Canada was limited but the need to intervene overseas probable. After providing for local defence and internal security a Mobile Force was envisaged which would be available to oppose enemy landings or, if necessary, provide a field force to serve overseas. Contingent A of the Mobile Force would consist of a Corps with one cavalry and two infantry divisions and a further four divisions would be available later. In strength the force closely matched that that the Otter Committee had suggested might be made available. In total these forces covered almost all the existing Militia but rearmament plans, in which the army held lowest priority, looked principally to the equipment of only the first two divisions. Early in 1939 the cavalry division was dropped from the Mobile Force when it became clear that Europe was the most likely destination for the Force. Detailed planning proceeded on the basis of mobilising the two infantry divisions on the outbreak of war but of not concentrating the second until the first had moved to an area of operations either in Canada or overseas. The composition of the divisions was pre-planned and units, staffs and commanders were nominated.[19]

v The Second World War

The first direct step along Canada's road to war took place on 25th August when 10,000 of the NPAM were called out on a voluntary basis to mount guards on railways and other vulnerable points and to man coastal defences. On 1st September mobilisation telegrams went out to form a Canadian Active Service Force.

The Canadian Active Service Force was formed by mobilising Permanent Force and NPAM units to form two divisions, although 2 Division was not to be concentrated at this stage. Constitutionally the CASF was not part of the Militia, although made up of units mobilised from the Militia. Membership was voluntary and men in mobilised units who did not wish to remain were released. However in all respects other than the constitutional the CASF was closely related to the Militia and units were simply active-service battalions of the NPAM regiments. This point received expression in July 1940 when mobilised battalions were designated the 1st Battalions of their regiments with the unmobilised portion designated as the 2nd Battalion.

To make up battalion establishments of 800 all ranks units had to be completed by enlistment and this route eventually provided about half of the strength. The position of rural units was particularly difficult and under mobilisation instructions some were mobilised as composite units, enlisting from sister units in the vicinity. Specified age limits were 18–45 and at first men were enlisted for one year only. Later in the year men had to be invited to re-attest for service for the duration of the war. Although men came in in satisfactory numbers shortages of accommodation, clothing and equipment hampered the Force's growth and on 11th October recruiting had to be suspended for all units of 2 Division. Before the end of September it was decided that 1 Division should go overseas as soon as possible and in December it crossed to Britain with the expectation of being ready to go to France in mid-1940. After the departure of 1 Division no further significant military events took place for some months. Although recruiting for 2 Division was resumed in March 1940 it was not concentrated until May when, with the prospect of the division being in France before the end of the year, it was decided to go ahead with the formation of a Corps Headquarters and associated troops. At the same time it was decided to form a third division for service either in Canada or overseas. This leisurely progress was interrupted by the German victories of May 1940 when a whole series of requests was received by the Canadian Government. Before the end of May a battalion embarked to relieve the British garrison in Jamaica; others went to Newfoundland where a garrison of brigade strength was maintained to the end of the war. The destination of 2 Division was now a matter of urgency. The Canadian Government was reluctant to sanction its sailing until 3 Divisioin was assembled, partly because of fears for the safety of the Pacific coast, but after a diversion to Iceland 2 Division arrived in Britain in the autumn of 1940.[20]

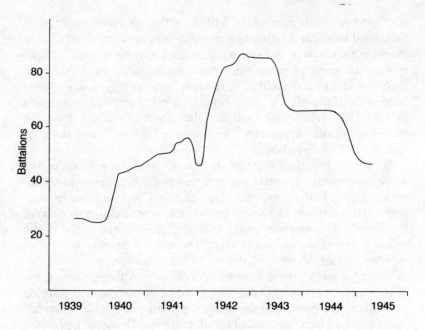

Figure 4.3. Canadian Army – Mobilised Infantry Battalions: 1939–45. Sources: PRO/WO/179 (Index). PRO/WO/193/13 and 14. Unit histories.

To supplement Canada's forces a Veterans Home Guard was formed in May, composed of over-age men, and this later became the Veterans Guard of Canada. Full-time companies later served in the West Indies and part-time reserve companies were formed. On 27th May the units to form a fourth division were mobilised although the division was not complete until June 1941. Five motorcycle regiments were mobilised from the cavalry in July to form a mobile reserve for home defence, with a further nine battalions being mobilised for local defence. (Figure 4.3) At the legislative level the National Resources Mobilisation Act, which received Royal Assent on 21st June, gave the Canadian Government wide powers over the population and its property, although the introduction of compulsion for service outside Canada was specifically excluded.[21]

In July 1940 Major-General Crerar was appointed Chief of General Staff after completing nine months in Britain as National

Defence Headquarters representative. The programme he initiated envisaged three divisions and an armoured brigade in Britain by the spring of 1941, with 4 Division to follow. 3 and 4 Divisions and the armoured brigade would be replaced by others for home defence. He suggested that five to seven divisions, of which one or more might be armoured, could be the largest force Canada was able to raise for overseas, supplemented by a further two, perhaps composed of compulsory service men, at home.[22]

Towards the end of 1940 General Crerar and Colonel Ralston, Minister of National Defence, visited Britain where it was made clear that, after 3 Division, the assistance of an armoured division and a tank brigade would be most valuable. Accordingly the formation of 1 (later 5) Canadian Armoured Division was pressed ahead at the expense of 4 Division which contributed units to the other formation. 3 Division, 5 Armoured Division and 1 Tank Brigade all crossed to Britain in 1941.

In the middle of 1941 planning commenced for the 1942 programme, preceded by the Adjutant-General's estimates that there was manpower sufficient for eight divisions, two of them at home, and to maintain them for five years. The formation of 6 Division was approved in July and in September preliminary planning was undertaken to convert 4 Division to an armoured role. In the prevailing optimism about the manpower position the Canadian Government agreed to a British request for a brigade of two battalions to join the garrison of Hong Kong. With five divisions now overseas, or earmarked for there, the higher command of these formations was now a matter of interest. Five divisions would be too many for a Corps and it was suggested that an Army Headquarters should be formed. This was a complex question involving the integration of such a structure into that of Britain, as well as being expensive in manpower terms. Consultation was lengthy but in January 1942 it was announced that 1 Canadian Army would be created during the year. The optimism about the Canadian manpower position was not maintained for long. On 16 October a Labour Supply Investigation Committee reported that 609,000 men between the ages of seventeen and forty were available for the armed services but added that 'drastic measures' would be needed to secure their services. It was becoming evident that Canada would be able to maintain no more than five divisions overseas.

The outbreak of the war against Japan, together with the entry of the United States into the war and a very great increase in German activity off the east coast, added to the requirements for home defence. To provide coastal garrisons many of the units of 4 Division were called upon and the conversion of that formation to armour was put back for several months. On the Pacific coast the feeble state of the defences gave rise to disquiet and although direct threat was remote public anxiety became acute. The formation of 7 Division was approved on 18 March 1942 and within a few days an eighth division was sanctioned. To complete these formations almost all the remaining Militia units were mobilised. The second Battalions of regiments which had mobilised were formed into Reserve Brigades with a local defence role. To complement these forces a Home Guard-type unit, the Pacific Coast Militia Rangers, was formed to patrol the west coast. The disposition of the major formations was to have 6 and 8 Divisions on the Pacific coast with 7 Division in the east. The threat of invasion was more apparent than real and 7 and 8 Divisions were broken up in the autumn of 1943, personnel being used as drafts for the formations overseas. One brigade of 6 Division took part in the operations in the Aleutians from July 1943 to January 1944 before that formation, too, was broken up to provide drafts for the Canadian Army in Europe, now entering the final campaigns of the war. Only seven infantry battalions remained in Canada and Newfoundland.[23]

Turning to general manpower questions, on mobilisation each unit had been responsible for recruiting to complete its own establishment but pre-war plans provided for the formation at an early date of Recruiting Depots to provide reinforcements. Detailed instructions laid down criteria to be applied, including a bar on the recruitment of those with special skills who might be more profitably employed elsewhere. Although physical requirements were eased, the minimum age for enlistment was raised to nineteen before the end of 1939.

The passing of the National Resources Mobilisation Act introduced a new factor and brought in elements of dualism which persisted until the end of the war. Overseas service was on a voluntary basis but compulsion could be applied for service in Canada. A National Registration in August 1940 called for personal details of all over sixteen and following this 29,750 single men were called up for thirty days of training in October, with further groups being

called out in November and January 1941. The period was really
too short to be useful and, in any case, tended to train more men
than were needed. From March 1941 5000 men were called up
each month for four months' training and in April sanction was
given to retain trained men already in service. This was followed in
July by the recall of the men who had been called out earlier for the
month's training. Under the changed circumstances of 1942 the
Government sought release from its earlier pledges that conscripts
would not serve overseas and after a referendum had shown a
decisive national vote in favour of the Government the clauses
restricting conscripts to home service were deleted. Quebec
maintained its traditional position in the referendum with a 75%
vote against the Government. In the event the Government did not
choose to apply its new powers until November 1944.

For the Active Service Force it was not until early 1941 that
the first man-power stringencies were experienced. Men were
still coming forward but not in the numbers needed to complete
the expansion programme. A broadcast appeal for 6000 men per
month made in April was followed by a recruiting campaign in
May to bring in 32,000 men over the next two months. After a slow
start the campaign met its target and probably contributed to
the optimism about the man-power position which then prevailed.
The introduction of compulsory service indirectly assisted general
service recruiting since many preferred going overseas to remaining
on guard duty in Canada for the duration.[24] From the middle of
1943, however, recruiting for overseas began to slow down, to
show that the limit for voluntary enlistment was approaching,
and that before the army had been in serious action. The heavy
casualties incurred in Italy and France in 1944 caused a short-term
crisis in maintaining the strength of the army in the war theatres.
On 23rd November 1944, after a long and bitter debate in the press
and Parliament, the Prime Minister announced that 16,000 NRMA
men would go to Europe. There was 'some rowdyism' in Quebec
but 6 Division and unattached units were sent over to be broken
up.[25] As can be seen from Figure 4.4 the Canadian Army reached
its maximum strength at the end of 1943 and suffered little decline
later, indeed the number of general service men continued to increase into 1945. The problems of 1944 were problems of deployment rather than shortage.

On mobilisation the training of recruits was undertaken by the

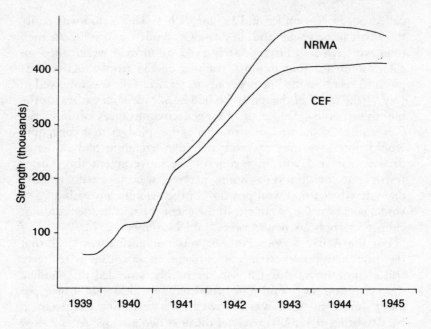

Figure 4.4. Canadian Army Strength: 1939–45. Source: C. P. Stacey, *Six Years of War*, Queen's Printer, Ottawa, 1955, Appendix A.

units themselves and to train reinforcements fourteen centres were set up in the Districts. Further centres were set up when the thirty-day programme for NRMA draftees was introduced. From March 1941 both types of centre were re-grouped as Primary and Advanced Training Centres but from 1943 both types of centre were combined. At the same time enlistment into specific corps was discontinued and recruits were allotted to corps according to aptitude and need.

The provision of officers caused little problem at the beginning of the war and during the successive mobilisations of the Militia since each unit brought its own officers with it. From November 1940 all officer candidates had first to complete a period in the ranks before being considered. The expansion of the army with the subsequent disbandment of 7 and 8 Divisions gave a surplus of officers in the junior ranks which made it possible to lend 673 of them to the British Army for service in North-west Europe.[26]

There was no official women's corps in the Canadian Army during the Great War although discussions were well advanced when the end of the war terminated further action. Discussions were resumed in 1939 but the Canadian Women's Army Corps was not formed until March 1942, at first as an auxiliary corps but later as a Corps of the Active Militia. As with the corps in other Dominions duties were of a clerical, administrative or domestic nature. The first drafts for the United Kingdom left in 1942 and subsequently the CWAC served in Italy and North-west Europe. Strength stabilised at about 13,500 from the end of 1943.

By the summer of 1943 there were three infantry and two armoured divisions and two tank brigades in Britain, when it was decided to reduce an armoured division's establishment to a single armoured brigade, matching the change which had taken place in British formations a year earlier. This gave four independent brigades equipped with tanks and two were broken up. Although two brigades of 2 Division suffered heavily in the raid on Dieppe in August 1942, by mid-1943 the position of the Canadian Army had many anomalies. Some units had been formed for active service as far back as 1939 but had seen little action. From a political point of view it was desirable that Canada should be seen as taking an active part in the war and Canadian formations were included in the troops taking part in the invasion of Sicily, being built up to a Corps for service in Italy.[27] This diversion of a significant force away from the main theatre weakened the forces available for 'Overlord' although little discussion appears to have taken place. 1 Canadian Army therefore entered the North-west European campaign with British as well as Canadian Corps under command. 1 Canadian Corps was recalled from Italy in 1945 to take part in the final stages of the war in Germany.

With a large proportion of the Canadian Army employed overseas for long periods the question of home leave assumed increasing importance as time went on. A trickle of men returned on compassionate grounds and on official duties but in February 1944 the Director-General of Medical Services suggested that on psychological grounds home leave should be granted to all who had been overseas for more than 4½ years. This suggestion was inopportune, for the major operation of the war was impending and all authorities were reluctant to see the departure of trained and experienced men. The subject was raised again in April by the Commander of 1 Corps who was becoming concerned about deteriorating morale, particularly amongst married men who feared for the survival of their homes. As an ameliorative measure men who had been wounded three times, or those twice wounded who had been away from Canada for three years, were to be posted home for six months but few qualified. In November a leave plan was published which released men who had served for five years with service in an active theatre counting double. Although it had been intended that those who went on leave should return to their units, of the first 2000 only fifty did so. This was legitimised in the spring of 1945 when it was decided that only specialists would return overseas. By now the war was nearly over and in June the scheme was absorbed into the repatriation programme. Certainly it would appear that under the ruling scheme there would have had to be significant reductions in the formations overseas had the war continued into 1946.[28]

Turning to the war in the Pacific, 6 Division was for some time earmarked for possible operations in the Kurile Islands but with the departure of the Division for Europe and disbandment the project lapsed. At a conference of Commonwealth Prime Ministers in London in May 1944 a Canadian contribution of one division for the closing stages of the war against Japan was suggested but this was not confirmed until May 1945 when the Cabinet approved in principle the formation of a division to American standards and with American equipment. Volunteering commenced promptly and since priority in repatriation was given, volunteers from 1 Army came to 90% of all who volunteered. Age limits for the Pacific force were 19–33 and by July the division's establishment was complete, with three months' reinforcements. Assembly commenced in August and 6 Division, as it was known, would have moved to the United States for training if the war had not ended.

The Canadian experience in both wars tended to follow that of Britain and India in that the total strength of the army rose to a maximum in the later stages of the war. From an organisational point of view the British experience was repeated in that in both wars contraction ensued after two or three years. In the Great War this was due, in part, to the reinforcement system in use but the short life of 5 Division indicated that manpower reasons were also responsible. For the Second World War it is possible to say that the army was not expanded at all. The formations which were placed in the field were almost all found by embodying Militia units which provided the cadres, in some cases very large cadres, on which the army was built. The formations overseas were maintained until the last six months of the war through voluntary methods and, in all, the methods used in the Second World War provide an efficient contrast to the 'call to arms' of 1914.

Notes

1 J. Gooch, *The Plans of War*, Routledge and Kegan Paul, London, 1974, pp. 6–7, 131–6, 166–8.
   Cd. 3527, Papers V and VI.
   Cd. 3523.
   R. A. Preston, *Canada and Imperial Defence*, U. of Toronto Press, 1967, pp. 31–2, 38–42, 288–98.
2 Gooch, *Plans of War*, pp. 137–40.
3 Cd. 4948.
   Gooch, *Plans of War*, Ch. 5.
4 Ibid., pp. 149–55.
   Preston, *Canada and Imperial Defence*, pp. 404–6, 445–53.
   D. Morton, *The Canadian General Sir William Otter*, Hakkert, Toronto, 1974, pp. 263–73, 294–5.
   G. W. L. Nicholson, *Canadian Expeditionary Force*, Queen's Printer, Ottawa, 1962, pp. 7–9.
5 Ibid., pp. 11–4.
6 Ibid., pp. 17–19.
7 Ibid., pp. 25–8.
8 Ibid., pp. 19–20.
9 Preston, *Canada and Imperial Defence*, pp. 467–8.
   D. Morton, 'Junior but sovereign allies', *J. Imperial and Commonwealth History*, VIII, 1979, pp. 56–67.
   Nicholson, *Canadian Expeditionary Force*, p. 29.
10 Ibid., pp. 109–10.
11 Ibid., p. 110.
12 Ibid., pp. 230–1, 381.
   R. Blake (Ed.), *The Private Papers of Douglas Haig*, Eyre and Spottiswoode, London, 1952, p. 266.
   Sir Charles Lucas (Ed.), *The Empire at War*, II, Oxford U.P., 1923, p. 210.
13 Nicholson, *Canadian Expeditionary Force*, pp. 114, 205–7.
   Lucas, *Empire at War*, p. 153.
   Morton, 'Junior but sovereign allies', pp. 59–61.
   Preston, *Canada and Imperial Defence*, pp. 477–82.
14 Nicholson, *Canadian Expeditionary Force*, p. 213.
15 Ibid., pp. 217–21, 343.
   Lucas, *Empire at War*, pp. 17–18.

16   Nicholson, *Canadian Expeditionary Force*, Ch. 11.
     Lucas, *Empire at War*, pp. 44–7, 56–7.
17   C. P. Stacey, *Six Years of War*, Queen's Printer, Ottawa, 1955,
     pp. 4–5.
     Morton, *The Canadian General*, pp. 355–60.
18   Stacey, *Six Years*, pp. 10–13.
19   Ibid., pp. 30–1.
20   Ibid., pp. 77–8.
     W. L. S. Churchill, *The Second World War*, II, Cassell, London, 1949,
     p. 236.
21   Stacey, *Six Years*, p. 82.
22   Ibid., pp. 88–9.
23   PRO/WO/106/4879.
     Stacey, *Six Years*, pp. 167–71.
24   Ibid., pp. 115–6.
25   PRO/Cab/66/40. WP(45) 7.
26   Stacey, *Six Years*, p. 139. (f.n.).
     L. F. Ellis, *Victory in the West*, I, H.M.S.O., London, 1962, p. 132.
27   C. J. C. Moloney, *The Mediterranean and Middle East*, V, H.M.S.O.,
     London, 1973, pp. 590–1.
28   Stacey, *Six Years*, pp. 428–31.

Chapter 5
Australia

i *The Australian Army to 1914*

Military forces were slow to develop in Australia. Nineteenth century Australia was remote and division of the Continent into six colonies did not encourage coordination for defence. A small volunteer association was formed in New South Wales as early as 1801 but this was disbanded eight years later, setting a pattern to be followed for the next century as the different colonies formed a succession of more or less transient corps. From the 1850s Australian opinion began to discern a threat in French and later Russian and Japanese expansion in the Pacific and each colony legislated for militia or volunteer forces. The colonies were undecided as to whether or not to concentrate on naval or military defence and, for the naval services, their relationship to the British service.[1] In 1885 New South Wales offered a force to the British Government for service in the Sudan, setting a precedent which was followed in later years as the Boxer rising and the Boer War were to show. In the latter conflict no fewer than fifty-seven contingents were sent by one or other of the colonies.

Following the establishment of the Commonwealth of Australia on 1st January 1901 the individual forces of the colonies came under central control. These were not inconsiderable, numbering 27,000 men in the various permanent, volunteer and militia forces. Under the Defence Acts of 1903 and 1904 all Australian men aged 18–60 were made liable for service in the Commonwealth in time of war and a Volunteer Militia of some 23,000 men was formed. With Britain's attention becoming increasingly focussed on Europe, Australian defence needs seemed increasingly to depend on a 'citizen army' based on universal military service.

Legislation to introduce compulsory military service was passed in 1909 but the Act was not implemented until after a visit of inspection by Kitchener in January 1910. Further Defence Acts were then passed and the new scheme came into operation in 1911 and 1912. Men aged 18–25 were liable for eight days' training per year in one of the units of the Australian Military Forces, with cadet training for the over-12s, whilst the over-25s would form a reserve. About 17,000 eighteen-year-olds were expected to be called up each year and by 1919 the 'citizen force' would have reached a maximum strength of 80,000 with a permanent cadre of about 3000. Existing members of the old militia were allowed to complete their terms of service, ending in 1914. In all by 1914 the AMF comprised twenty-three Light Horse regiments and fifty-three infantry battalions.[2]

So far as defence policy is concerned the supremacy of the Royal Navy protected Australia from serious threat of invasion throughout the 19th century. However from 1902 Britain's increasing preoccupation with European affairs and the concentration of the Fleet in Home waters was coupled with Japan's evident ambitions in the Pacific. The Imperial Conference of 1909 envisaged the formation of a Pacific squadron to which the 'colonies' would contribute and in the November a Bill providing for the establishment of an Australian naval force was placed before the Federal Parliament. For the army, although Australia accepted the principle of an Imperial General Staff very little was done to implement the proposal. Theoretically Australian defence policy was considered by a Council of Defence but since this body did not meet higher planning was ineffective.

Planning for the AMF up to 1914 envisaged only local defence and contingency planning for an expeditionary force was specifically prohibited by successive Defence Ministers. However in 1912 consultations with Major-General Godley, the New Zealand GOC, were permitted when he visited Australia. A broad agreement was then reached that if either Australia or New Zealand was invaded a joint contingent of 12,000 Australians and 6000 New Zealanders would be formed, organised as an infantry division. This informal agreement became the basis of the first offer of forces made by Australia in 1914.

ii *The First Australian Imperial Force*

As war approached in 1914 public statements in support of the British Government were made by leaders of Government and opposition parties on 31st July. Newspapers gave great prominence to offers of assistance made by Canada, it being widely believed that 30,000 men had been offered. No immediate action was taken by Australia although on 2nd August AMF units were called out to defend ports and installations. The following day the Cabinet decided to offer troops to Britain and although the advice of the Director of Military Operations was that 12,000 men could be ready to sail in six weeks the Prime Minister, taking account of the exaggerated reports from Canada, thought that 20,000 would be a more worthy contribution. The first response from Britain was unfavourable but acceptance followed on 6th August. The following day the Australian Government was invited to mount an operation against the German radio station at Rabaul, in the Bismarck Archipelago, and an Australian Naval and Military Expeditionary Force was formed. This diversion occupied a force of about a brigade until February 1915.[3]

By 1914 the militia had been formed for three years and was in the main made up from youths aged 19–21. As a defence force for service in the Commonwealth it could not be sent abroad without legislative and other action. It was therefore decided to raise the Australian Imperial Force as a force separate from the AMF as a whole. Recruitment was voluntary from the 19–38 age group and although it was anticipated that the majority would have had previous military experience or training in the event it was found that about 30% had no previous military background. Height and other physical standards were particularly rigorous and had to be relaxed for later contingents. Contrasting the situation in Canada, about 80% of those recruited were born in Australia. The composition of the AIF was to be an infantry division and a Light Horse brigade and particular attention was paid to the territorial composition of the force. A brigade each was drawn from the larger states of New South Wales and Victoria with the third brigade from the smaller states. Units were given specific areas to recruit from to make the territorial links as strong as possible. Recruiting was formally commenced by Proclamation on 10th August and men came in rapidly. The services of a fourth infantry brigade and two more Light Horse brigades were offered by the beginning of October. To officer the AIF, the Commander, Major-General Bridges, selected his brigadiers who then chose their unit commanders, the unit commanders selecting their own officers. For later contingents officers were chosen by Selection Boards but after Gallipoli promotion from the ranks became the basic system.[4]

Alarms connected with the location of the German naval squadron in the Pacific delayed the AIF's embarkation and in October it was decided that, combined with New Zealand's expeditionary force, it would travel to Europe via the Cape as a reserve for dealing with the rebellion there. However the situation in South Africa stabilised and, in view of the unfavourable experiences of the Canadians on Salisbury Plain, it was decided that the combined force would travel to Egypt to train there before going on to Europe in 1915. The force arrived in Egypt in December 1914 where it was joined by Major-General Birdwood, who had been appointed by Kitchener to command the Australian and New Zealand Army Corps. Originally it was intended that ANZAC Corps would be composed of a cavalry and two infantry divisions but for the time being it contained the Australian division and a combined ANZAC Division containing two infantry and two mounted brigades. One of each of these brigades was Australian.[5] The possibility that ANZAC Corps might be needed for an attack on Gallipoli reached the Corps on 24th February 1915 and the attack was launched on 25th April. 1 Australian Division and 4 Australian Brigade had then been formed for seven months, a month longer than had been 1 Canadian Division when it crossed to France.

From December 1914 Australia was asked to send reinforcements of 15% per month for infantry units overseas and 10% for cavalry but this target was easily achieved and in February 1915 the Australian Government was able to offer 5 and 6 Brigades and 4 Light Horse Brigade. Two months later 7 Brigade was offered. These brigades all sailed in May and June and were formed into 2 Division in August, shortly before they crossed to Gallipoli. 4 Light Horse Brigade arrived in Egypt with only one regiment mounted (13 Light Horse Regiment). This unit went to 2 Division and the remainder joined the other three Light Horse Brigades which had been dismounted and sent to Gallipoli.[6] The commander of 2 Division, Major-General McCay, was chosen by Generals Birdwood and Legge, in command of the AIF from May, who had their choice approved by Lord Kitchener with the concurrence of the Australian Government.

Following the news of the Australian landing in Gallipoli there was a considerable upsurge in enlistment and in June the Commonwealth Government was able to offer a new brigade plus double reinforcements in October and November. On 25th November a further 50,000 men were offered organised as nine infantry brigades.[7]

The withdrawal of ANZAC Corps from Gallipoli, with the consequent reduction in battle casualties, coincided with the arrival in Egypt of 8 Brigade and the reinforcements promised by the Australian Government. Taking account of the number of men in hand Lieutenant-General Godley, commanding the NZEF and officiating commander of ANZAC Corps, proposed in January 1916 that two new Australian divisions should be formed from unallotted troops. This was opposed by the Staff on grounds of the difficulty of finding sufficient officers but the project was revived within a few days by General Birdwood who had resumed command of the Corps. The basis of Birdwood's proposal was that an ANZAC Army should be formed. As in Godley's scheme two new Australian divisions could be formed while the New Zealand Brigade, which also had reinforcements in hand and in sight, could be expanded to a division. General Murray, commanding British troops in Egypt, supported the proposal as did the Australian Government which offered to form an additional division in Australia. The War Office turned down the ANZAC Army idea but, pending approval of the expansion proposals, the formation of the new divisions commenced. 4 Brigade was taken away from ANZAC Division, which would be expanded into the New Zealand Division, and with 8 Brigade provided two of six brigades needed. The others were found by dividing 1–4 Brigades to form duplicate 12–15 Brigades for 4 and 5 Divisions, all being then filled up with the reinforcements from Australia. 3 Division was formed in Australia and began to assemble in Britain in July 1916.[8]

The doubling of the AIF was not completed without difficulty. Experienced artillerymen were scarce even in the original AIF, since both of the original ANZAC divisions were on low artillery establishments. Although the men could be found, training could not overcome all of the deficiencies in skill. To provide the increased number of officers, many men were commissioned from the ranks, either being sent to Officer Training Schools or being promoted in the field. Generally men commissioned stayed with their old units. In spite of all problems 1 ANZAC Corps with 1 and 2 Australian Divisions and the New Zealand Division crossed to France in March and April. In June it was followed by 2 ANZAC Corps with 4 and 5 Australian Divisions.[9]

The Light Horse Brigades remained in the Middle East and it is convenient to summarise their subsequent development at this point. Concurrently with the duplication of the infantry divisions the three surviving Light Horse Brigades and a New Zealand mounted brigade were formed into an ANZAC Mounted Division. In addition there were three unbrigaded Light Horse Regiments, together with an Imperial Camel Brigade which was formed in December 1916 and which included three ANZAC battalions. In January 1917 4 Light Horse Brigade was reconstituted and with 3 Brigade from ANZAC Mounted Division and two Yeomanry Brigades formed into an Imperial Mounted Division. When one of the Yeomanry Brigades left the Division in June 1917 it was restyled the Australian Mounted Division. The second Yeomanry Brigade left the Division in March 1918 to leave it composed of only 3 and 4 Light Horse Brigades. In June 1918 the Camel Brigade was broken up and the Australian elements were mounted as two new Light Horse Regiments, forming a new 5 Light Horse Brigade. The third unit of 5 Brigade was French.

The establishment of an Australian GHQ to administer the AIF and maintain a watching brief over the policies under which it was employed differed in many respects from Canadian experience. The latter's London Headquarters grew into virtually a miniature War Office but the Australian overseas headquarters remained purely an administrative body, with policy decisions being referred to Sydney. An Australian base was established in Egypt in January 1915 as part of the Staff of Lieutenant-General Maxwell, commanding British troops in Egypt. A Major-General Spens was sent out by Kitchener to join Maxwell's Staff and assist in the training of ANZAC drafts with a British staff. The inter-action between this initiative and the Australian staff which had already been set up for this purpose led to the Australian Government advising the British that an Australian officer would be appointed to command its troops in Egypt and be responsible for their administration and training. The Australian Government had recognised that it could not surrender responsibility for its own people. Indeed the Commonwealth Government was asserting that the AIF was not part of the British Army but was an independent army under the ultimate control of the Australian Government. In mid-1916 the Australian base was transferred to Britain where it absorbed depots set up mainly to look after convalescent wounded from Gallipoli. The Administrative Headquarters, AIF, in London was commanded by General Birdwood who was appointed to command the AIF in September 1916. To supply reinforcements for the AIF Training Groups and Depots in England fed holding units in France.[10]

Recruitment for the Australian Imperial Force proceeded at a satisfactory level until well into 1916. Physical and other criteria for enlistment were, though, reduced from February 1915 when the original height standard of five feet six inches was reduced to five feet four inches and the age limits enlarged to 18–45. Successive reductions brought the height standard down to five feet in April 1917. The general policy regarding recruits was that they should be sent overseas as soon as possible to train in the theatres in which they would serve and, except at times of rapid enlistment, only small numbers of troops were held in Australia.[11]

Public pressure for a more active organisation to promote recruiting began to develop early in 1915 and the question of introducing conscription was raised in Parliament in April and again two months later. On both occasions the proposal was rejected. In July a recruiting campaign was introduced in Victoria, a state in which enlistment was considered to be especially backward, and subsequent recruiting drives were launched in other states. A 'war census' in July called for information on all males aged 18–60 and this showed that there were still 244,000 single men available. Their details were passed to local recruiting organisations to contact all who had not volunteered. Although Prime Minister Fisher declared in September that he was opposed to conscription he proposed to make a postal appeal to each man aged eighteen to forty-four. Indeed the conscription question was becoming an emotive and divisive issue in Australian politics. Some sections of the public were in favour, others, including many Trade Unions, were against and even the Cabinet was divided. State War Councils were set up and assigned recruiting quotas and intensive canvassing of potential volunteers took place. The intensity of the canvassing became a further factor in provoking opposition to conscription.[12]

The entry of Australian troops into the line in France, together with the heavy casualties suffered in the Pozieres battle in July 1916, hastened the call for conscription. A telegram from the Colonial Secretary on 24th August asked for a special draft of 20,000 infantry plus 25% reinforcements in each of the following three months. With recruiting for the AIF now running at 6000 per month such reinforcements were simply not in sight. A proposal to break up 3 Division, still in Britain, was rejected but 233 men were taken from each battalion in September. Only conscription could supply the men now being called for but the strongly held opposing views of many sections of the public gave little confidence that the measure would be supported. The Government's response was to announce that a referendum on the issue would be held, while making yet another call for volunteers in September, this time for 32,500 men. Anticipating a positive vote, in October all unmarried men aged between twenty-one and thirty-five were called up under the existing Defence Acts for service within the Commonwealth. The referendum was held on 28 October. The vote in three states was in favour, three against. The adverse vote in New South Wales was the deciding factor. 1,087,557 voted in favour of conscription, 1,160,133 against. Those called up earlier in the month were released, although perhaps as many as 5000 of them chose to enlist for overseas.[13]

The failure to bring in conscription, together with the Australian experiences in France, brought in two elements which persisted until the end of the war. The first was the continuing difficulty in keeping the AIF up to strength, the second was an intensification of the belief that Australian troops should fight together under their own commander. On a visit to Haig in May 1916 Prime Minister Hughes expressed the view that the ANZAC troops should be regarded as an army and that Birdwood should command it. At the same time he mentioned the possibility that a sixth division might be formed. The Canadians already fought together, as a precedent, but the Australian five divisions were too many for a single Corps and too few for an Army. With the New Zealanders they made up two Corps and fought divided. The sixth division suggestion was repeated by the Australian CGS but, bearing in mind the reinforcement difficulties already faced by the Australians, the Army Council rejected the idea.[14] The project was revived in February 1917 when Britain asked Australia for an extra division and this time a brigade began forming in the United Kingdom to act as a cadre for future expansion. The casualties suffered at the battle of Bullecourt in April were, however, such that the project had to be abandoned.[15]

In July 1917, in a message to the Colonial Secretary, the Australian Government again returned to the question of the grouping of the Australian troops but these urgings were accompanied by a steady decline in the fighting strength of the Australian divisions. By October each was above 3000 under strength with little likelihood of replenishment across the winter. Transferring the mounted units from Egypt was considered but this was rejected because of the vital role they were playing there. However the weakness of the Australian formations was itself instrumental in bringing about one of the Australian ambitions. In November 1–3 and 5 Divisions were at last grouped as an Australian Corps with General Birdwood in command. The under-strength 4 Division acted as a reserve. To help meet the chronic manpower shortage another referendum on conscription was announced in November. In anticipation of a successful result Lord Derby, the British War Secretary, wrote to Haig suggesting that if the Australians were able to form a sixth division they might be grouped as a Command of two Corps each of three divisions. It will be recalled that about this time a similar suggestion was being made in connection with the Canadians. However the voting on 20th December still showed opposition to compulsory service with 1,015,159 for and 1,181,747 against. The Command proposal died. It was becoming clear that some units and formations would have to be broken up sooner or later but for the present all remained in being, even the four-battalion brigades being retained.[16]

After the failure of the referendum, attempts were made to revive volunteering but the souring of views caused by the divisions of the referendum campaigns produced much resistance. There was even confusion and debate as to how many men were really needed and eventually an enquiry under the Chief Justice was set up. This reported in March 1918 that 5400 per month would maintain the AIF's strength but 8233 per month would be needed to make up deficiencies. These figures were accepted as recruiting targets but even the lower figure was never attained.[17]

The intensive operations early in 1918 brought further fears about the future of the Australian troops in France. The Australian Prime Minister was now concerned that if the war continued into 1919 and the Australian representation was reduced to two or three divisions Australia would have diminished influence in peace negotiations. The first Australian disbandments took place in May when three battalions were broken up. To conserve remaining strength the Prime Minister suggested to the CIGS that home leave should be granted to original members of the AIF and that the whole Corps should be transferred to a milder climate for the coming winter. In another way, though, Australian aspirations were being satisfied when Lieutenant-General Monash, an Australian officer, was appointed to command the Australian Corps in May. General Birdwood remained in command of the AIF as a whole. September brought further reductions when the disbandment of a further eight battalions was ordered and the first draft for home leave, 3600 men, sailed for Australia. But the end of the war was in sight. 1 and 4 Divisions were withdrawn from service to await reinforcement from the trickle of men coming from Australia but the other three kept on to the end.[18]

In attempting to maintain five infantry divisions and five mounted brigades in service it is clear that without conscription Australia faced an impossible task. After 1916 Australia's experience of volunteering repeated that of Canada to a considerable degree, although the manpower problems of the latter were eased to a considerable extent by conscription. Both countries paid the price of internal disunity for introducing compulsory service as a political issue. Under voluntary enlistment Australia raised 416,809 men during the war against Canada's 469,557 out of male populations of 2·3 and 3·8 millions. In so far as gross population figures indicate recruiting potential, Australia would appear to have obtained a better result than Canada but at the end of the war the latter was only attempting to maintain four divisions in the field, not six.

Discussion of Australia's manpower problems in quantitative terms is hampered by the lack of statistics. No strength figures for the AIF appear to have survived and British sources are suspect. Basing estimates on the latter, the AIF's strength in February 1918 was 198,333 against a strength of 178,342 in November. However similar calculations for Canada's forces give an under-estimate of 8–12% when compared with Canadian sources. Canada had larger numbers of troops employed away from the Canadian Corps on such duties as forestry and railways, making it easy to 'lose' Canadian troops in others' statistics. Even so the discrepancies are too large to give other than a general impression that the AIF's strength was decreasing significantly across 1918.[19] The 'divisional slice' for the AIF in November 1918 was probably a little over 30,000. On the one hand this seems to indicate a remarkable efficiency in the handling of limited manpower but reserves were few and had the war continued into 1919 contraction in the number of formations must have ensued. The low 'slice' indicated, too, that the Australian Corps, like the ANZAC Corps before, needed the support of the ancilliary services of other countries. With the Australians employed to a very great extent as front line troops the AIF earned a superb reputation as a fighting force, greatly enhancing the sense of Australian nationality and self-esteem.

iii   *The inter-war years*

During the war just finished the Australian Military Forces, the Militia, continued annual training much as in peacetime, being called out briefly in 1916 and 1918 when attack by raiders was feared. In 1918, before the end of the war, the AMF was re-modelled to duplicate the structure of the AIF, with reserves, but this was not maintained for long. Faced with the heavy burden of expenditure on development and viewing the League of Nations as a potent instrument for lasting peace, in 1921 a further reorganisation of the Militia eliminated the reserve component, leaving only the units for five infantry and two cavalry divisions.

   Further events in 1921 and 1922 rapidly produced more reductions in Australia's defences in general and in the Militia in particular. At the Imperial Conference in 1921 it was announced that Britain had decided to construct a main fleet base at Singapore. Hypothetically a naval force based there would be on the flank of any thrust on Australia and New Zealand, adding to their security. Although some views were expressed at the time and later that if such a threat developed it would be at a time when Britain herself was threatened nearer home and would be unable to spare a fleet, Australia adopted the CID's defence policy ready-made. The Washington Conference on fleet limitation which followed in 1922 also appeared to be an optimistic move. Although tacitly the agreement implied that the Royal Navy accepted that it no longer held maritime supremacy, and the associated Four Power Treaty which replaced the former Anglo-Japanese Alliance was a weaker instrument in curbing Japanese ambitions, both were seen at the time as further moves towards disarmament and peace.

After the Washington Conference Australia took steps to reduce the RAN, at the same time reducing the strength of the Militia to 31,000, little more than a cadre for the seven divisions, whilst halving the army's permanent staff to 1600.

The Imperial Conference of 1923 confirmed Britain's intention to develop the Singapore base and at the same time confirmed that Australia's defence policy would be a dependence on maritime power. Such resources as could be spared would be devoted to naval construction.[20]

In October 1929 a Labour Government took office and this event was immediately followed by further reductions in military expenditure. Compulsory training for the Militia was abandoned and in its place a new voluntary militia was created. The new force had an establishment of 35,000 but enrolled strengths in the following years varied between 26,000 and 29,000. The abolition was based on political theory but the coincidental collapse of the New York Stock Exchange ensured that economic necessity would confirm the reductions. Between 1934 and 1937 a very modest programme provided for a partial mechanisation of the Militia but such preparations held a very low priority in Australian policy. In 1937 an analysis of defence policy described its basis as being participation in Empire naval defence to protect trade and deter invasion and raids, coupled with local defence. For the army three scales of mobilisation were envisaged. In the first coastal defences would be manned, in the second two divisions and seven brigades would be needed to repel raids. In the final situation an enemy, probably Japan, would be threatening invasion and all seven divisions would be mobilised, mainly being concentrated to defend the Sydney area.[21]

The deteriorating situation in Europe had its corresponding effects in Australia. In November 1937 the influential Returned Soldiers League called for the formation of a reserve of ex-soldiers to carry out local defence duties and in March 1938 a considerable increase in defence spending was announced, spread over three

years. Major priorities were still assigned to the naval and air forces
but the Militia's establishment was doubled. In a recruiting campaign in the latter half of 1938, after Munich, the strength of
the Militia increased to 43,000 by the end of the year and then on
to 70,000, the target, by March 1939. A list of Reserved Occupations and Industries was prepared and a National Register was
undertaken.[22] An inspection of Australian defences by Major-
General Squires, a British officer, recommended that a regular force
of two infantry brigades should be formed and this proposal was
accepted in March 1939, when it was announced that two battalions would be formed as a first step. Amendment to the Defence
Acts was necessary since these restricted permanent forces to
artillerymen and technical troops. Indeed, in the previous year
when a small contingent had been recruited as a garrison for
Darwin they had been recruited as artillery, although equipped and
trained as infantry. Another legislative step taken at this time was
to extend the definition of Australian territory to include Papua and
Norfolk Island, extending the area within which a compulsorily-
enlisted Militia could serve.[23]

A policy change soon followed a change of Government in April
1939. In August it was announced that the regular force would not
be raised but a special force of Militia would be raised in its place.
This would be 14,000 strong and it would train for thirty-two days
per year. For the rest of the Militia training would be increased to
sixteen days per year with additional training for officers and
NCOs.

At the outbreak of war the Australian Army comprised 3500
permanent staff with 70,000 militiamen. They were organised in
two cavalry and four infantry divisions, three independent brigades
and two recently formed Armoured Car Regiments. 'Substantially
the force was armed with the weapons which the AIF had brought
back in 1919'.[24]

iv   *The Second AIF*

The first actions to commence the Second World War began on
25th August when coast defences were manned on a skeleton basis
and a 'precautionary' stage was adopted on 2nd September when
the formal steps were taken to call out the militia. Two days later
parties of militiamen were called up, 10,000 at a time, for guard

duties until relieved by Garrison Battalions which had been formed of old soldiers. No immediate action was taken to form further forces although the Government was invited to consider whether or not British garrisons in South-east Asia might be relieved by Australian brigades or that Australian divisions should be sent to the main theatre. The attitude of Japan was the crucial factor. If the Government decided against dispatch of Australian forces it was requested to hold formations in readiness to reinforce South-east Asia. On 15th September the Prime Minister, Mr Menzies, announced that a division would be formed for service either at home or abroad. The division would be formed on the same geographical basis as 1 Division in 1914 and enlistment would be open to men aged 20–35. At the same time he advised that the militia would be called out in two drafts, each of about 40,000, for a month's training.[25]

The formation of 6 Division commenced at a leisurely pace. It was intended that the Division would be assembled in November but after an initial rush men were slow to come in. The operation of the list of reserved occupations prevented the enlistment of some and there was doubt about the Division's future employment. Government statements, too, seemed to indicate that air forces were of greater importance. About half of the recruits were expected to come from the militia and the sense of lack of urgency was enhanced by a Cabinet decision not to fill gaps in the militia caused by enlistment, nor those caused by the withdrawal of men in essential occupations. It was further decided that married men who had completed their month's militia training could transfer to the reserve.[26]

Major-General Blamey was chosen to command 6 Division and, as in 1914, he chose his brigadiers who in their turn chose unit commanders who chose their own officers. No direct affiliation with militia units was attempted although it would appear that an indirect one grew up in the early stages. Militia organisation was a replica of that of the old AIF and the decision to form 6 Division on the old AIF pattern ensured that the organisations were parallel. While the Division was forming a long debate ensued about its employment. All of the old arguments about the Japanese threat were repeated but at last, on 28th November, the Cabinet reached its decision. The first elements of 6 Division sailed from Sydney on 9th January 1940 and headed for Suez.[27]

In October 1939 the Cabinet decided that compulsory training for the militia would be re-introduced from 1st January. The first draft called up would be unmarried men 21 years of age, the objective being to maintain the militia at a strength of at least 75,000. No initial training was prescribed although shortly afterwards the militia units were called out for three months' training.

In February 1940 the Cabinet approved the formation of 7 Division, destined to follow 6 Division for the Middle East where they would unite as 1 Australian Corps. In that same month the Defence Department's Manpower Committee estimated manpower needs to mid-1942 as a little over 150,000 – an indication of how small an ultimate expansion was then envisaged. While 7 Division was forming the second and third brigades of 6 Division sailed for the Middle East and while the last of these convoys was in transit the entry of Italy into the war effectively closed passage of the Red Sea. The convoy, containing 18 Brigade and other troops, was diverted first to Cape Town and then on to England where they arrived in June. The Australian Government was anxious about the splitting up of their forces but acquiesced in the diversion and the Australians provided a welcome reinforcement for Britain in the days following.

Even though recruits for 7 Division were only coming in slowly, on 22nd May the Commonwealth Government approved the formation of 8 Division. The crisis of mid-1940 changed the situation greatly. In June nearly 50,000 men offered their services, the number being swelled by raising the maximum age limit to 40 and by reducing the height standard to five feet. During the third week in June it was decided to form a fourth AIF division and even a fifth seemed possible. With men enlisting from the militia in large numbers there were risks that the home defence forces were being unduly depleted and on 19th July recruiting for the AIF was temporarily suspended. The Government's intention at this time was to build up a home defence force of about 250,000 men, including the 30,000 or 40,000 AIF men likely to be under training in Australia at any one time. An Australian Army Reserve was also formed. Part A contained volunteers up to forty-eight years of age who trained with the militia: Part B, in two groups, either served in a Garrison Battalions Reserve or in a Volunteer Defence Corps which was administered by the Returned Soldiers League as a Home Guard.[28]

The troops diverted to Britain in June included reinforcement drafts from which a brigade was improvised and it was decided to draw on these troops to form the elements of 9 Division which would assemble in the Middle East. To complete the Division a brigade was drawn from 8 Division, a new brigade being formed in Australia. 7 Division began to move from Australia to the Middle East in October while the brigades from Britain were transferred a month or two later. The diversion of the brigade of 6 Division had thus instituted what became a wholesale transfer of brigades from division to division and units from brigade to brigade which retarded the preparation of the AIF for service. However by March 1941, when 6 Division embarked for Greece, the Australian Corps in the Middle East was well on the way to becoming the largest homogeneous Commonwealth force in the theatre. The Australian divisions remained there until the outbreak of war with Japan when 1 Corps, with 6 and 7 Divisions, sailed for South-east Asia and then on to Australia. 9 Division remained to take part in the Alamein battles before returning in the early part of 1943.

v   *The defence of Australia*

The German victories of 1940 aroused disquiet in Australia as to whether or not Japan might take advantage of those victories to improve her position in the Pacific. In Australia a National Security Act in June authorised control over all persons and property in the service of the Commonwealth. This apparently allowed full industrial conscription but application was akin to that in Britain in the Great War, with industries being protected and transfer of workers only allowed with permission from the Department of Munitions.[29]

Towards the end of June a request was received for a division to reinforce Singapore and although the use of 7 Division for this was discussed, that formation eventually went to the Middle East. However the weakness of Malaya's defences remained under review and early in 1941 one of 8 Division's brigades went there, to be followed by another and the divisional headquarters later in the year. Contingency planning at this time was concerned with the establishment of air bases to the north of Australia and three battalions were earmarked for the defence of Rabaul, Timor and Ambon. Thus 8 Division, originally intended to join its fellows in the Middle East, was now committed to South-east Asia. The formation was lost in Malaya in February 1942 while the detached battalions of the third brigade were lost piecemeal in their island garrisons.[30]

In the early part of 1941, following British emphasis on the development of armoured formations, it was decided to form 1 Armoured Division as part of the AIF with the intention that it should follow the infantry divisions to the Middle East. The outbreak of war with Japan caused a review of its future, as will be noted later.

Australia was not immune from the pressure to form raiding forces and a mission arrived from Britain in November 1940 to advise on training requirements. A Training Centre opened in February 1941 and four Independent Companies were formed later in the year with four more in 1942. Although one company was lost in the islands in 1942, the others served in New Guinea until absorbed into the dismounted Divisional Cavalry Regiments of the AIF divisions in 1943. Parachute training commenced as part of the Independent Company organisation and a battalion began forming in March 1943. It was warned for duty from time to time but never used. The battalion served briefly with the occupation forces in Singapore in 1945 and 1946.

After the AIF enlistment phase of mid-1940 the strength of the militia had fallen to around 60,500 and the age group for compulsory training was extended to cover all unmarried men and childless widowers aged 18–35. A month's training had been ordered in 1939 and a further three months' in 1940. This was followed by orders to undergo a further ten weeks' early in 1941 and then, in July 1941, by orders that 'trained soldiers' of the militia should carry out three months' training each year, while recruits would train for six months. Although the piecemeal nature of this training reduced its value all units of the militia now had cadres of officers and NCOs serving full time and quite significant numbers were in service at any one time as units occupied the training grounds in succession. With incipient signs of manpower shortage, a Manpower Priorities Board was established in July 1941 to monitor the distribution of labour. AIF strength was now expected to approach 250,000 and the formation of a Women's Army Service was approved in August although recruitment did not commence until January 1942.[31]

On the outbreak of war with Japan the militia was called out on 9th December 1941 and two days later the Cabinet decided to extend conscription to married men aged 18–35 and childless married men and widowers aged 35–45. Enlistment for the AIF, which had been running at 5000 per month, doubled but did not reach the heights of June 1940 for in January the Government prohibited transfers from the militia. The Manpower Priorities Board was reconstituted into a Manpower Directorate with wide executive powers. One of its first acts was to institute a new National Register of all over the age of sixteen. A supplementary register in April 1943 extended the coverage to include 14-year-olds. At a survey in April 1942 the Manpower Directorate indicated that 318,000 men and women were needed for the armed forces and essential industry. Only 130,000 were available. The needs could only be met by increased employment of women, reduction of less essential industry and by downwards revision of the Services' programmes.[32]

With the mobilisation the number of units in service grew rapidly and the militia concentrated to defend the populated areas (see Figure 5.1). The rapid success of the Japanese offensives, coupled with the attack on Darwin on 19 February and subsequent raids, appeared to indicate the imminent invasion of Australia and further forces were concentrated in the Northern Territory and Queensland, which seemed to be the areas immediately threatened. Even before the end of 1942, though, the Japanese naval defeats, the evident threat developing through New Guinea and the diminished risks of direct invasion indicated that the number of units and formations in Australia was excessive and some contraction ensued. The Volunteer Defence Corps grew rapidly in strength as danger approached and exceeded 90,000 by May 1942. It was stood down progressively from mid-1944.

The troops originally available to defend New Guinea were heterogeneous. The oldest was the New Guinea Volunteer Rifles, formed from local residents in September 1939, and this was joined by the first elements of a Papuan Infantry Battalion in June 1940. From July 1940 units composed of militia volunteers for tropical service reached Port Moresby, totalling three battalions by January 1942. A further militia brigade reached Port Moresby in May and another went to Milne Bay in July. Brigades of 7 Division began to arrive in New Guinea in August. The New Guinea Volunteer Rifles

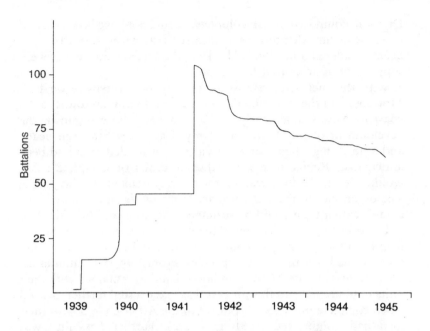

Figure 5.1. Mobilised Australian Infantry Battalions: 1939–45. Sources: Australian Official Histories. Unit histories.

and Papuan Infantry Battalion were extensively used for reconnaissance and further units were raised later.[33]

The two Cavalry Divisions of the CMF mobilised in December 1941 but a mechanisation programme was put in hand immediately and in March 1942 they became Motor Divisions. Six months later they became 2 and 3 Armoured Divisions, a Tank Brigade being formed at the same time. Tanks were available in fair quantity from the United States and local production and equipping went ahead rapidly. However even before the programme was complete the reduced risk of invasion and the limited use of armoured formations in jungle warfare produced a review of policy and reductions commenced. The Armoured Divisions were all broken up in 1943 and only one armoured brigade remained. In retrospect it would appear that the Australian armoured forces were greatly over-expanded but they would have been invaluable in the event of invasion. One Australian recorded his regret that 1 Armoured

Division, composed of AIF volunteers, could not have been released to serve in the Mediterranean theatre. This never seems to have been considered officially and by 1943 the Mediterranean was well-supplied with armoured formations.[34]

With the successful repulse of the Japanese offensive on Port Moresby, and the Australian and American follow-up to the north coast of New Guinea early in 1943, a new phase began in the development of the Australian Army. Casualties had been heavy and a much higher rate of replacement was needed than had been anticipated. Replacements, whether as drafts or complete units, would need to be fully trained for the requirements of the jungle. The organisation of the Australian Army had been expanded to a greater extent than could be sustained and units and brigades had to be broken up. The division of the Army into two sections did not help for although the AIF could be used anywhere the CMF could only be used in Australian territories. From July 1942 militiamen could transfer to the AIF on condition that they remained with their units until needed and this process was taken a step further in 1943 when complete units could transfer to the AIF if 65–75% of their men had volunteered (see Figure 5.2). Further flexibility was obtained through a Defence Act of February 1943 which re-defined the zone in which the militia could be employed as being south of the equator and between the easterly meridians of 110 and 159 degrees.[35]

From November 1942 a jungle warfare training centre was set up at Canungra in Queensland to train drafts who had completed basic training. At Atherton a large centre was established to facilitate the training and retraining of units and formations before they entered or returned to New Guinea or other jungle warfare areas. The system developed provides an interesting contrast to that of the Indian Army faced with a similar problem.[36]

Returning to general manpower questions, in September 1942 overall authority passed to a War Commitments Committee which, reporting in January 1943, noted that 35,000 persons would be needed each month with only 10,000 available. In March, observing that the Army was 79,000 under establishment and that it needed 12,500 men per month, the Cabinet minuted that reductions in the number of fighting formations would be needed. March was, indeed, the month in which the Australian Army reached its greatest strength but with a population only two-thirds that of

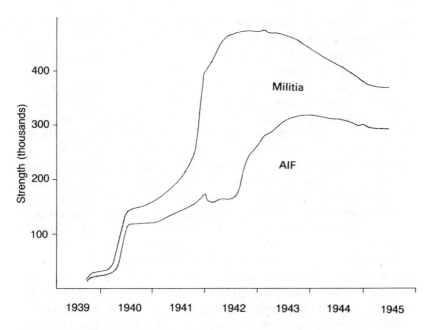

Figure 5.2. Australian Army Strength: 1939–45. Source: Information from Australian Central Army Records.

Canada it was attempting to maintain roughly the same number of men under arms. The Army's programme, presented in April by the C-in-C, General Blamey, was for nine infantry and two armoured divisions with an armoured and a tank brigade. Six of the infantry divisions were needed for New Guinea.[37] Manpower economies could be made by employing the Volunteer Defence Corps for coastal defence but some reduction was inevitable.

The considerable Australian victories of June 1943–February 1944, which resulted in clearing the Japanese from the eastern half of New Guinea, was followed by a phase of reduced activity in 1944. Control of operations passed to the United States and Australian divisions returned to the mainland for rehabilitation, leaving the equivalent of two divisions on garrison duties. It was at this time the Australian Army received a request for officers to serve with the Indian Army, a figure of 600 being mentioned, and 168 were seconded.[38] Another enquiry was for the services of airborne troops, if these were available, since India was attempting to form an airborne division. The Australian Parachute Battalion was, however, committed to South-west Pacific Area and it was said that it could not be spared.

During 1943 Australia's manpower position continued to deteriorate. In addition to supporting naval, air and land forces in the war against Japan, and to some extent against the Germans, Australia's industrial and agricultural base was supplying American forces in the South-west Pacific with many of their necessities. In October 1943 the Cabinet ordered the Army to release 20,000 men to industry and agriculture by June 1944. Before this process had been completed a planned reduction of the Army was confirmed by the Cabinet in July 1944, which would reduce it to six divisions and two armoured brigades by mid-1945. Reporting to the Cabinet in May 1944, the CGS said that the Army would be able to carry out its commitments provided it received 1500 men and women per month but the Cabinet decided to allot only 1345. With a monthly wastage of 4000 this ensured that there would be a further fall in strength and this was enhanced when, on 2nd August, the Prime Minister advised the C-in-C that he intended to cut the Army by another 30,000 by mid-1945. These discussions took place while the future role of the Australian Army was in doubt. Three of the six divisions were from the militia and, while containing many men who had volunteered for the AIF, they contained many who had not. They could not be employed north of the Equator. The employment of the CMF divisions was settled on 12 July 1944 when the Supreme Commander ordered that Australian formations would relieve American in containing Japanese forces remaining in the Solomons, New Britain and on the north coast of New Guinea. These commitments would need an AIF division as well as the militia.[39]

The employment of 1 Australian Corps. containing the two remaining AIF divisions, caused considerable discussion. Allied strategy for the closing stages of the Japanese war was unclear and the pace of the war was tending to out-run plans. On the British side, in 1944 the war in Burma was at its height and there was uncertainty about when troops would be available after the defeat of Germany. There was uncertainty about whether British effort should be towards South-east Asia or through the Pacific, based on Australia. On the American side there was reluctance to accept

British aid in the final stages, coupled with doubt as to whether it could be developed in time to be effective. The adoption of a British Pacific strategy would apply a great strain on Australia's economy, for perhaps half a million troops would be based there, and this could well demand a further reduction in the Australian forces themselves. 1 Australian Corps was already allotted to South-west Pacific Command and for a time it was proposed that it would take part in the invasion of the Philippines but a firm role only emerged in February 1945. The Corps would capture Borneo and from there would probably go on to Japan. All this was placed in the melting pot when, in April, the Cabinet decided that the Army and Air Force would release 50,000 men by the end of the year, in addition to ordinary wastage which was estimated at 20,000.[40]

By the end of 1944 the original AIF volunteers had been serving for four or five years and as a first stage for providing relief to long-service men it was decided that those who had enlisted before they were twenty-one and who had three years service could be released, while those who wished to complete courses in badly needed skills, such as medicine, the sciences or engineering, could be released after one year. The conditions under which the total of 80,000 men referred to in August 1944 and April 1945 would be released were discussed in mid-1945. Hitherto releases had been governed by the needs of industry, as determined by the Manpower Directorate. General Blamey submitted that a proportion of the releases should be allocated to men who had served for more than five years, those who were over thirty-five and had served for three years and to the over-45s. On 31st May, however, the Cabinet decided that all who had served for five years should be given the option of discharge. With one AIF division in action in New Guinea and two more about to invade Borneo the implications of this decision were similar to those concerning 'Python' and the invasion of Malaya but the decision was too near to the end of the war to significantly accelerate the discharge of men with long service.[41]

In the light of the end of the war against Germany, on 16th May the C-in-C suggested that the Australian contribution to the war could be reduced to three divisions and this was confirmed by the Cabinet in June. One division, with two brigades, would be employed in New Guinea and the Solomons, one division in New Britain, a brigade could be available for South-east Asia which would leave one division for operations against Japan.

At the beginning of the war Australia saw the conflict as one in which she could participate on 'limited liability' terms and the formation of the AIF appears to have been a natural response to this assumption. Although the AIF was formed as a separate force from the militia it drew heavily on the latter, especially for its leaders. The crisis of 1940 did not entirely dispel the 'limited liability' hypothesis, although with a potential threat from Japan considerable elements of the militia were mobilised for training. With the outbreak of war with Japan the militia was mobilised in full. The threat to Australia was now close and the degree of mobilisation was not one which could be sustained. Once the threat had passed men had to be released to return to civil life. It was ironical that while planning was going on to mount large campaigns from Australia in 1945 and 1946 the main thrust of Australian internal planning was increasingly turning towards postwar reconstruction.

In June 1945 the Australian Army contained 365,000 men, 80% of them volunteers, and this force was sustaining twenty-one brigades. It was therefore taking some 52,000 men to place the equivalent of a division in the field, indicating a relatively smaller 'tail' than existed in many other armies. Although this could indicate a high degree of organisational efficiency the operations in which the Australian Army was engaged were operations in which a high degree of mechanisation was a hindrance rather than a help. Further, although communications to the front line were difficult the distance from the main bases in Australia was not great and the Army had no need to create an infrastructure for its bases as was necessary in the Middle East or in India. However the war being fought was an infantry war with the inevitable high rates of wastage and a fully developed training and reinforcement system was a necessity. Even so a 'divisional slice' of 52,000 appears for the times to have been very modest.

So far as the organisation of the Australian Army was concerned the cycle of development repeated that observed earlier with both Britain and Canada in that contraction ensued in the later years of both wars. Manpower experience was different. In the Great War, having to depend entirely on voluntary enlistment, strength dwindled towards the end. In the Second World War the Government deliberately limited enlistment from mid-1943 and applied a policy of selective demobilisation from later in that year.

Notes

1 R. A. Preston, *Canada and Imperial Defence*, U. of Totonto Press, 1967, pp. 96–102.
  G. St. J. Barclay, *The Empire is Marching*, Wiedenfeld and Nicolson, London, 1976, pp. 6–26.
2 Sir Philip Magnus, *Portrait of an Imperialist*, John Murray, London, 1958, pp. 244–5.
  Army List, 1914.
  C. E. W. Bean, *Australia in the War*, I, Angus and Robertson, Sydney, 1921, p. 34. E. S. Scott, XI, 1936, pp. 191–5.
3 Bean, *Australia in the War*, I, pp. 29–31.
4 Ibid., pp. 37–42, 54.
5 Field Marshal Lord Birdwood, *Khaki and Gown*, Ward Lock, London, 1941, pp. 238–40.
  Bean, *Australia in the War*, I, pp. 117–8.
6 Bean, *Australia in the War*, II, 1924, pp. 419, 423–4.
7 Bean, *Australia in the War*, III, 1929, pp. 7–9.
8 Ibid., pp. 36–42.
  Birdwood, *Khaki and Gown*, p. 299.
9 Bean, *Australia in the War*, III, p. 53.
10 Preston, *Canada and Imperial Defence*, pp. 482–5.
  Bean, *Australia in the War*, II, pp. 401, 418. III, pp. 146, 158–66.
11 Scott, *Australia in the War*, XI, p. 439.
12 Ibid., pp. 310–12.
  Bean, *Australia in the War*, III, p. 10.
13 Ibid., pp. 865–8.
  Sir Charles Lucas (Ed.), *The Empire at War*, III, Oxford U. P., 1924, p. 34.
  Scott, *Australia in the War*, XI, pp. 339–57.
14 Bean, *Australia in the War*, III, pp. 155–7.
15 Bean, *Australia in the War*, IV, 1933, p. 15.
16 Bean, *Australia in the War*, V, 1936, pp. 3, 9–11.
  Scott, *Australia in the War*, XI, pp. 412–27.
  R. Blake (Ed.), *The Private Papers of Douglas Haig*, Eyre and Spottiswoode, London, 1952, p. 266.
17 Scott, *Australia in the War*, XI, pp. 443–4.
18 Bean, *Australia in the War*, VI, 1942, p. 877.
  Lucas, *Empire at War*, p. 166.
19 War Office, *Statistics of the Military Effort of the Empire*, H.M.S.O., London, 1922, Table facing p. 64 and pp. 146, 155.
20 G. Long, *To Benghazi*, Australian War Memorial, Canberra, 1952, pp. 4–5.
21 Ibid., pp. 12–4, 21, 24–5.
  Cmd. 6923.
22 S. J. Butlin, *War Economy, 1939–42*, Australian War Memorial, Canberra, 1955, pp. 14–8, 228–34.
23 Long, *Benghazi*, pp. 27–9.

24 Ibid., p. 40.
25 Ibid., pp. 35, 39.
26 Ibid., pp. 65–6.
27 Ibid., pp. 42–3, 64–5.
28 D. McCarthy, *Kokoda to Wau*, Australian War Memorial, Canberra, 1959, p. 3.
29 Butlin, *War Economy*, pp. 235–6, 249–52.
30 L. Wigmore, *The Japanese Thrust*, Australian War Memorial, Canberra, 1957, pp. 19–20, 24, 59.
    W. L. S. Churchill, *The Second World War*, III, Cassell, London, 1949, pp. 591–2.
31 McCarthy, *Kokoda to Wau*, pp. 1–2.
    Butlin, *War Economy*, pp. 475–81.
32 McCarthy, *Kokoda to Wau*, pp. 11, 13.
    S. J. Butlin and C. B. Schedvin, *War Economy, 1942–45*, Australian War Memorial, Canberra, 1977, pp. 13–22, 39–41.
33 G. Long, *The Final Campaigns*, Australian War Memorial, Canberra, 1963, pp. 82–3.
34 PRO/WO/193/13 and 14.
    McCarthy, *Kokoda to Wau*, pp. 452–3.
    D. Dexter, *The New Guinea Offensives*, Australian War Memorial, Canberra, 1961, p. 18.
35 Ibid., p. 16.
36 Ibid., pp. 228–9.
37 Ibid., p. 13.
    Butlin and Schedvin, *War Economy*, pp. 43–6, 353–8.
38 Dexter, *New Guinea Offensives*, pp. 781–2.
39 Long, *Final Campaigns*, pp. 21–2, 31–2.
    Butlin and Schedvin, *War Economy*, pp. 360–6, 686–7.
40 J. Ehrman, *Grand Strategy*, V, H.M.S.O., London, 1956, Chs. 11 and 12, VI, Chs. 6 and 8.
    Long, *Final Campaigns*, pp. 13–4, 28, 34.
    Butlin and Schedvin, *War Economy*, p. 700.
41 Long, *Final Campaigns*, pp. 390–3.

Chapter 6
New Zealand

i New Zealand's Army to 1919

British sovereignty was proclaimed in New Zealand in 1840, as part of the colony of New South Wales, and separate status was accorded in May the following year. The first militia and volunteer forces were formed between 1843 and 1845 although it was not until the Maori Wars of the 1860s that there was any considerable expansion. Volunteering was particularly strong in New Zealand and although militia enactments remained until 1911 as early as 1881 the Army List shows fourteen yeomanry units with over eighty rifle volunteer corps. The first elements to serve overseas did so during the Boer War when ten contingents embarked for South Africa.

New Zealand became a Dominion in September 1907 and, paralleling events in Australia, a review of defence preparations was undertaken. As in the case of Canada and Australia, ultimately New Zealand's defence depended on the strength of the Royal Navy. Differing from the other two, however, as the strength of Britain's navy became concentrated in Home waters New Zealand's response was not to establish its own naval service but to offer to pay for an additional battleship for the Royal Navy. This offer was made in March 1909, before the Imperial Conference of that year, and after the Conference the warship became designated as one of the vessels to join the proposed Pacific squadron in which it would have joined the ships of the new Australian Navy.

In New Zealand a Defence Act of 1909 introduced a military service liability on all males between seventeen and fifty-five years of age. Preliminary arrangements for the scheme were inspected by Lord Kitchener when he visited the country for a month in 1910, shortly following a similar visit to Australia.[1] The new system, which came into force in 1911, was based on a Territorial Force in which all men aged 18–25 were enlisted after prior training in a cadet force. After Territorial service a man would transfer to the Reserve for five years and then become a member of a Rifle Club until reaching the age of fifty-five. The Rifle Clubs provided a supplementary scheme for those, such as residents of rural areas, who did not have access to a Territorial unit and, indeed, the Rifle Clubs trained about 35% of all those liable for Territorial service. It was anticipated that a peace establishment of 30,000 would be reached in 1915 after which the Reserves would fill until 87,000 men were available. Administratively New Zealand was divided into four Districts, each of which produced an infantry brigade and a mounted rifles brigade. It was specifically provided that the TF could volunteer for overseas service.[2] A permanent cadre of 625 officers and men supervised training.

Major-General Godley was appointed to New Zealand as GOC and Chief of the local section of the Imperial General Staff in 1910. The latter, however, remained an ephemeral body since at that time only two New Zealand officers had enjoyed Staff training. No expeditionary force was contemplated but, as noted in the previous Chapter, in 1912 the GOC reached an informal agreement with Australia that in an emergency New Zealand would provide 6000 men for a joint force. The following year Kitchener suggested to Godley that an expeditionary force might be needed for service in Europe.[3]

As war approached in 1914, as early as 31st July Prime Minister Massey indicated in the House of Representatives that in the event of war an expeditionary force would be prepared. The offer was formally made on 7th August and accepted on the 12th. On the 6th the New Zealand Government was invited to occupy Samoa and this was done by mobilising a composite Territorial battalion which remained there until April 1915.

The New Zealand Expeditionary Force was organised under the command of Godley as a division containing a brigade each of infantry and mounted rifles. Units were formed by instructing each Territorial unit to supply a company or a squadron, thus linking the NZEF intimately with the pre-existing units of the New Zealand Army. The Expeditionary Force sailed on 15th October and, joining up with the Australian Imperial Force, landed at Alexandria on 3rd December. In Egypt the NZEF was joined with 4 Australian Brigade to form the ANZAC Division and training continued until the Division, less the mounted brigades, crossed to Gallipoli in April 1915. The mounted brigades were dismounted and followed a month later.[4]

Back in New Zealand the enlistment of reinforcements continued at a satisfactory rate and the first draft of 2000 sailed on 14th December 1914. Volunteers were registered and called for every two months until September 1915, after which calls were made monthly. The first Maori contingent began training in October 1914 and sailed for Egypt in February 1915. With the news that the New Zealanders were in action a fresh phase of expansion commenced when the Governor-General called for volunteers to form a New Zealand Rifle Brigade. The response to this was favourable and two battalions reached Egypt in October 1915, followed by two more in March 1916. A National Registration Act covered all males aged 17–60 and those aged between nineteen and forty-five were invited to express their willingness to serve overseas. 112,778 of the 303,704 who responded expressed their willingness to serve, which appeared to show that there were adequate reserves to support the Expeditionary Force.[5]

The return of the Australian and New Zealand troops from Gallipoli, together with the arrival of the Rifle Brigade and the accumulation of reinforcements, resulted, as was outlined in the last Chapter, by the suggestion that the existing forces should be doubled. Lengthy discussion followed between the War Office, Egypt and the New Zealand Government but the latter finally gave its approval on 17th February 1916 and the formation of the new brigade started. This was in all respects a duplicate of the original brigade, although some of the cadres were found from the mounted rifles, which were also heavily drawn upon to form the extra artillery units which were needed. The New Zealand Division crossed to France in April 1916, leaving the Mounted Rifles Brigade in Egypt where it served in the ANZAC Mounted Division until the end of the war.[6]

A small base was established in England in 1915 to look after convalescents from Gallipoli and this was enlarged to a full Administrative Base in 1916, a Reserve Brigade being formed to provide reinforcements for the Division in France. The Division itself was enlarged in March 1917 when, for a time, the reinforce-

ment position was such that it became possible to form a fourth
brigade. The extra brigade was disbanded in February 1918 but
few manpower problems were suffered in the last two years of the
war and in November 1918 a New Zealand Tank Battalion was
forming in readiness for 1919.

In New Zealand a Military Service Act came into force on 1st
August 1916. This placed all men aged 20–46 in a NZEF Reserve
of two divisions, those with family responsibilities being placed in
the second division. Men in the first division were subject to ballot
at monthly intervals to find drafts for the NZEF, the ballot being
extended to the second division from November 1917. The
Military Service Act was applied to Maoris from June 1917 but the
first ballot was not held until ten months later.[7]

The Military Service Act passed through Parliament with little
opposition but some opposition developed in the country at large
over the following months. Strikes were called, particularly in the
docks and mines, and the authority of the Government to impose
conscription for overseas service was challenged in the courts. The
Appeal Court decided in favour of the Government and the
disruption quietened by mid-1917.

In sum, the mobilisation of the NZEF and its expansion to a
division and an independent brigade appears to have caused few
problems. Although compulsory service had to be resorted to, the
earlier Registration indicated that it would enjoy some measure
of popular support and it did not have the divisive effects which
campaigns for similar measures inflicted on Australian and Canadian politics. In retrospect the industrial disturbances of 1916 and
1917 seem to have been quite minor. Although the formation of the
fourth brigade for the New Zealand Division could be seen as an
over-expansion the step was taken deliberately as a temporary
measure and no harm was done by the subsequent contraction. The
formation of an Expeditionary Force strongly founded upon the
Territorial Force appears to have been a more successful expedient
than the 'new army' methods adopted in Canada and Australia.
British statistics give a strength of 60,775 for February 1918 and
63,879 for November but, as suggested in the case of Australia,
these figures may be under-estimates by some 10%.[8]

ii   The New Zealand Army, 1920–45

In many respects the development of defence policy in New Zealand during the inter-war years followed the pattern already discussed in connection with Australia. From 1921 the proposed main fleet base at Singapore was held to provide protection against the only conceivable threat in the Pacific, that evidenced by Japan's expansionist policies, and New Zealand's attention was mainly directed towards maritime forces. As in the case of Australia there were doubts about Britain's ability to send a fleet in some grave emergency and further doubts that Singapore might prove to be too distant from either Australia or New Zealand to provide an effective shield. To an even larger extent than Australia New Zealand's defence policy followed that established in London. This subordination is demonstrated by New Zealand's naval forces which, constituted in 1913 and designated the New Zealand Division, Royal Navy, did not achieve separate status until October 1941.

For the army, the 1920s were a period of reduction with such funds as were available being allocated elsewhere. By 1923 the number of mounted rifles regiments had been reduced from twelve to nine and infantry battalions from seventeen to twelve. Following the economic crisis of 1929, compulsory training for the Territorial Force was abandoned in October 1930 and the force reduced to six battalions and three mounted regiments. Strength in 1934 was 210 permanent staff and 9270 volunteers.

The deteriorating world situation of the 1930s was marked by the formation of a Territorial Special Reserve in 1937. To some extent this was intended as a measure of relief for the unemployed and it gave five months' training, including vocational training, to men aged 18–30 who were then eligible either for the regular forces or the TF. Further expansion of the reserves took place in 1938 with the establishment of a National Military Reserve open to former soldiers.[9]

In April 1939 a conference was held in Wellington between British, Australian and New Zealand military representatives to discuss defence in the Pacific. The possibility of New Zealand supplying garrisons for Fiji and other islands was mentioned but few concrete proposals were made. The British member, Major-General Mackesy, was invited to report on the state of the New Zealand land forces. His main recommendations were that a regular brigade should be formed and that the Territorial Force should be expanded. In May Prime Minister Savage asked Parliament to increase the Territorial establishment from 9500 to 16,000 with an extra 250 men for the coastal defences. At the same time he asked for the registration of all men aged 20–55 in the National Military Reserve but little was accomplished before the outbreak of war.[10]

On 30th August 1939 reserves were mobilised to man coastal defences and guard vulnerable points. Although it remained to be decided what New Zealand's contribution to the war would be, on 6th September the Prime Minister announced the formation of a Special Force of 6000 men for service either at home or abroad. Recruitment was open to men aged 21–35 who would enlist for the duration of the war plus twelve months. It was intended that after training for three months the Force would be released on unpaid leave if not required by then. Recruiting opened on 12th September when 5419 enrolled and there were 14,983 applications by 5th October. Before the end of the month it was decided that New Zealand should contribute a division to the Imperial forces. The first echelon, or brigade, assembled on 3rd October and, as in 1914, Territorial units were given the task of sponsoring companies, with each Military District producing a battalion. Command of what became 2 New Zealand Division was given to Major-General Freyberg, a British officer who had spent his youth in New Zealand. The second and third brigades assembled in January and May 1940 with leaders being given two months' training with earlier contingents.[11]

In November 1939 New Zealand's Deputy Prime Minister visited Britain where it was decided that the first brigade would move to Egypt as soon as practicable and that 2 Division should be ready there by September 1940. The second brigade, which included an extra Maori battalion, left New Zealand in May 1940 and was one of the formations diverted to Britain when the entry of Italy to the war for a time closed the passage of the Mediterranean.[12] The brigade, with the Australian troops which arrived at the same time, formed a valuable addition to Britain's defences in the crisis period after the fall of France. The stay of the New Zealanders was brief and they sailed to join their compatriots in the Middle East, their arrival completing 2 Division for the third brigade arrived in Egypt in September 1940.[13]

Late in 1939 and early in 1940 a Schedule of Reserved Occupations was compiled and the Social Security Department completed a register of all males aged 16 and over. In light of the Schedule men with skills in the prime industries were removed from the Expeditionary Force, as were men with more than two children. In April 1940 the upper age for enlistment was raised to forty whilst on 30th May it was announced that compulsory service would be introduced. Volunteering for the NZEF continued to 22nd July, by which time 59,644 had registered.[14] Recruitment of Maoris opened on 5th October and remained on a voluntary basis throughout the war. Initially only single men aged 21–35 were enlisted but this was later extended to include married men with up to two children.

On 5th June 1940 the New Zealand Government announced that an additional brigade would be formed for service in Fiji, commencing what became a significant dispersion of New Zealand's limited strength. It is proposed first to outline developments in the western theatre before returning to the problems of home defence and the Pacific.

2 New Zealand Division remained in the Mediterranean theatre for the remainder of the war, taking part in the campaigns in Greece, Crete, the desert and in Italy. To support it a Training Brigade was formed in Egypt in 1941 as a core for the New Zealand base. The heavy casualties suffered by the Division in the retreat to the Alamein position and the fighting on that line in 1942 instituted a review of the formation's organisation. New Zealand's manpower reserves were becoming depleted and at the same time there was dissatisfaction concerning the armoured support the Division had received from British formations. It was consequently decided to re-form one of the brigades as an armoured formation and it was with this structure that the Division fought in Italy. As a result of the desert crises of 1942, New Zealand's Middle East base was reorganised as an improvised 6 Division for the defence of the Nile Delta and this title was retained until the middle of 1944. 2 Division crossed to Italy in October 1943 and remained there until the end of the war.[15]

The outbreak of war with Japan began a debate on the form and location of New Zealand's part in the war which lasted until the end of the war itself. With New Zealand seen to be under threat of invasion there was a natural belief that New Zealand's own soldiers should be recalled for its defence and although assistance was obtained from America the view persisted.[16] New Zealand simply did not have the manpower to make a major contribution to both wars and she was a country of the Pacific not of Europe. In April and May 1943 the Cabinet and Parliament discussed at length where New Zealand's effort should be made. 2 Division had been overseas for three years of hard-fought campaigning and it was felt that some relief should be given. Eventually it was decided that the Division should remain where it was but that leave should be given to 6000 long-service men. The decision implied that New Zealand's part in the Pacific war would have to be limited.[17] By then 3 New Zealand Division was in service in the Solomons and the debate resumed in January 1944 when it was obvious that one of the divisions would have to be broken up. The British Prime Minister and the British Chiefs of Staff pressed for the retention of 2 Division in Italy, at least until after the fall of Rome, but no decision was reached for some months. Of the 7000 men who eventually returned under the 1943 leave scheme few returned to service, on grounds of unfitness or hardship, and for some time there was concern about whether 2 Division could retain its fighting qualities.[18] The decision was finally made in September 1944. 3 Division would be broken up and a new leave scheme was instituted for 2 Division under which 9000 men were relieved in the last months of 1944 and early 1945.[19]

Returning to the Pacific theatre, this was left at the point at which New Zealand despatched a brigade to Fiji in June 1940. The pre-war garrison there had consisted of a Defence Force whose main element was a Territorial battalion of the Fiji Regiment. A second battalion was formed in July 1940, by which time a company was on full-time duty. A proclamation made all Fijian males aged 18–36 liable for military duty and three groups of a hundred men were called out in succession for three months' training. In New Zealand itself 30,000 men were called out for three months' training with the Territorial Force in the year ending June 1941 and four new battalions were formed for full-time service.[20] Concurrently a Tank Brigade began forming with the intention that it should join 2 Division in the Middle East. Diversions took place with the need to form defence forces for Tonga, Samoa, Rarotonga and Fanning Island, while in June 1 Fiji Regiment was formed for full-time service with 2 Fiji Regiment as a part-time Territorial unit.[21]

With the outbreak of war with Japan 4600 coast defence troops were mobilised on 15th December 1941, when 11,000 of the Territorial Force and National Military Reserve were also called out. Further mobilisations soon followed and the number of men in service grew rapidly (see Figure 6.1). The Military Districts were reconstructed as 1, 4 and 5 Divisions whilst 100,000 Home Guards were available for local defence. During January 1942 the Government approved the formation of a second brigade for Fiji, improvised from reinforcements for the Middle East. The two brigades remained there until relieved by an American division in June and August, when they returned to New Zealand as the major formations in a newly forming 3 Division. 3 and 4 Fiji Regiment were formed during 1942 and two Fijian battalions fought in the Solomons in 1943 and 1944 under American command.[22]

In July 1942 Admiral Ghormley, Allied Commander for the South Pacific Area, suggested that in the forthcoming offensive

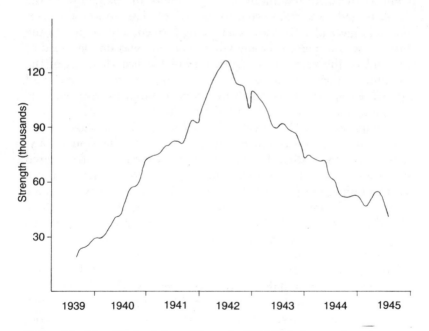

Figure 6.1. New Zealand Army Strength: 1939–45. Source: Statement on the Strength of the Armed Services (IWM file K16104).

operations New Zealand might be able to provide follow-up and garrison troops. 3 Division, with only two brigades, was available for this and it moved to New Caledonia in November.[23] Further distractions appeared when garrisons were called for for Tonga and Norfolk Island and although the Cabinet approved the formation of a third brigade for 3 Division finding the troops proved an intractable problem. The use of a Fijian brigade was considered at one time but the Division was still only two brigades strong when it entered the Solomons campaign in September 1943. As noted earlier it was broken up a year later.[24]

As may be seen from Figure 6.1 the New Zealand Army reached its greatest strength in the middle of 1942 and thereafter declined. Once the threat of Japanese invasion was seen to have decreased a partial demobilisation of the Territorial Force commenced in January 1943. In October 1942 a Women's Auxiliary Army Corps was formed to take over ancillary tasks and ease the manpower burden. This grew to reach a strength of 3000 but contractions soon followed. In the middle of 1943 one of the battalions of the Tank Brigade was transferred to the Middle East to join the armoured brigade of 2 Division, then being formed, and the rest of the brigade was dispersed. Home Guard training was discontinued at the end of the year and in March 1944 the last elements of the Territorial Force stood down. Recruiting for the WAAC had ceased, except for some small numbers required for overseas service, and the Corps was being allowed to fade.

The question of New Zealand's part in the closing stages of the war against Japan was linked with the future of 2 Division in Italy. The retention of that formation in the western theatre caused decisions to be deferred for a considerable period. Although in a visit to London in June 1944 Prime Minister Fraser was said to be in favour of joining a British offensive based on Australia nothing was done for a year. In July 1945 a New Zealand division of two brigades was listed as one of the formations to be based on India for operations in South-east Asia but that appears to have been little more than a speculation. At about the same time it was being proposed in New Zealand that a division for service in the Pacific could incorporate a Fijian brigade. Not until 7th August did the British Chiefs of Staff receive a telegram offering a New Zealand contingent of two brigades for operations against Honshu. The first atomic bomb had been dropped on Hiroshima the previous day.[25]

To outline the development of the New Zealand Army during the Second World War has been particularly difficult. The Army was called upon to undertake a wide variety of commitments and with limited resources was at one and the same time trying to maintain a division in the west, build up a striking force for the Pacific, provide island garrisons and defend the homeland. When this task proved beyond its capacity the Army rapidly shrank to the division in Europe. A suggestion made by the British Chiefs of Staff in 1944 that 2 Division should return from Italy after the fall of Rome to provide a cadre for a force to serve in the later stages of the Pacific war was not followed up. Although British planning for Commonwealth participation in the invasion of Japan continued to feature a New Zealand Division it seems doubtful if such a formation would have materialised. Had the war continued it is probable that the New Zealand contribution would have been reduced to air and naval forces.

Notes

1   R. A. Preston, *Canada and Imperial Defence*, U. of Toronto Press, 1967, pp. 453–6.
    Sir Philip Magnus, *Portrait of an Imperialist*, John Murray, London, 1958, p. 245.
2   PRO/WO/32/4819.
    General Sir Alexander Godley, *Life of an Irish Soldier*, John Murray, London, 1939, pp. 142–4.
    New Zealand Year Book, 1915, Government Printer, Wellington, 1915, pp. 288–95.
3   Godley, *Life*, p. 148.
4   F. Waite, *The New Zealanders at Gallipoli*, Whitcombe and Tombs, Auckland, 1921, pp. 2–4.
    H. T. B. Drew (Ed.), *War Effort of New Zealand*, Whitcombe and Tombs, Auckland, 1923, Essay by S. J. Smith.
    Sir Charles Lucas (Ed.), *The Empire at War*, III, Oxford U. P., 1924, p. 232.
    Godley, *Life*, pp. 154–5.
5   Drew, *War Effort*, pp. 2–13.
    Lucas, *Empire at War*, p. 238.
    New Zealand Year Book, 1916, Government Printer, Wellington, 1916, p. 199.
6   H. Stewart, *The New Zealand Division*, Whitcombe and Tombs, Auckland, 1921, pp. 5–10.
7   Lucas, *Empire at War*, p. 243.
    New Zealand Year Book, 1916, pp. 201–3, 1918, p. 229.
8   War Office, *Statistics of the Military Effort of the Empire*, H.M.S.O.,

London, 1922, Tables pp. 146, 155 and facing p. 64.
9   W. G. McClymont, *To Greece*, Department of Internal Affairs, Wellington, 1959, p. 3.
    British Army List, 1939.
    Annual Report of the New Zealand CGS, 15.6.40. (IWM file K11825).
10 O. A. Gillespie, *The Pacific*, Department of Internal Affairs, Wellington 1952, p. 7.
11 McClymont, *To Greece*, pp. 3–5.
    Report of the CGS, 15.6.40.
    P. Singleton-Gates, *General Lord Freyberg*, Michael Jospeh, London, 1963, pp. 102–4, 187–9, 251–3.
12 An additional brigade was improvised during the stay in Britain.
13 McClymont, *To Greece*, pp. 5–6, 35.
14 Report of the CGS, 15.6.40.
    McClymont, *To Greece*, p. 45.
15 I.S.O. Playfair, *Mediterranean and Middle East*, III, H.M.S.O., London, 1960, pp. 348–51.
    PRO/WO/212/573 – 602.
16 W. L. S. Churchill, *The Second World War*, IV, Cassell, London, 1951, pp. 169–72.
    Gillespie, *Pacific*, p. 103.
    Singleton-Gates, *Freyberg*, p. 242.
17 Gillespie, *Pacific*, pp. 105–7.
    Singleton-Gates, *Freyberg*, pp. 254–7.
18 PRO/Cab/79/70 and 76.
    Gillespie, *Pacific*, pp. 195–6, 202.
    Report of the CGS, 10.8.44. (IWM file K11825).
    Singleton-Gates, *Freyberg*, pp. 287–9.
19 Gillespie, *Pacific*, p. 202 and Appendices 7–9.
    Report of the CGS, 16.7.45.
20 Gillespie, *Pacific*, pp. 22–3.
    R. A. Howlett, *Fiji Military Forces*, Crown Agents, London, 1948, pp. 15–16, 24.
    Reports of the CGS, 15.6.40 and 15.6.41.
21 Gillespie, *Pacific*, p. 42 and f.n.
    Howlett, *Fiji Military Forces*, pp. 29–30.
22 PRO/WO/106/3386 and WO/193/13.
    Gillespie, *Pacific*, p. 45.
    Howlett, *Fiji Military Forces*, pp. 30–6.
    Report of the CGS, 21.7.42.
23 Gillespie, *Pacific*, pp. 73–5.
24 Ibid., pp. 83, 318.
    Howlett, *Fiji Military Forces*, pp. 54–5.
25 Sir Arthur Bryant, *Triumph in the West*, Collins, London, 1959, p. 218.
    PRO/Cab/79/36 and 37.

Chapter 7
South Africa

i *The Union Defence Force to 1919*

In August 1914 South Africa was the newest of the Dominions, having been created as recently as May 1910. The military history of the Union was, however, lengthy, extending back to the Dutch East India Company in the seventeenth century. Throughout the nineteenth century a succession of small wars demanded the mobilisation of forces and these were followed by the Boer War and the Zulu Rebellion of 1906. Participation in overseas campaigns was negligible.

The traditional South African military organisation was the Boer commando, a mounted militia. In the Orange Free State and Transvaal each electoral district, forty in all, produced a mounted unit on summons, all fit men being liable for service. In Cape Province a militia system held sway, although this does not appear to have been invoked after 1880. Ballots were held but it would appear that units for the various campaigns formed as 'Volunteers' or 'So-and-so's' Horse. In Natal a voluntary system prevailed until the passing of a Militia Act in 1903. In general, the picture is one of a succession of small units being formed for specific emergencies, the units being disbanded once the emergency was over. In the more settled areas a few units acquired a more permanent status from the 1850s, supported by militarised police forces.

The Defence Act of 1912 authorised a Union Defence Force in five sections; Permanent, Coast Garrison and Citizen Forces with a Naval Volunteer Reserve and an Army Special Reserve. After the Great War the Air Force was formed as part of the UDF. All male citizens of European descent between the ages of seventeen and sixty were liable to serve in southern Africa in defence of the Union.

Those aged between seventeen and twenty-five had to train for a
month in each of four years but the Active Citizen Force need only
contain 50% of those eligible, the ballot only being resorted to if
the number of volunteers was less than this percentage. Indeed the
ballot was not needed until after the Second World War. Citizens
not called up received training in Defence Rifle Associations.

The Permanent Force was based on five South African Mounted
Rifles Regiments, originally the military police forces of the former
colonies and numbering 2500 in all. They had an external defence
and internal security role in support of the civil police which itself,
under the Police Act of 1912, was liable to support the regular
military forces in time of emergency. The Active Citizen Force
contained nineteen regiments of mounted rifles, fourteen of dis-
mouted rifles, which would be mounted as and when animals were
available, and twelve infantry battalions. The establishment of the
ACF and Coast Garrison Force was 25,000.[1]

Alone among the Dominions the Union contained a British garrison in 1914 and on 4th August the Union Government offered to
relieve it, using Permanent Force units. The British units left South
Africa on the 10th. On the same day the Government undertook to
take part in a joint naval and military expedition against ports and
radio stations in German South-west Africa. Individual units of
the ACF were called out for service on 24th August and this was
followed on 9th September by the mobilisation of the whole Force.
In reporting this to Parliament the Prime Minister formally revealed
the Government's undertaking to institute operations against
South-west Africa. This was hotly contested in the Senate and,
although the opposition was heavily defeated in a vote, the
projected invasion was a major factor in the South African rebellion
which broke out on 9th October. By the middle of December the
outbreak was over although sporadic incidents continued for
another two or three weeks.[2]

The occupation of South-west Africa was the first campaign
undertaken by the UDF and although it was announced on 20th
September that only volunteers would take part, after the rebellion
this was rescinded. The rebellion delayed the original plans for the
operation which was finally mounted in December. Ten mounted
and four infantry brigades were employed, involving most units of
the Permanent and Active Citizen Forces, while four of the
mounted brigades were found from the Defence Rifle Associations.

With the end of the campaign in July 1915 all of these forces were demobilised, leaving the Permanent Force for the defence of South Africa and a Garrison Battalion in South-west Africa. 30,000 troops were mobilised to put down the rebellion while about 70,000 took part in the South-west Africa campaign. The latter also required 35,000 men for Native Labour Contingents.[3]

In April 1915, before the campaign in South-west Africa had ended, the Governor-General raised the question of further aid for the British Government and on 11th May the Colonial Secretary cabled that any assistance South Africa could give would be welcome. A new phase of development now commenced. Towards the end of June the South African Government had to advise that, while prepared to raise a contingent, it was unable to pay for it and although recruiting for a South African Brigade commenced in July discussion on financial matters rumbled on until the end of 1916.[4] The Brigade was thus on a different basis from the contingents raised by the other Dominions in that the latter were in essence overseas contingents of the Dominions' armies while that of South Africa was fundamentally a mercenary force. Not that that implied that those enlisting did so from commercial motives. British Army pay was lower than that paid by the other Dominions and, indeed, was lower than that of the UDF. The Brigade arrived in Britain in October 1915 and, after a brief visit to Egypt, it joined 9 (Scottish) Division in France in April 1916.

While the South African Brigade was being formed the Union Government was asked for a small body of troops to garrison Nyasaland and two battalions were raised. They served in Central Africa until August 1917. A further initiative, in July 1915, was an offer by the Union Government to form a coloured infantry battalion for overseas service. This offer was accepted and a Cape Corps Battalion was formed for service in East Africa, where it arrived in February 1916 before going on to Egypt early in 1918. A second Cape Corps Battalion served in Central Africa from 1917 to 1918. All of these units were paid for out of British funds.[5]

On 9th September 1915 the Governor-General asked if a South African mission could be sent to East Africa to report on the operations taking place there. The mission did not return until November by which time the Government had already agreed to send an infantry brigade and a mounted brigade. Other infantry and mounted brigades followed early in 1916, where the four took part in the offensive operations of that year organised as 2 and 3 East African Divisions. The operations were substantially successful but 12,000 troops had to be invalided in 1916 and the last South African troops left that theatre in October 1917. Again the contingent was a charge on British funds.[6]

To recruit for the South African Brigade in France, 144 War Recruiting Committees were set up across South Africa with a target of 15% reinforcements per month. With recruiting for East Africa also going on, enlistment for Europe was suspended in March 1916 but the heavy casualties sustained by the Brigade in July soon caused a resumption. Indeed in September recruiting for East Africa was discontinued to leave the field clear for recruiting for France. In February 1917 and again in January 1918 the Governor-General expressed to Parliament the hope that the South African contingent might be increased but in February 1918 the number of reinforcements available in South Africa was down to 379. Heavy casualties were again sustained in March 1918 and for six months the South Africans in the Brigade had to be concentrated in a composite battalion.[7]

The insatiable demands for labour in France were also responded to by South Africa. A Native Labour Corps and a Cape Coloured Labour Corps were formed in 1916, 13,500 men being recruited, with further contingents coming from the High Commission Territories of Basutoland and Bechuanaland.[8] A white labour battalion was also sent to France. 3600 transport drivers were enlisted following a War Office request in February 1917, while railway operating companies were raised for East Africa and France, forestry and engineer companies for the western theatre and artillery for France and Egypt.

The contribution of South Africa to the Great War was different in kind from that of the other Dominions. Although the Union Government promptly agreed to mount the campaign in South-west Africa, the following rebellion indicated that the Government enjoyed but little support from some sectors of the community. This was understandable. The Boer War had been over for a scant dozen years and the divisions which created that war, as well as those created by the war itself and the subsequent peace, had had little time to heal. From 1915 the Government was content to act as a provider of troops to contract and to furnish such other assistance as might be called for from time to time. The attitude was in marked contrast to the Imperial role played by General Smuts and other Union leaders of the time.

At the 1911 census, South Africa contained 244,000 men of European descent aged 20–40. South African statistics for the number of men who served during the war are bedevilled with inconsistencies and double-counting but it is probable that 160,000 served at one time or another.[9] Allowing for those needed for essential occupations and the unfit, the proportion of the population recruited for active service is remarkably high considering the divisions within the country. Rather more than 80,000 of the coloured population enlisted but only the 8000 who were recruited for the Cape Corps were combatants. The fundamental assumption, so fundamental that it was not even discussed, was that under no circumstances should the 'natives' be armed and trained. Available evidence is that the Cape Corps was formed at the instigation of the Union Government but this appears to have been regarded as a limited experiment, with the units being moved out of South Africa as soon as they were complete.

ii   *The Union Defence Force 1919–45*

The reductions inevitable after a long war commenced in 1920 when four of the five Permanent Force units were disbanded and the last one only survived until 1926. Although this left the ACF as the army of South Africa, reductions followed here also, since between 1926 and 1929 an infantry battalion, fourteen mounted rifles regiments and all of the dismounted rifles were disbanded. Economy was, of course, the order of the day and compulsory training for the ACF was abandoned in 1932.

Improving economic factors allowed a modest expansion from 1933 in which eight new Dutch-speaking infantry battalions were formed, partly to restore the national balance of the army since it had been mainly Dutch-speaking units which had been disbanded in the 1920s. Continuous training was resumed in 1934, when also a Special Service Battalion was formed in the Permanent Force to give training, including vocational training, to unemployed youths aged 17–22. Enlistment was for one year, after which a youth could sign on for a further period or enter civil employment. The Italian occupation of Abyssinia in 1936 inspired a reexamination of South Africa's defence policy since with only modest advances

South Africa would come within air striking range of Italian bases. No land-based threat was envisaged and the role of the UDF was seen as meeting an enemy on African soil in bush warfare. The ACF was reorganised into nine brigade groups, with the Defence Rifle Associations available as a mounted supplement.[10]

On 3rd September 1939 coastal defences at the major ports were manned and Parliament was summoned to meet the following day. A Government motion implying that a policy of neutrality should be observed was defeated by eighty votes to sixty-seven and on 5th September General Smuts took over as Prime Minister. The following day South Africa declared war on Germany. The narrowness with which the vote leading to South Africa's declaration of war had been won meant that in many respects South Africa's internal position was similar to that in 1915–18. Support for the war was far from unanimous and, indeed, some sectors of the public were actively opposed to the war. In the circumstances any part that South Africa might play was heavily dependent on voluntary effort.[11]

In September 1939 the Permanent Force was 3353 strong against an establishment of 5385 and the Citizen Force's 14,631 men contrasted with an establishment of 15,646. The Defence Rifle Associations had 122,000 members although their Director-General estimated that only 18,300 were fit for service. No large scale expansion was envisaged although the Special Service Battalion would be expanded to a brigade. In October an Essential Services Protection Corps was formed for guard duties from men aged over forty-five.

Before the end of September the CGS, Lieutenant-General Sir Pierre van Ryneveld, proposed to the Prime Minister that a Mobile Field Force should be formed. This would consist of two divisions found from the ACF with each containing three infantry brigades, a mounted brigade and an armoured regiment. Corps troops included two mounted and two dismounted brigades. Artillery establishments were especially large and the Field Force, with the coastal defences, would need 140,000 men. Although these proposals were not formally accepted it will be seen they were influential in determining the subsequent mobilisations and the structure of the force created. No overseas expeditions were contemplated although in December the British Government suggested that contingency plans might be worked out for a move of South African troops to Kenya.[12]

During the early months of 1940 all ACF units were called out in succession for a month's training and in February the Special Service Brigade was reconstructed as a Field Force Brigade. In Parliament on 7th February General Smuts declared that it was the Government's intention to extend operations to East Africa and practical expression was given to this on 29th March when officers and men were invited to take a new oath to be prepared to serve anywhere in Africa for the duration of the war. A few days earlier a telegram from London had asked if a brigade could reinforce Kenya as soon as shipping was available. General Smuts's reply was that a brigade group would be ready by the end of June.[13]

On 11th May 1940 orders were issued to mobilise units to form 1 South African Brigade and, although few assembled with more than 650 men against an establishment of 926 all ranks, the German victories in France soon inspired a wave of enlistments. This did not imply that the long term manpower prospects were bright for current estimates by the Adjutant-General were that with voluntary enlistment only 110 – 115,000 men were likely to be available out of a population of about 320,000 European men between the ages of twenty and forty. With a policy, implicit rather than explicit, that the 'natives' should not be armed, the establishments of the Field Force could not be completed. The alternatives were either to reduce the size of the Field Force or to extend recruiting to the non-white population. It does not appear that the problem was faced in those terms. Instead a series of measures was instituted on an ad hoc basis to meet manpower shortages as they arose. For the time being the mobilisations continued, with four brigades being mobilised in June, when the Field Force Brigade became 2 Brigade, and three more in July. In June, also, a Mounted Commando Division was formed from members of the Defence Rifle Associations. On 11th June South Africa declared war on Italy and during July 1 Brigade arrived in Kenya with 1 South African Division being assembled there before the end of the year.[14] 2 and 3 Divisions were assembled in South Africa in October and November.

The war in East Africa was being conducted in a region devoid of the facilities to be found in a developed country and, as the only formation in the theatre with European personnel, 1 South African Division was soon called upon to provide technicians. Men were needed for road, railway and harbour construction, surveying, forestry, provision of water supplies and the development of motor transport, medical and other services. These demands could only be met by draining the combatant units, which were already suffering from lack of reinforcements. With the successful conclusion of the campaign it was decided that 1 Division would be transferred to Egypt. This decision caused some dismay for it would appear that the troops expected leave in South Africa before commencing a new campaign. However signals between East Africa, South Africa and the Middle East established that the Division was to move as speedily as possible. It arrived in the Middle East in May 1941 where it was joined by 2 Division. 3 Division remained in South Africa as a drafting formation. No attempt was made to unite the divisions in the Middle East in a South African Corps, the view being expressed that the South Africans did not want all of their eggs in one basket.[15]

As a measure to relieve the manpower shortages a Cape Corps and an Indian Services Corps, later the Indian and Malay Corps, were formed before the end of 1940. Both were originally intended to provide Motor Transport and Pioneer Companies and they were amalgamated in December 1942. They were joined by a Native Military Corps which was intended for pioneer and labouring duties. Although formed for non-combatant duties they were soon employed on a wider range of tasks, including the guarding of prisoners of war camps, while those serving as drivers with 1 Division had to be armed for their own protection even before the Division left East Africa. Although a British rather than a South African Corps, an African Auxiliary Pioneer Corps, later the African Pioneer Corps, was formed in the High Commission Territories of Basutoland, Bechuanaland and Swaziland in 1941. This carried out labouring duties and its members were used to dilute British anti-aircraft units in Italy from 1944.

With virtually all of the ACF dedicated to overseas service, a Reserve Brigade was formed from men not fit for active service to undertake guard duties in South Africa. This was joined by the formation of the National Volunteer Brigade, the Mines Engineer Brigade, the National Reserve Volunteers and, later, the Coast Defence Corps, all of them part-time forces for local defence.

The Women's Auxiliary Defence Corps was another Corps which appeared in 1940. The Women's Auxiliary Army Services

Corps was the military section; at first recruited only to provide drivers, duties were later extended to general administrative services. Recruits were at first attested for service in Africa and the first drafts left for East Africa in September. A 'Home Town Service' section was formed later. As part of the run-down of South Africa's military effort the headquarters of the WAAS was closed down in March 1944. Total WADC enlistments came to 21,265.[16]

The first South African armoured units dated from the first half of 1940 when a light tank company and armoured car and motor-cycle companies were formed. These were grouped into a battalion in May but the companies travelled independently to East Africa later in the year. In March 1941 South Africa agreed to provide armoured car units for the Middle East and across the year a dozen regiments were formed, mainly from the Mounted Commando Division, but also by mechanising some under-strength infantry battalions. In view of the shortage of men for the infantry divisions, a shortage which became even more acute when 1 Division's 5 Brigade was over-run in November, the creation of a large arm-oured car force appears to have been ill-advised as a waste of scarce man-power resources.

As soon as they arrived in the Middle East the possibility of converting 1 and 2 Divisions to armour was raised. Both lacked reinforcements but equipment to convert them was scarce to the point where Major-General Theron, the UDF's General Officer, Administration, in the Middle East, warned General Auchinleck about the criticisms which would arise if they suffered losses before being fully organised and equipped. It will be recalled that a similar warning was expressed about this time in connection with the use of Indian troops.[17]

South Africa's manpower problems became acute during 1942. During April 3 Division in South Africa began converting to an armoured division with two armoured brigades and, interestingly, two Cape Corps battalions were attached to serve as motor battalions. This took place only a month after General Smuts had caused an outcry in Parliament when he stated that if the Japanese invaded he would be prepared to arm the non-white population.[18] Needless to say the stay of the Cape Corps battalions with 3 Division was brief. Formation of a 4 Division commenced using the part-time National Volunteer Brigade and the National Reserve Volunteers, while discussions were resumed regarding the replacement of 1 and 2 Divisions by armoured formations. The capture of 2 Division at Tobruk in June caused these plans to be re-cast. Over 10,000 men had been lost from the South African forces, 9000 of them European. Although a brigade of 3 Division was made available to garrison Madagascar from June to December the Division was broken up before the end of the year. In November firm decisions were taken to withdraw 1 Division from the Middle East and replace it with an armoured division. The Alamein victories, followed by the expulsion of enemy forces from the African continent, both simplified and complicated the questions facing the South African Government concerning its future participation in the war. The African victories facilitated the withdrawal of 1 Division and gave a breathing-space for decision-making but the movement of the war away from Africa meant that a totally new phase of development had to commence.[19]

At the beginning of 1943 a new oath for general service was introduced and recruiting for Africa service was discontinued. So far as the organisation of the Army was concerned the situation was far less clear. In future, both in South Africa and overseas, the Army would consist principally of armoured formations but the number of these which could be raised and maintained remained in doubt for a considerable period. Shadowy formations appeared briefly in the Orders of Battle, to disappear as it was realised that the men for them did not exist. 1, 4, 5 and 6 Armoured Divisions were the major formations. 1 Division was intended as a mobile force for home defence and for some time it was suggested that a motor brigade for it should be raised from the Rhodesian African Rifles but in July 1943 it was decided that the formation would be reduced to the only brigade that had been formed. In effect the brigade became a feeder for 6 Division, moving to Italy and being disbanded in May 1945. 4 and 5 Divisions were part-time home-service formations, equipped with armoured cars, of which the nebulous 5 Division was broken up in the middle of 1943.[20] 6 Armoured Division began forming in the Middle East in February 1943. It was at first intended that it would have two armoured brigades with an infantry component found from the Cape Corps but in June it was decided that it should be purely a European formation.[21] The Division reached Italy in April 1944 and fought through to the end of the war but its manpower position remained precarious to the end. In May 1944 Field Marshal Smuts again raised the question of arming coloured soldiers, to have his sugges- tion vetoed by the Cabinet.[22] The last chance of solving South Africa's manpower problems, in some measure, had gone.

In many ways the problems of South Africa in the Second World War repeated those of the Great War. Within the country there was little support for the war and participation had to be on a voluntary basis. The forces that could be raised for active service were bound to be limited and even before the end of 1940 there were fears that an over-expansion was being attempted. The loss of 2 Division in 1942 meant more to South Africa than simply the loss of two brigades and a divisional headquarters. The conclusion of the war in Africa marked, from many points of view, the end of the war for the Union. 6 Division fought in Italy but it is very doubtful if it could have been sustained into 1946. From 1943 onwards South Africa's part in the war depended very much on the motivation of individuals and, as individuals, the response was considerable. In addition to 6 Division almost 1500 officers were seconded for ser- vice with the British Army[23] while a Reserve Brigade and Cape Corps battalions served in the Middle East in the last year of the war. For their own reasons the South African Government decided to restrict membership of fighting formations to European person- nel only, although the number of non-Europeans in the Army grew as they were recruited to take over wider ranges of guard and other duties. For some of these tasks units were, in fact, armed. The duties, however, fell short of participation in combat against European troops. Whether the South African Government should, or should not, have mobilised the non-European population for war is a larger question than should be answered here.

Notes

1 Sir Charles Lucas (Ed.), *The Empire at War*, I, Oxford U. P., 1921, pp. 227–9.
  British Army List, 1914.
2 W. K. Hancock, *Smuts*, I, Cambridge U. P., 1962, pp. 379, 383–93.
  Lucas, *Empire at War*, IV, 1925, pp. 373–6, 389.
3 Hancock, *Smuts*, p. 396.
  Lucas, *Empire at War*, IV, pp. 319–20, 437.
  Union of South Africa and the Great War, Government Printing Office, Pretoria, 1924, p. 212.
4 *The Union and the Great War*, p. 65.
  Lucas, *Empire at War*, IV, pp. 469–70, 511–2.

5   Ibid., p. 512.
6   The Union and the Great War, pp. 66, 82.
7   Lucas, Empire at War, IV, pp. 513–4.
    War Office, Statistics of the Military Effort of the Empire, H.M.S.O.,
    London, 1922, p. 155.
8   War Office, Statistics, gives 25,111 for the NLC and 1899 for the
    CCLC.
9   181,862 – Union and the Great War, p. 212.
    146,515 – Union Year Book, 1919, Government Printer, Pretoria,
    1920, p. 411.
    136,070 – War Office, Statistics, p. 772.
10 N. Orpen, East African and Abyssinian Campaigns, Purnell, Cape
    Town, 1968, pp. viii, 335.
    H. J. Martin and N. D. Orpen, South Africa at War, Purnell, Cape
    Town, 1979, pp. 10–16.
    British Army List, 1939.
11 Hancock, Smuts, II, 1968, pp. 315–23, 330–1.
    Orpen, East Africa and Abyssinia, pp. viii–ix.
    G. Tylden, Armed Forces of South Africa, Afrikaner Museum,
    Johannesburg, 1954, p. 27.
12 Orpen, East Africa and Abyssinia, Appendix 4.
13 Hancock, Smuts, II, p. 333.
    J. A. I. Agar-Hamilton and L. C. F. Turner, The Sidi Rezeg Battles,
    Oxford U. P., 1957, p. 72.
14 Martin and Orpen, South Africa at War, pp. 59–60, 72–4.
    IWM file K35593.
    Orpen, East Africa and Abyssinia, p. 52.
15 Ibid., pp. 63–4, 85, 219–20, Appendix 8.
    Hamilton and Turner, Sidi Rezeg, pp. 74, 81.
    Hancock, Smuts, II, p. 360.
16 Tylden, Armed Forces, p. 212.
    Martin and Orpen, South Africa at War, pp. 304, 346.
17 Hamilton and Turner, Sidi Rezeg, pp. 82–4.
18 Hancock, Smuts, II, pp. 370–1.
19 J. A. I. Agar-Hamilton and L. C. F. Turner, Crisis in the Desert,
    Oxford U. P., 1952, p. 221.
20 PRO/WO/193/13 and WO/32/10193.
    Martin and Orpen, South Africa at War, pp. 149 ff., 222–6.
21 PRO/WO/32/10193.
    Martin and Orpen, South Africa at War, pp. 164–5, 224.
22 Hancock, Smuts, II, p. 412.
23 C. G. Kerr in Foreword to Orpen, East Africa and Abyssinia, p. iv.

Chapter 8
Colonial forces

To outline the development of the forces raised in the Colonies across the two World Wars would be a lengthy task. Individually many of them were small, perhaps insignificant, but collectively they formed a considerable body. Generally they performed subsidiary tasks or were merged with the forces of one or other of the Dominions but those raised in East and West Africa grew to some size in both wars and are worth special notice. The West Indies provided a large contingent in the Great War and Burma an equally large one in the Second War. Finally, brief mention may be made of one or two smaller contingents to stand as example.

i West Africa

At the start of the Great War the forces in West Africa were made up of three elements. In the Gold Coast there were six volunteer corps formed from European residents. The West African Regiment, under the control of the War Office, provided the garrison of Freetown, where there was also a battalion of the West India Regiment. The largest element was the 7500 men of the West African Frontier Force which was controlled by the Colonial Office. The WAFF had been formed from the police forces of the four West African colonies and in 1914 it consisted of the five battalions of the Nigeria Regiment, one of them mounted, a battalion of the Gold Coast Regiment, the Sierra Leone Battalion, the Gambia Company and artillery and engineer units. As in the Indian Army the WAFF embodied ideas of 'martial' classes, with Hausas and Yorubas as the favoured groups in Nigeria and similar preferences in the other colonies.[1]

In 1914 the Gold Coast Regiment mobilised on local initiative on

31st July and on the outbreak of war a swift campaign, mounted with the aid of the civil police, brought about the occupation of Togoland before the end of August. More serious operations were needed to invade the Cameroons, eventually involving twenty-six companies including elements of the West Africa and West India Regiments. French and Belgian troops were also involved, as well as the Indian 5 Light Infantry which arrived shortly before the campaign was completed in February 1916.

The end of the Cameroons campaign was followed by a call for service in East Africa. There, as noticed in the last chapter, South African troops had suffered heavily from disease, and it was hoped that West Africans would prove as resistant as local troops were proving. The Gold Coast Regiment served in East Africa from July 1916 to September 1918 and a Nigerian Brigade from December 1916 to February 1918. Thus far no organisational expansion of the WAFF had been attempted. This changed in September 1918 when recruiting commenced for two brigades, one each from Nigeria and the Gold Coast. They were destined for the Middle East but the end of the war came before they were ready.[2]

The West African Frontier Force suffered the usual reductions across the 1920s, although a Gold Coast Territorial Battalion was formed in 1930. In 1935, with the outbreak of war between Italy and Abyssinia, the possibility of the WAFF reinforcing East Africa was revived and a reorganisation gave the Nigeria Regiment three battalions on full establishment and two on half, with the Gold Coast Regiment having one of each. It was planned that on mobilisation the cadre battalions would duplicate themselves and eventually there would be a brigade each from Nigeria and the Gold Coast. Officers would be found from a European Reserve Force, formed in 1933, and from Rhodesia.[3]

With the outbreak of war the two brigades began to form and fortuitously nine months were available before they were required to go to war, which allowed the Gold Coast Brigade to complete its complex expansion. Arriving in East Africa in June 1940 the West African Brigades joined East African Brigades in 1 and 2 (later 11 and 12) African Divisions before returning to West Africa late in 1941. In West Africa itself no further expansion was attempted until the crises of 1940. Then, being surrounded by potentially hostile French territory, a rapid expansion commenced although a British brigade had to be assembled there as a mainstay of the defence for some months. No less than thirteen new battalions were formed in the second half of 1940 and eight more in 1941.[4]

The problems involved in such a large scale expansion were considerable. Local sources were unable to find the number of officers needed, although some were found from the United Kingdom and some from the Polish Army.[5] NCOs were especially difficult to find and language problems remained acute since officers and NCOs were often unfamiliar with the dialects spoken by their troops. With a largely illiterate population, the recruitment of men for skilled and semi-skilled tasks was a constant problem. Internal communications in the West African colonies were not well developed and early in 1941 the establishments of West African Brigades were altered to include an Auxiliary Group of carriers.[6]

Between December 1940 and April 1941 three brigades were formed in West Africa with two more coming early in 1942. Britain's 55-division target of 1940 included two African divisions, which presumably were the two in East Africa. By January 1941 four African divisions were referred to but by February this had come down to three, although the Prime Minister's Directive of March 1941 listed three East African and a West African division. By October, however, only two African divisions are mentioned.[7] No divisions were, in fact, formed in West Africa at this stage and by late 1942 the Allied victories in North Africa, coupled with the favourable developments in the French territories, implied that forces in West Africa were excessive in view of the threats they faced. Across 1942, however, it was being suggested that the cross-country mobility provided by porter transport might make West African troops useful in Burma and in January 1943 Headquarters, West Africa, was requested to prepare two divisions for that theatre.[8]

81 West African Division sailed for the Far East in July 1943, followed by 82 Division in May 1944. 81 Division arrived in India at the time when a large expansion of Special Force was in view and a brigade was allocated to the Force until it was broken up in 1945. Both Divisions were employed in the Arakan and although the troops were easily unsettled by minor set-backs they performed satisfactorily on what was essentially a secondary front. 81 Division was withdrawn from Burma in February 1945 and although at first included in the troops listed for the invasion of Malaya it was decided to repatriate it in September. With the end of the war there

was reluctance to retain in India unemployed troops who were regarded as being unsuitable for internal security duties and both divisions were back in West Africa by September 1946.[9]

During the Second World War the West African forces were expanded to four times their pre-war size which was a remarkable achievement bearing in mind the unfavourable circumstances under which it was made. After the failure of the Arakan operations of 1943 the arrival of the West African troops appears to have been looked forward to as an answer to the Japanese tactics and much was expected of them. However by the time they arrived the Indian Army was well on the way towards finding a solution of its own and the West African Divisions simply became two more formations.

ii   *East Africa*

In 1914 the forces in East Africa were of the same character as those in West Africa although lacking the Imperial Service units. From the point of view of defence, the colonies of Nyasaland, Uganda and East Africa were linked through the King's African Rifles, which was the counterpart of the West African Frontier Force. By 1914 it comprised three battalions, one from each colony, and, as in West Africa, some classes and clans were preferred for recruitment. 1 Battalion, for instance, recruited only from the Yao, Atonga and Angoni peoples. The only volunteer units were one each in Uganda and Nyasaland.[10]

The outbreak of war found these scanty forces faced by much larger ones in German East Africa but reinforcements from India soon arrived. In East Africa an East Africa Regiment and a corps of Mounted Rifles were formed from 1800 volunteers, while Town Guards were formed in the principal centres. No attempt was made to expand the KAR but early skirmishes, conducted by small columns only a company or two in strength, were not such as to indicate that large forces were needed. The failure of the assault on Tanga tended to confirm this attitude and in January 1915 a defensive policy was ordered. However wastage from sickness was high and with a long campaign in view the locally raised volunteer forces tended to dwindle away. Settlers called for conscription but a survey indicated that under a hundred men were not either already serving or covered by possible exemptions. A Registration Ordinance was published in September 1915 and a Compulsory Service Ordinance three months later, although the latter was not applied until March 1917 when 300 settlers were called up.[11]

Lieutenant-General Smuts assumed command in East Africa in February 1916, taking over an augmented force charged with the destruction of the last of the German forces remaining in Africa. Since whether the campaign was short or long additional troops would be needed, if only to act as a garrison force, an expansion of the KAR was authorised in April. By the end of 1916 the very high sickness rates suffered by European, South African and Indian troops were such as to indicate that future operations could best be conducted by locally raised troops and another wave of expansion commenced. From February 1917 the possibility of raising troops for Egypt was discussed but the pressure of current operations caused decisions to be deferred. The new units raised at this time included two from enemy prisoners, a fact which under-lines the true mercenary nature of many of the colonial forces.[12] By April 1918 there were twenty-two KAR battalions in service and the question of East African units serving in the Middle East was re-vived, two brigades being asked for. No action was taken before the end of the war.[13]

In 1914 the strength of the KAR was 2400 and by November 1918 this had grown to 35,500. To support this relatively modest body of troops no fewer than 201,431 carriers were enlisted in East Africa with 178,819 in Uganda between 1914 and 1917 and 123,325 in Nyasaland in 1917 and 1918.[14]

In the inter-war period events roughly followed those in West Africa. A Kenya Defence Force was created in 1927 and in 1936 a Territorial Kenya Regiment was formed. A reorganisation of the KAR in 1937 saw three battalions raised to first-line strength with another three as cadres for future expansion. 7 King's African Rifles formed as a Territorial unit in Uganda shortly before the outbreak of war as an experiment which might have been followed in the other territories.

In 1939 the first stages of mobilisation took place as early as 19th July, when 2 KAR mobilised in aid of the civil power, and general mobilisation followed on 22nd August. On the outbreak of war two brigades were formed to defend the northern frontier and the first stages of expansion commenced. Defence Forces were formed in Uganda, Tanganyika and Nyasaland while the Kenya Regiment sponsored an armoured car regiment. In October 1939 contingency plans envisaged the use of a brigade for the Persian Gulf area, while a battalion might be needed for Aden or Somaliland.[15]

With the entry of Italy into the war and the arrival of the two West African brigades, 11 and 12 African Divisions were formed incorporating the two East African Brigades. These, with 1 South African Division, were responsible for the campaigns which resulted in the occupation of Italian East Africa. 11 Division was disbanded at the end of the campaign in November 1941 but 12 Division served as a garrison formation until April 1943. The opening of an active war on the African continent was the signal for a very great expansion of the East African army. One new battalion was formed in 1939, seven in 1940, ten in 1941 and no less than seventeen in 1942 and 1943, although by then some reductions were also taking place. These forces were deployed on a range of garrison duties in East Africa, including the blockade of French Somaliland, while two brigades were called on for the Madagascar campaign of 1942. Garrisons were also needed for the Seychelles and Mauritius after Japan entered the war and one or two units served in the Middle East.[16]

From 1943 the main focus of attention was the war in the Far East. In March 1942 an East African Brigade arrived in Ceylon and later that year, concurrently with the decisions to employ West African troops, an East African Division was called for to serve in Burma. 11 East African Division finally assembled in Ceylon in June 1943, followed by two brigades intended as reserves. The units of the five brigades were mainly found from the KAR with two battalions from Northern and one from Southern Rhodesia. The Division took part in the campaign in Assam from June 1944 to April 1945 while the independent brigades, despite their reserve status, fought in Arakan. The Division was training for a new campaign in Burma at the end of the war and it returned home early in 1946.

iii   The West Indies

The West Indies had a long military tradition going back to the earliest years of settlement in the 17th century. Mostly the forces were based on militias but they were joined in the Napoleonic period by the West India Regiments, which were Imperial regiments recruited in the West Indies. By 1914 only two battalions of the West India Regiment remained, one as the garrison of Jamaica and one at Freetown. 1 West India Regiment sent two companies to the Cameroons before it was relieved by 2 Battalion in 1915. The latter went to East Africa from July 1916. Apart from the West Indies Regiment there were fourteen local defence forces on the various West Indian islands in 1914, those of British Guiana and Bermuda being based on a militia while the rest were recruited from volunteers. Strengths were, however, low. The Trinidad Light Infantry was 160 strong while the associated Light Horse had 100 men.[17] Many of the police forces either had a defence role or were given one during the war. On the outbreak of war steps were taken to enlarge these forces since German cruisers were at large in the Atlantic and landings were feared. Once this threat had disappeared many of the little units disappeared also, leaving such Imperial garrisons as were stationed in the West Indies. These comprised the West India battalion in Jamaica plus the garrison of Bermuda. The British battalion there was relieved by a Canadian unit in 1914 and a succession of Canadian units served there until a British Territorial battalion arrived in 1916. Some harbours were given artillery defences, mainly manned by Royal Marines, from 1917.

Local defence preoccupied the West Indies for the early months of the war but the Governor of Jamaica raised the question of a West Indies Contingent with the War Office and recruiting commenced in May 1915. The original contingents were accepted from Jamaica, Barbados, British Guiana and Trinidad but this was later extended to the other islands. The first contingent of 550 men reached Britain in August 1915, although a formal recruiting campaign did not commence in Jamaica until September. Volunteers came in steadily but about 80% were rejected on medical grounds and a Compulsory Service Act and Registration Act were passed by the Legislative Council, coming into force in June 1917. By then a succession of contingents had sailed but priority for shipping was now being given to the transport of American troops across the Atlantic. Enlistment was suspended in August 1917 and finally terminated in May 1918 when drafts under training were disbanded. Compulsion was not applied in the other islands although Saint Kitts and others introduced a system of enlistment bounties.[18]

In the United Kingdom the West Indian contingents were formed into a British West Indies Regiment of which the first battalion was raised in October 1915.[19] In April 1916 a British West Indies Brigade was sent from Britain to Egypt, where it was broken up in July. Two battalions remained in the Middle East to the end of the war, mainly serving on the lines of communication but fighting in the campaign of 1918. The remaining ten battalions served as pioneers on the Western Front and in Italy, with small contingents also serving in East Africa and in Mesopotamia. Total recruitment for the British West Indies Regiment came to 15,200 of whom about two-thirds came from Jamaica.[20]

In the inter-war years little of military significance interrupted the Caribbean calm. The West India Regiment was disbanded in 1927, after which a British unit provided the Jamaica garrison. At the start of the Second World War the West Indies were not disturbed until 1940 and no attempt was made to develop the individual defence forces. From May 1940 a Canadian battalion relieved the British unit in Jamaica and a succession of Canadian units occupied that station until 1946. For the rest, the shadow of the United States seems to have been regarded as sufficient protection and this attitude was reinforced when the development of American bases was authorised from September 1940. During 1941 and the early part of 1942 full-time defence companies were formed, based on the old defence forces, with two full-time battalions in Trinidad, where there were extensive oil installations to protect.

The entry of the United States into the war, together with the German U-boat offensive, brought active war to the West Indies and with it a review of the defences. In January 1942 a full-time battalion was mobilised in Jamaica with another in Guiana and later in the year a visit of inspection from the War Office resulted in further increases and the establishment of an overall organisation.[21] The existing defence companies were expanded or amalgamated into battalions and from January 1943 North and South Caribbean Forces were established to control the units. Home Guards were also formed at this time. Thus, after three and a half years of war, a coherent defence scheme was established.

It was not until late in 1943 that it was proposed to form a West Indian contingent for overseas service. The Caribbean Regiment was then formed and after training in the United States it arrived in Italy in September 1944, before going on to join the garrison forces in the Middle East. Although the idea of forming further units was briefly entertained only one battalion was created.[22]

Relative to the events of the Great War developments during the Second seem to have been small and late and it is unclear why this should have been so. In 1939 there was little threat to the West Indies but undue reliance was placed on the indirect protection afforded by the United States. Once the development of American bases commenced the protection was more direct and the demands for labour for construction reduced the numbers available for defence. Accepting that weapons were in short supply more could have been done earlier to provide for self-defence. Commando-type raids could have been mounted which, while not militarily damaging, might have been politically embarrassing.[23]

iv *The Burmese Army*

In 1914 Burma was administered from India and there were no indigenous Burmese forces. The Indian Army expansions were extended to Burma, though, and in 1916 a Kaching Company was formed as part of the Burma Military Police, as well as a corps of Burma Pioneers. By 1918 these had become 85 Burma infantry and five battalions of 70 Burma Rifles. The Indian Army's 1922 reorganisations grouped these as 20 Burma Rifles, which became the basis of Burma's army when separation from India took place in April 1937. The forces then transferred were quite considerable. They comprised three battalions, a Territorial battalion and a training battalion of Burma Rifles, five battalions of the Burma Auxiliary Force, six of the Burma Frontier Force and three of Burma Military Police. The composition of the Burma Rifles was largely Chins, Kachins and Karens, while the BFF and Military Police contained large elements of emigre Sikhs, Punjabis and Gurkhas. After separation there was a demand for larger Burma representation in the army and recruiting was extended to this class, an additional battalion being raised.

After the outbreak of war two additional Territorial battalions were raised and another in 1941. Four new Burma Rifles battalions were formed between April 1940 and February 1941, of which 7 Battalion came from the Police and 8 Battalion, made up of Sikhs and Punjabi Mussalmans, from the BFF. Supporting arms and modern weapons were lacking and development here was confined to a new company of Burma Sappers and Miners and the conversion of the Rangoon Battalion BAF into a Heavy Anti-aircraft Regiment. From November 1940 service in the Auxiliary Force was made compulsory for all European British subjects of military age.[24]

In July 1941 Burma Division was formed with two Burma Brigades and after the campaign in Burma in 1942 these were re-formed as 39 Indian Division. Burmese soldiers were given the option of discharge when the retreat reached the Burmese frontier and only 2 Burma Rifles survived to join Special Force, while Chin Hills Battalion, BFF, remained as a reconnaissance unit on the frontier. The Burma Rifles earned an unhappy reputation during the campaign but they suffered from the same problems of over-expansion as did the Indian Army at this time, as well as seeing their homeland being over-run by another alien force.

The remnants of the Burmese Army which were not discharged were taken onto the Indian establishment as the Burma Regiment, organised in two brigades. The original establishment was quite ambitious with six infantry battalions, reconnaissance and training battalions and two garrison battalions but by 1944 the brigades were broken up and only three infantry and two garrison battalions remained.[25]

Another thread in the development of the Burmese Army is provided by the Burma Defence Army. This was formed under Japanese auspices in August 1942 and became the Burma National Army before defecting to the Allies in March 1945. It became the Patriotic Burma Forces in May.[26]

The formation of a new army for Burma commenced in January 1945 and development occupied a considerable amount of time and discussion because of Burmese political ambitions and uncertainty about the future. By the end of the year five battalions of Burma Rifles had been re-formed, incorporating the former 2 Burma Rifles and elements of the PBF and Burma Regiment. They were joined by the Chin, Kachin and Karen Rifles, formed mainly from levy corps which had been raised to fight the Japanese.

v   *A summary*

Sufficient has been said to indicate that the military contributions made by the colonies during the two World Wars were considerable and varied. To give in detail the efforts made by each and every colony would be redundant for the purpose of this discussion, although many are of intrinsic interest. Looking generally at the colonial involvement, two principal factors may be distinguished. One of these is the question of labour and the other is the nature of the threat to which the different colonies were exposed.

During the Great War operations on the Western Front, in the Middle East, East Africa and Mesopotamia were very demanding for labour of all forms and large numbers were called for to support the fighting formations. A major colonial contribution was made in this field, the world being scoured to find men. Even the leased territory of Wei-hai-wei recruited 45,000 for a Chinese Labour Corps for France with a similar number coming from Tsingtao.[27] At the same time the direct threat to many of the colonies was slight and few men, if any, needed to be devoted to local defence. This contrasted with the situation in the Second War when many colonies were exposed to direct attack and defensive forces had to be raised, the demand for crude labour being much less. A case in point is that of Fiji which between 1914 and 1918 raised 250 volunteers for the British and New Zealand Armies, as well as sending a Labour Corps to France and Italy. In the later war a considerable force had to be raised in Fiji for its own defence.[28]

By 1918 the manpower shortages of Britain were such that British forces were being concentrated on the main theatre and in the Middle East and Salonika Indian troops were taking over. At that period colonial troops were being earmarked for service in the Middle East and one might speculate that if the war had continued into 1919 a phase of 'colonialisation' would have ensued, with colonial troops replacing Indian, releasing the latter to serve on the Western Front again. In the later war colonial troops were employed in active theatres from an early date and that contribution was contained in pre-war planning. East and West African troops were employed with success in a major campaign against what was then regarded as a secondary enemy before moving on to the Far East. Their contribution in Burma was not without reverses but it was of value and part of the final defeat of the Japanese.

Notes

1   A. Haywood and F. A. S. Clarke, *History of the Royal West African Frontier Force*, Gale and Polden, Aldershot, pp. 49, 88–9.

2   Ibid., pp. 252–3.
    Sir Charles Lucas (Ed.), *The Empire at War*, IV, Oxford U. P., 1925,
    pp. 43–4, 134.
3   Haywood and Clarke, *RWAFF*, pp. 325–6.
4   PRO/WO/173 – Index.
5   W. L. S. Churchill, *The Second World War*, III, Cassell, London,
    1950, p. 686 gives 'about 400'. Haywood and Clarke, *RWAFF*, p.
    373 gives 'some 200'.
6   Ibid., pp. 365–71.
7   Churchill, *Second World War*, III, pp. 452–3, 654, 701.
    PRO/Cab/66/15.
8   Haywood and Clarke, *RWAFF*, p. 373.
    S. W. Kirby, *The War Against Japan*, II, H.M.S.O., London, 1958,
    p. 361.
    Churchill, *Second World War*, IV, 1951, p. 752.
9   Kirby, *War Against Japan*, III, 1961, p. 154, IV, 1965, p. 345, V,
    1969, pp. 64, 89.
10 H. Moyse-Bartlett, *King's African Rifles*, Gale and Polden, Aldershot,
    1956, pp. 138, 158–9.
11 Ibid., p. 293.
    Lucas, *Empire at War*, IV, pp. 210–1.
12 C. Hordern, *East Africa*, I, H.M.S.O., London, 1941, p. 513.
    Moyse-Bartlett, *KAR*, p. 335.
13 Ibid., p. 414.
14 Lucas, *Empire at War*, IV, pp. 214, 238, 270.
15 Moyse-Bartlett, *KAR*, pp. 475–6, 480.
16 PRO/WO/212/265 – 273.
    PRO/WO/169 – Index.
17 Lucas, *Empire at War*, I, 1921, p. 258.
    NAM file 6207 – 17.
18 Lucas, *Empire at War*, II, 1923, pp. 346–50, 377.
19 Army Order 4/1916.
20 Lucas, *Empire at War*, II, pp. 335, 350.
21 PRO/WO/32/10092.
    PRO/WO/212/481–2.
22 PRO/WO/32/11753.
23 Churchill, *Second World War*, IV, p. 789.
24 Kirby, *War Against Japan*, I, 1957, pp. 8–9.
    J. Lunt, *Imperial Sunset*, Macdonald, London, 1981, pp. 355–60.
25 IO/WS/21233 and 26559.
26 Sir William J. Slim, *Defeat into Victory*, Cassell, London, 1956,
    pp. 474–5, 504–9.
27 Lucas, *Empire at War*, V, 1926, p. 454.
28 Lucas, *Empire at War*, III, 1924, pp. 393–5.

Chapter 9
Expanding and contracting armies

The previous chapters have summarised how the countries of the Commonwealth responded to the challenges of 1914 and 1939 and how they placed considerable armies in the field. Many points of similarity in the way in which the armies developed will have been noticed. To a superficial view this is not unexpected. The history of the Dominions and colonies was a part of British history and tradition. In their formative years the military forces of those territories had been subject to British influence in varying degrees and from the Colonial Conference of 1907 deliberate efforts were made to integrate the colonial forces, in whole or in part, into the Imperial forces. Yet looking in detail at the way in which the forces developed, although the final result was similar the manner in which that result was achieved was significantly different from Dominion to Dominion and colony to colony. Indeed almost the only common element is the wave of sentiment which inspired the developments of 1914. Once that wave was spent the paths diverged.

The manpower and organisational problems experienced in the development of the armies were many and varied. Manpower and organisational problems inter-relate and are rarely separable. In the ideal situation organisational planning precedes manpower planning but the former commonly needs adjustment because of manpower limitations and the planning process then becomes one of successive modification, with the organisation being adapted to suit the men and the men being adapted, or selected or trained, to fit the organisation. In the case of the armies the expansion problems existed at a multiplicity of levels and to facilitate discussion three broad levels may be distinguished. At the constitutional level there were the problems created by the place of the army in the community at large and how it was visualised in the context of the

212   *The Commonwealth armies*

nation and its policies. At the institutional level there were the
problems arising out of the overall structure of the army, such as
the integration of full-time and part-time forces or the balance
between different arms. Finally there were the internal problems of
the army itself concerning the distribution of men between the
various arms, how they should be trained and the organisational
units into which they should be grouped. Too much should not be
read into this hierarchy, since a single problem could exist and have
its effects at all levels. The class composition of the Indian Army,
for instance, had its implications in how that Army was perceived
by the Indian people as a whole, how the Army was recruited and
trained and how the Army was organised to accommodate the
different classes.

i   *The army and the nation*

The Commonwealth Armies of 1914 fell into three groups. One
was the British Regular Army which was seen in part as a striking
force for use oveseas, the second was made up of the British Territorial Force and the defence forces of the Dominions while the third
consisted of the internal security forces of the various colonies. The
Indian Army did not easily fall into this grouping for it was, in part,
a de facto reinforcement to the striking force, while the remaining
portion was committed to local defence and internal security in
India.

Numerically the largest of the groups was that of the Territorial
Force and the Dominions' forces. The terms under which these
were raised and maintained are instructive. The legislative provisions governing all of them were restrictive and all were specifically
raised for the 'defence' of the various countries with, usually, terms
which geographically limited where they could be employed. The
assumptions under which all were raised attempted to distinguish
between 'offensive' and 'defensive' war with, perhaps, the one
being seen as 'bad' and the other 'good' and ignoring that to defend
one's home on its doorstep is to see it reduced to dust and ashes.
Raising military forces, especially in peace-time, is the art of the
possible, since the effort must be publicly acceptable, but the
constitutions adopted made the pre-war forces an imperfect
foundation for the post-1914 expansion. Perhaps as important as
the legislative limitations were those imposed by what the

limitations were seen or believed to be. In South Africa in 1914 the proposed use of the 'defensive' Union Defence Force for offensive operations in South-west Africa was a significant factor in the outbreak of the Rebellion. In Canada the Militia could have been made available for overseas service in the defence of Canada but operations in Western Europe were not seen as being operations in the defence of Canada, as such, and the Canadian Expeditionary Force was raised as a 'New Army'. Although the imperfections of these forces were seen and recognised during the Great War little attempt was made between the wars to remedy them. In Britain, although the Territorial Army was recruited with 'general service' liability, until 1939 it existed on the Statute Books as a home defence force, a totally anomalous situation. In the Dominions the 'home defence' principles of the forces were retained although in 1943 an Australian Defence Act extended the Commonwealth Militia's area to one bounded by geographical coordinates which allowed a militiaman to 'die in Dutch New Guinea but not in American Luzon, in Portuguese Timor but not in British Borneo'.[1] The retention of these limited terms of service can only be explained by the 'never again' attitudes of the inter-war period in Britain and, perhaps, in the Dominions by a feeling, sub-conscious rather than expressed, that to maintain limited service armies retained for them a greater range of choice regarding participation in a future war. The growth in the importance of the air arm, too, sowed doubts as to what the role of an army would be in a future war. Again, in the Second World War, what the terms and conditions of an army, or part of it, were believed to be rather than what they really were had some effect in that, for example, there is evidence that the Indian Territorial Force was reorganised for general service in 1941 partly because personnel believed themselves liable to serve for only two years. In another incident, in East Africa towards the end of 1941 a brigade designated for service overseas had to be replaced when its members asserted that they should be allowed to volunteer afresh for such service.[2] Members of 1 South African Division expected to return to South Africa at the conclusion of the East African campaign in 1941.[3]

When a nation is under a threat which is seen to be immediate, or is embarked upon a major war and committed to raising a mass army, sooner or later the question of compulsory service will arise. In a democratic society a Government governs only by consent and it is perhaps inevitable that the degree of consent for universal service will vary directly with the nearness of the threat. In war a Government requires powers of direction to allocate its citizens not only to fill out its armies but also to control their deployment between the different Services and industry to reduce the economic damage resulting from indiscriminate recruitment and to control the deployment of those with scarce talents. This lesson was hardly learned in Britain from 1914 onwards and the relative success of the application of compulsory service in the later war owed much to the earlier experience. In the Dominions the threat was not immediate until 1941, and then only for some, and the imposition of compulsory service in them was more difficult than in Britain, where the threat of direct attack was more apparent and more immediate. At best the application of compulsory service is potentially divisive and is likely to alienate sectors of the community which see themselves as having separate interests from the majority. In Britain during the Great War the threat of direct attack was relatively slight, though much feared, and the application of compulsory service was halting and clumsily administered so that it was believed to be unjust and inequitable. Industrial unrest followed, marked by a series of damaging strikes. In the Dominions the threat of direct attack was remote and the risks of internal division much more acute. Although New Zealand was able to introduce compulsory service measures in 1916, doing so with some demonstrations against them, the divisive effects were much more evident in Canada where the introspective French-Canadian community was opposed to the measure. In Australia opposition to compulsion was sufficiently great to prevent its introduction and in South Africa, after the experience of the Rebellion, the application of compulsory service was not even considered. During the later war Britain appeared to be under threat of immediate attack and conscription provoked little opposition, as happened later in Australia and New Zealand when Japanese attack appeared to be immediate. Canada, more remote, experienced little difficulty in applying conscription for home service but the extension of this to overseas service in 1944 reactivated the divisions of 1917 and 1918. South Africa, with significant sections of the populace opposed to any part in the war, did not attempt to apply conscription at all.

When recruiting an army under voluntary conditions the evidence is that the initial call will produce a flood of applicants but that thereafter the number coming forward will rapidly tail away to give numbers insufficient to replace wastage. Given some significant event, such as the Anzac landing at Gallipoli or the crisis of 1940, a repeated appeal will again bring forward many volunteers but a further repetition of appeals will have little result. One of the theoretical advantages of introducing compulsory service is that the initiative for intake to an army is transferred from the motivation of individuals to the requirements of the Armed Services, which can then call men forward as they need them. British experience of the Second World War, however, suggests that the point of initiative goes to the authority distributing manpower which drafts men as and when they can be released from industry. This certainly provides a central point to which representations for men can be made but it is likely that a particular Service will still not receive men as it would wish to have them. Some elements of flexibility may be regained, however, since compulsion may encourage volunteering, as the Canadians found in 1942. Volunteers may be encouraged, too, by such devices as allowing some choices of Service to those who anticipate their call-up.

The introduction of compulsory service, when once decided upon, is a lengthy proceeding since essential pre-requisites are a national registration and a listing of occupations which are of national importance. Indeed, the creation of such a schedule was, perhaps, the most important piece of planning in Britain between the wars. An over-riding problem, however, is the national defence priority which will determine the distribution of men between the different Services and industry. In the First World War the army was predominant, with the Royal Navy in a supporting role and the air forces as subsidiary services. Industrial production was geared accordingly. In the Second World War the decision to allocate a major offensive role to the Royal Air Force not only increased the size of that force at the expense of the army but demanded an industrial development which still further reduced the number of men available for the fighting Services. The predominance given to an air-based strategy after the fall of France in 1940 was logical, since few alternatives were available, but the acceptance of that strategy, with limited resources, ensured that only a relatively small army could be built up. Further, the high casualties suffered in the bomber offensive reduced the supply of potential officers available for the other two Services and contributed to the British Army's officer shortage of 1944. The shortage was alleviated by second-ment from the Dominions but it is notable that the Commander-in-Chief of the Indian Army ascribed the cessation of expansion of that Army to a shortage of officers, rather than to any other cause.

With a continental commitment envisaged for the British Army before 1914 it is remarkable that pre-war planning did not at least encompass contingency plans to expand the army on the basis of national service. Compulsory service had been a political issue since the turn of the century and although the measure was without pre-cedent in Britain there was an active 'lobby' for the introduction of conscription. What is even more surprising is that so little was done between the wars to prepare for the introduction of such a measure. Certainly the CID's Manpower Committee established a manpower strategy, or series of strategies, which could be applied but it was not until February 1939 that the War Office started to study how the army could be enlarged if and when national service was introduced. In the Dominions compulsory service, for home defence, was the basis of the forces of two countries in 1914 and available, although not enforced, for Canada and South Africa. However, all abandoned compulsory service between the wars. So far as the provision of expeditionary forces is concerned, the preparations made by the British Army are well known. Before 1914 Canada, Australia and New Zealand had plans for forces to serve overseas and, although these were not followed in detail in August 1914, they at least provided an outline of what forces could be produced with little advanced warning. By 1939 only Canada envisaged a Mobile Force for service outside the Dominion.

Once the need to expand the armies was recognised in 1914 the methods by which this could be done were limited. The pre-1914 armies consisted of small Regular forces supported by home-service troops. The options available for creating an expanded army were:

a. The introduction of conscription, coupled with redrafting the service conditions of the home-service forces.
b. Canvassing the home-service units to find out which were willing to volunteer for general service.
c. Forming general-service units on the basis of the home-service forces.
d. Forming 'New Armies' on such cadres as could be collected from the Regular and home-service troops.

In the Great War the first option was politically unacceptable, while the preconditions of a national register and an outline of what were and what were not believed to be essential occupations were not available. The development of an army on the basis of compulsory service, even if acceptable, would require a considerable period of time which might not be available. The British decision in 1914 was to base expansion on the fourth option while concurrently pursuing the second. The Canadian and Australian choice was also to take the fourth option, although with very strong cadres found from the home-defence forces. New Zealand took the third option as did South Africa, in effect, for the South-west Africa campaign although changing to the 'New Army' option from 1915.

For the Second World War, so far as Britain was concerned, the pre-war duplication of the Territorial Army and the introduction of compulsory service ensured that the first option was followed. Only Australia chose to use the 'New Army' route from 1939 with the other Dominions choosing to use the third option as the main line of development.

The evidence as to which method of expansion was the more efficient is inconclusive. The British Territorial Army before 1914 was expected to be fit for service after six months from mobilisation and a similar period was allowed the Kitchener Armies. In the event the British 'New Army' divisions were ready in nine months on average, and the Territorial divisions in a similar period in spite of many difficulties. 1 Canadian Division landed in France in 1915, just six months after being formed, and 1 Australian Division and the New Zealand Brigade landed on Gallipoli seven months after mobilisation. In the later war 6 Australian Division was fourteen months old when it was committed to its first campaign. Since, in general, in the early stages of a war it is likely that forces will be committed when they are needed, whether fully trained or not, much will depend on circumstances as to whether or not a formation is considered 'ready for service'.

Because of the method of expansion used the British Army's main organisational expansion took place with the duplication of the Territorial Army before the start of the Second World War and little expansion took place afterwards. Similarly it is worth noting that the expansion of the Canadian and South African Armies in the Second World War took place by mobilisation within the framework of the pre-war forces and few new units were raised. After the fifth AIF division was formed in 1941 subsequent Aus-

tralian expansion was by the mobilisation of Militia units. In peace-
time the role of an army is to provide a potential striking force and
also the cadres upon which a much larger organisation can be
built.[4] By this criterion it would appear that the structure of the
British Army was much more successful in 1939 than it was in 1914
although this was due in large part to the political gesture of the
duplication of the Territorial Army. The pre-war forces of the Dominions performed adequately as a base for expansion in both
World Wars. The Indian Army of 1914 did not at all provide a base
for expansion but was much improved by the reorganisation of
1922.

ii *The structure of the army*

The overall constitution of the Commonwealth armies into Regular and home-service components added a great deal of com-
plexity to the systems which had to be developed to expand and
maintain them during the two wars. In Britain, Regulars and
Territorials existed side by side until 1916, necessitating parallel
recruiting, training and drafting systems until then. Up to that time
it was not possible to use potential drafts for one to feed the other
in case of need. One of the early acts of September 1939 was to
eliminate this duplication and to all intents and purposes the
Territorial Army became absorbed into the Regular Army for the
duration of the war. In the Dominions the Regular forces were
small and, indeed, by 1939 most did not even possess formed
Regular units. Canada was the only country to mobilise Regular
units for both wars, South Africa only mobilising its Regulars for
South-west Africa. In both of these countries the permanent forces
were very much a minority of those engaged. In Australia, after the
mobilisation of the Militia in 1941, two forces with dissimilar
terms and conditions of service existed side by side. Although AIF
and CMF men trained together much resentment seems to have
been caused by regarding AIF units as being superior to militia
ones.

In both World Wars the division of the armies into mobile,
mounted or armoured, units and formations and infantry appears
to have caused problems in that the balance between the two was
difficult to establish. In the First World War there was a considerable over-expansion of mounted formations. In Britain the great

number of second- and third-line Yeomanry units formed a strong
mobile force for home defence but there was little prospect of them
finding a role in the field. The Australian and New Zealand
mounted troops found employment in the Middle East but those of
Canada were largely converted to infantry.

In the Second World War the difficulty of establishing a balance
between armour and infantry became acute. The development of
mobile and armoured forces was the subject of considerable discussion between the wars and the considerable German successes
in the campaigns in Poland and France appeared to confirm the
views of those who claimed the pre-eminence of armoured warfare.
The extent to which the British Army was to become armoured
was confirmed by the Cabinet in August and September 1940 and
these decisions were broadly followed by the Governments of the
Dominions and India, which modified their own development
programmes to follow the British lead. The desert campaigns of
1940 to 1942 and the campaign in Russia appeared to confirm the
correctness of the British decision. In part the British development
was due to the view, stemming from the Great War, that
'mechanical appliances of all kinds rendered the deadly duties of
the infantry easier and less costly';[5] while in the circumstances of
1940, with Britain facing Germany on her own, the British shortage
of manpower was such as to need any practicable assistance from
mechanisation to redress the balance. Unfortunately the development of the campaigns against the Japanese and the later campaigns
against Germany in Italy from 1943 and France from 1944 did not
confirm the earlier experience. What was now wanted was infantry
and armoured units and formations had to be broken up to fill the
deficiency. Thus, general manpower shortages were compounded
by an incorrect assessment of the balance of the forces required.

The organisation of an army into divisions and brigades for
operational purposes is an essential organisational feature. The use
of these terms as a measure of army size is more dubious. When
a target for expansion is set as a number of divisions there is a
tempation to reach and retain the target by any means practicable.
Thus, there was a tendency to keep nominal 'divisions' in service in
name even when they had wasted. In 1916 the seventy-one British
divisions then included nine 'second-line' Territorial divisions for
home defence, 'of very little value',[6] while in July 1943 the CIGS
was bewailing the retention of 'emaciated' formations which could

not be maintained.[7] The 55-division target for the Commonwealth in the Second World War was originally conceived as a field army for deployment in France but by August 1940 it included brigades for local defence in Britain as well as forces raised or being raised for limited operations in Africa. Indeed after March 1941 the target was effectively abandoned and account was taken in terms of 'equivalent divisions' of the world-wide commitments now being undertaken by the forces of the Commonwealth. A large proportion of these forces was made up of garrison troops and others providing infrastructure services. Although their work was invaluable they had little prospect of meeting an enemy in the field.

iii   *Internal organisation*

The internal structure of army units and formations, particularly in the Great War, gave rise to a number of problems in deployment since different establishments were used to form what were intended to be inter-changeable organisations. In 1915 British Regular, improvised Regular, Territorial and New Army divisions were all on establishments which differed in material respects, while the Indian divisions were on a different establishment again. This created obvious problems when one formation was to relieve another. Although the establishments were later brought more into line there was a retrograde movement when Canadian divisional establishments were changed in the winter of 1917/1918, while Dominion establishments in general did not change when British divisions were reduced in February 1918. The differences in establishment between British organisations in 1914 extended to unit level, there being four large companies in a Regular battalion and eight small ones in a Territorial unit. The difference which probably caused the greatest problem at this time was that an Indian division was considerably weaker than a comparable British formation and had to be strengthened by posting additional British units.

Changing basic organisations is a process which requires a considerable period of time, especially in peace-time, when because of economies the weapons on which reorganisation is based are not available in quantity. In 1935 the British Army began to turn to a four rifle-company organisation for infantry battalions in place of the former one machine-gun and three rifle-company organisation. Four years later some units were still on the old organisation, while

Australian militia and Union Defence Force battalions still included a machine-gun company in 1942.

In 1909 agreement was reached that in principle the forces of the countries of the Commonwealth would be raised to common organisational patterns and this provided the pattern for the mobilisations of 1914. Although still maintained as a principle, the majority of the divisions raised by the Dominions in 1939 were to differing establishments. While British divisions consisted of three brigades of three battalions an Australian brigade of 1939 contained four battalions, while a Canadian brigade had a machine-gun and three infantry battalions. The South Africans proposed a divisional establishment which differed quite markedly from those of Britain and the other Dominions. Although the Canadian and Australian organisations owed their differences in part to the lack of modern automatic weapons, it could also be said that the 1909 agreement was breaking down as part of the general move towards greater independence.

In the Second World War great emphasis was placed on raising special forces for raiding and behind-enemy-lines operations. It was earlier noted that a number of Commanders who held high positions were averse to such developments, asserting that such functions could be accommodated within existing army organisations. It has already been seen that many of these organisations were reabsorbed into normal organisations by the end of the war. 3 Indian Division did not long survive the death of General Wingate, the British Commandos fought as light infantry in the final campaigns of the war, while the Australian Independent Companies were absorbed into normal divisional reconnaissance units. Field Marshal Slim's assessment was that such special forces:[8]

a. Reduce the quality of the rest of the army by skimming off the best soldiers.
b. Encourage the belief that certain operations can only be carried out by specially trained men.
c. Can only be employed for limited periods before they have to be withdrawn for recuperation.

One more could perhaps be added:

d. Special forces, because of the exigencies of the moment, will often be called on to carry out tasks allocated to more regularly constituted units, when they prove to be untrained and ill-equipped for those tasks.

Field Marshal Slim excluded only one type of operation from his analysis; that of operations by small parties behind the enemy's lines.

From many points of view forces raised for home defence with restrictive conditions of service are but another species of special force. The limited constitutions of the defence forces of the Dominions and the British Territorial Force have been referred to several times, the British National Defence Companies of the 1930s being another example. It is inevitable that after mobilisation any existing body of men is likely to be needed to serve in places and under conditions quite different from those envisaged when it was raised.

When new units were created, or part-time units mobilised, the unit was responsible for training its own men. The need for a training organisation to provide a flow of reinforcements and replacements was not foreseen in 1914 and it was found necessary to convert the Fourth New Army into such an organisation. In the Territorial Force 'second-line' and later 'third-line' units were used for this purpose and for the army as a whole the training organisation was in a continuous state of improvisation and evolution until late in 1917. The Canadian Army's reinforcement system had to be improvised in a similar manner, breaking up battalions raised in the first instance as service units for the Expeditionary Force. In this respect the systems devised by the other Dominions seem to have fared rather better. Second World War developments took advantage of the earlier experience and training organisations were formed or developed in the first stages of expansion except, perhaps, for South Africa where uncommitted units and formations were used. In the later war training demands reached greater heights with the need for specialised training and saw the organisation of such establishments as Battle Schools, the Indian Training Divisions and the Australian complex at Canungra.

A problem which was not fully faced in either World War was that of how long, in a non-professional army, can a man be expected to serve overseas without leave. With this, indeed, is coupled the related problem of just how long can such a man be expected to serve at all. With its tradition of long periods of overseas service without home leave, the British Army was slow to recognise that a problem existed and, in the event, the circumstances of the Great War were such as to reduce the nature of the problem. With the main British deployment taking place in France, regular home leave was practicable and the most serious problems in this field were those caused by retaining Territorials in India until 1919. By November 1918 troops from Canada, Australia and New Zealand had been overseas for four years and an Australian leave scheme had been instituted at the pressure of the Australian Prime Minister just before the end of the war. In the Second World War larger bodies of troops were employed overseas for long periods and the problem became both more widespread and more acute. The introduction of the British 'Python' scheme from January 1943, with later modifications, provided in the first instance for the return of those who had been overseas for more than six years but in 1945 the period was much reduced with, potentially, a crippling of projected operations. The Canadian and New Zealand Armies faced similar problems. Both instituted leave schemes for long-service personnel to find that for a variety of reasons very few of those who returned home for leave ever went back to active service. The return of the Australian divisions from the Middlie East allowed home leave to be given and by 1945 the demobilisation of long-service men was under way. The development of the war in the Allied favour from 1943 onwards permitted the relief of men with long service, although it is doubtful what would have been practicable had the war continued to run against the Allied cause. The end of the war came just in time to avert what would have been a severe problem.

iv *Over-expansion*

The intrinsic problem affecting the armies of Britain and the other members of the Commonwealth is illustrated by the graphs which are reproduced as Figures 1.1. and 1.2. The second of these shows that the number of battalions in service increased to a maximum in the middle of 1916 and decreased thereafter, while the text indicates that further reductions were on the way in 1919. A diagram for the number of divisions in service would demonstrate the same point. On the other hand Figure 1.1 shows that the strength of the British Army reached a high level in March 1918, when a sharp drop represents the transfer of men to form the Royal Air Force, after which the number of men available rises again. To a very large extent the development of the other armies examined repeats this sequence, this is to say fighting units and formations being disbanded on account of lack of men when, in fact, the number of men shown on strength returns is steady or even rising.

The exceptions to this process are few. For the Great War Figure 3.1 indicates that the organisation of the Indian Army was still expanding in 1918 while, had the war continued, it is probable that still further expansion would have followed. Similar remarks could be applied to the troops raised in East and West Africa. Thus, what could be considered the mercenary forces of the Commonwealth were still expanding in 1918. However, it should be remembered that no expansion of these forces was contemplated until 1916 so that insufficient time had elapsed to show any pattern other than that of expansion. In the Second World War the Indian Army reached a peak strength in terms of units or formations in 1942 or 1943 and thereafter declined (Figure 3.2), while in East and West Africa units were being disbanded from the end of 1941. In the Second World War, when the creation of new forces commenced much earlier than in the First, it would appear that the more usual pattern prevailed.

So far as the strengths of the armies are concerned exceptions from the 'normal' pattern are limited. For the Canadian Army Figure 4.2 shows a slight fall in the middle of 1918, due to a deliberate reduction in the rate of enlistment, while Figure 4.4 also shows a slight fall towards the end of the later war for similar reasons, although it is noteworthy that the number of 'general-service' men was still increasing in 1945. No reliable statistics are available for Australian strengths during the Great War although they were certainly declining towards the end. In the Second World War Figures 5.2 and 6.1 show that for Australia and New Zealand troops were being demobilised from 1942 or 1943, once the immediate threat of Japanese invasion was believed to be over. Figure 5.2 shows that for the Australian forces the demobilisations were effected more through the Militia than through the AIF. One of the factors in the Australian and New Zealand demobilisations was the belief that in those countries their mobilisations represented a greater load than that taken by other Allies and it is intended to examine the validity of this belief in later paragraphs. In both wars South Africa mobilised when local threats were believed to exist and reduced once those threats were eliminated.

Although, as has been indicated in previous Chapters, the individual circumstances surrounding the development of the

Commonwealth armies could be considered unique in each case there is evidence that those developments, in spite of the exceptions, fall into a pattern which is sufficiently regular to merit examination.

The strengths of the armies used in the various Figures are those officially returned in sources which were identified adjacent to the Figures themselves. They do not distinguish between 'effective' and 'ineffective' personnel and to do so would demand close definition of what is meant by each term. The number of 'ineffectives', including unrecovered wounded and sick, can make up a significant fraction of any statement of strength. Even though strength returns show constant figures, over a period the effective strength could well be declining, particularly if active operations are taking place so that casualties are being suffered or if the army, or some portion of it, is in unhealthy environments so that the number of sick is rising. Even so, it would be anticipated that one would eventually reach a position of stability at whch the number of 'effectives' was reasonably steady.

The number of men which a country can maintain under arms depends ultimately on the population of that country, although not on the total population since different countries have significantly different population structures. Differing birth-rates, death-rates, immigration and emigration are all reflected in the age distribution of a country's population. The question remains as to which demographic statistic gives a ready indication of a country's mobilisation potential. Regimental rolls, casualty lists and direct observation suggest that the fighting arms are principally manned by younger men and it follows that the 20–25 age group will probably provide the best indicator. This is the age group whose members are principally found in the fighting formations, while members of supporting arms tend to be older. Age is, of course, not the only criterion. Physical fitness is another principal factor, but this, too, is age related. Between 1939 and 1945 73.5% of all those aged 20–25 were found to be in the highest physical category. The younger were even fitter.[9]

The strengths of the various armies at the end of the two World Wars in relation to the male population age group 20–25 were as indicated in Tables 9.1 and 9.2. No detailed figures are available for the troops of South Africa but there were 31,560 white South Africans in East Africa in April 1941, rather more than 40,000 in the Middle East late in 1943 and 42,000 in the Mediterranean

Table 9.1   Great War: army strength and population

	20–25 male age group	Army strength November 1918	Ratio strength: age group
United Kingdom	1,704,423	3,759,471	2.21
Australia	230,125	178,342	0.78
		(max. 198,333)	(0.86)
Canada	385,855	362,774	0.94
		(max. 388,038)	(1.01)
India	13,154,601	573,484	0.04
New Zealand	49,692	63,879	1.29
South Africa (White)	65,726	18,796	0.29
		(max. 67,237)	(1.02)
(Other)	226,061		

Sources: Census Reports. Published Strength Returns.

Table 9.2   Second World War: army strength and population

	20–25 male age group	Army strength June/July 1945	Ratio strength: age group
United Kingdom	1,737,000	2,920,000	1.68
Australia	309,490	365,764	1.18
		(max. 473,790)	(1.53)
Canada	517,956	461,773	0.89
		(max. 479,147)	(0.93)
India	16,314,675	1,729,608	0.11
New Zealand	66,000	53,156	0.81
	(est.)	(max. 124,773)	(1.89)
South Africa (White)	94,670	n.a.	n.a.
(Other)	314,375		

Sources: Census Reports. Published Strength Returns.

theatre at the end of the Second World War. Total enlistments for full-time service were 132,194.[10]

Making allowances for the separate status and complexities of the Indian manpower situation and for the problems of South Africa it would appear that, except for the United Kingdom, the number of men in the armies represented a considerable proportion of the number available in the critical 20–25 age group. When, in the Second World War, the armies of Australia and New Zealand significantly exceeded that figure for a period the Governments of the day took steps to reduce the number of men in the armies concerned.

The size of the army any Government wishes to create is governed not only by the size of the available population but also by the numbers which have to be allocated to industry and also by the degree to which it is desired to expand the other two fighting Services. For the Great War only Britain devoted large numbers of men to the navy and air force and in November 1918 the total number of men in uniform was about 4,457,000, or 2·62 times the 20–25 age group. The extent of the Dominions' commitment to these Services is exemplified by the 5000 and 6000 men who were in the Australian and Canadian Navies, respectively, in 1918. In the Second World War all of the Dominions created naval and air forces of some size and in addition many individuals from the Dominions joined or were seconded to the British services. Approximate strengths at the end of the later war were as indicated in Table 9.3. The old Dominions used their manpower to enlarge their air forces rather more than Britain expanded the RAF, relatively speaking: indeed of the 487 squadrons under RAF command in June 1944 exactly 100 were from the Dominions.

Considering a country under full mobilisation conditions and wishing to raise a large army, the largest pool of fit men is to be found in the 20–25 age group. To this may be added the fit men in higher age groups and as many of the under-20s as it is thought

Table 9.3   Strengths of the Armed Services, 1945

	Army	Navy	Air Force	Total	Ratio total: 20–25 male age group
United Kingdom	2,920,000	783,000	950,000	4,653,000	2.68
Australia	366,000	34,000	170,000	570,000	1.84
Canada	462,000	93,000	215,000	770,000	1.49
India	1,730,000	30,000	29,000	1,789,000	0.11
New Zealand	53,000	11,000	33,000	97,000	1.47

Sources: Published Strength Returns.

advisable to include. This pool will be reduced by the number claimed by the other Services and by those it is desired to retain for industry. The size of the pool may be increased again, of course, by the inclusion of the partially fit, who can be used on less arduous duties. The values of these additions and subtractions will tend to be mutually cancelling although, so far as the additions and subtractions are concerned, their values will largely depend on the decisions of the Government of the day. Under the circumstances of the two World Wars the number of men available for the armies tended to approximate to the number of men in the 20–25 age group. What size of army, in divisions, could be formed from those men? It was earlier indicated that the usual 'divisional slice', the number of men needed to keep a division in the field, was of the order of 60,000. This represented 15,000 to 20,000 men in the division itself plus men counted as GHQ, Army and Corps Troops, supply and maintenance services, training and administrative organisations, garrisons and local defence troops as well as the provision of infra-structure services, such as road and railway building, for campaigns where those were inadequate. About 10% of the 60,000, on the basis of previous experience, could have been 'ineffective'. On this basis the number of 'divisions' which could have been formed is indicated in Table 9.4, together with the number of 'equivalent Divisions' actually in existence in 1918 and 1945. The 'Actual' figures for the British Army could also carry an addition to represent the British component of Indian formations.

Comparing the 'Actual' with the 'Theoretical' figures in Table 9.4 some of the difficulties experienced by the various countries in

Table 9.4   Number of Divisions, 1918 and 1945

	November 1918		June/July 1945	
	Theoretical	Actual	Theoretical	Actual
United Kingdom	28.4	64⅔	29.0	42
Australia	3.8	6⅔	5.2	7⅓
Canada	6.4	4⅔	8.6	6⅓
India	219.3	17	271.9	18
New Zealand	0.8	1⅓	1.1	1
South Africa (White)	1.1	⅓	1.6	1
(Other)	3.8	0	5.2	0

keeping formations in service may be readily appreciated. All of the countries listed, except India in the Great War, had by November 1918 and July 1945 already reduced their number of serving brigades and divisions and most were engaged in further reductions. The Australian Army in 1918 was engaged in a process of ad hoc contraction as individual units fell below effective strength, whilst in 1945 a reduction to three divisions was in view. The Canadian Army, with a relatively small number of serving formations, was maintaining its strength with not too much difficulty. New Zealand was able to maintain its four brigades in 1918 without trouble, although in 1945 the task of keeping a division of four brigades in service was proving to be a considerable strain, especially when coupled with doubts as to whether or not the place where the division was employed was really in New Zealand's best interests. In South Africa, with in both Wars a substantial section of the population opposed to participation, difficulty was being experienced in keeping the formations deployed up to strength. By this criterion Kitchener's seventy divisions could not have been sustained, although the 1939 British estimate of thirty-two divisions was a reasonably practicable target.

The forces deployed by India bore no relation to those which could have been formed, on the basis of population. Also on the basis of population a number of formations could have been placed in the field from the non-white population of South Africa. Both of the World Wars arose, in the first place, out of a conflict between European powers with, in the later War, Japan entering as a developed nation with many of the interests, economic and political, of a European power. The causes and consequences of these Wars thus impinged on the peoples of dependencies only so far as their interests coincided with those of their nominal rulers. For India, the Gold Coast, Uganda, the Bantu races of South Africa and the indigenous peoples of the colonies the Wars were not national as they were for the British or for the sections of white South Africa which supported the Wars. So far as national aspirations were concerned it could even be seen, by some, that the defeat of Britain or her Allies would benefit the dependent peoples, as was witnessed by the formation of the Indian National Army under the Japanese. To impose a national mobilisation on many of the colonial peoples would have involved cutting across many traditional customs, practices and barriers so that it could have demanded a degree of

coercion which would have been morally and politically unacceptable and economically counter-productive. The forces raised in
India and the colonies, and in non-white South Africa, were thus
formed on a voluntary basis from those sectors of the population
which had evolved a tradition of military support and cooperation,
of respected individual and collective relationships, some extending
over several generations. The 'martial races' concept was, from the
point of view of, say, an Indian nationalist, an expression of alien
domination. From the point of view of the ruling power it was a
part rational, part emotional, practical convenience hallowed by
shared experience with the members of those 'martial classes'. In
practical terms, too, if large numbers had come forward to enlist in
the dependencies, where general levels of education were low,
considerable, perhaps disproportionate, resources would have had
to be devoted to training over a long period. Such expansion as was
undertaken in India, the colonies and non-white South Africa was
a compromise solution to the general problem of raising the
greatest forces practicable to win wars between countries of the
developed world.

The case of the British Army in both World Wars demands
particular consideration since even in 1918 and 1945, after considerable reductions in the number of formations placed in the field,
many more divisions and brigades were in service than could
theoretically be maintained. In 1918 the Army contained a number
of men double that of the 20–25 age group and in 1945 nearly as
many. The implications are that the Army contained numbers of
men from younger age groups, some too young for active service,
and considerable numbers of older men, among whom the
proportion of those falling short of Grade I standard rises rapidly
with age. Formations made up of these men, or containing significant proportions of them, would tend to waste rapidly on active service unless an outstandingly close matching was achieved
between individual men and the tasks they had to carry out. The
extent to which similar practices are followed by an enemy then
becomes critical in case a relative qualitative inferiority becomes
apparent. In short, even in 1918 and 1945, after the earlier reductions, the British Army was attempting to keep in service many
more formations than could be maintained efficiently.

The number of active service formations which can be maintained for long periods appears to be indicated by the number of

men allocated to the army from the 20–25 age group. It remains to consider the occasions when this number can be exceeded. Two sets of circumstances appear to present themselves. The first of these occurs during the mobilisation stages at the beginning of a war. In both World Wars new units were formed, or part-time units mobilised, with the units themselves responsible for training their men. Since, in the mobilisation stage, training facilities have to be developed from peace-time to war-time levels the formation of additional units, brigades and divisions to carry out the training processes reduces the pressure on limited training facilities. At the same time the number of men requiring training during the early stages, when several age groups are being called up simultaneously, is much greater than will be the case in later stages when only one or two age groups are called up at a time. The formation of surplus units to carry out basic training is thus a useful expedient, preventing the development of separate training facilities which will later become redundant. The difficulty, on the experience of both Wars, would appear to lie in recognising that surplus units and formations have been created which will naturally be reduced in the course of time, rather than trying to maintain them with inadequate manpower resources. The second contingency in which greater expansion can occur is when the homeland is under threat of imminent invasion, or appears to be. Under this circumstance the 'divisional slice' may be considerably below the 60,000 of previous experience. In the homeland many of the infrastructure services probably exist already and, if the emergency is genuinely imminent, facilities, such as training, having a longer term commitment may be dispensed with. The circumstances under which Canada, Australia and New Zealand expanded their organisational structures in late 1941 and early 1942, or in which Britain expanded hers in the summer of 1940, broadly conform with this pattern. Outside the Commonwealth similar examples may be found from Germany in 1944 and 1945 and Japan in the later year. Indeed under desperate circumstances the question becomes one of grouping any forces that might be scraped together without too much regard for establishments, for which men with appropriate experience and training, and equipment, may be lacking.

So far the size to which the armies were expanded has been considered only in relation to a static system in terms of the limitations imposed by population. It is in fact a dynamic system subject to a constant inflow of men on the one side and a constant outflow on the other. The inflow, or enlistment, and the problems faced by armies and Governments in attempting to maintain it, was related in the previous Chapters. So far as the outflow is concerned, some reference has also been made when considering the problems of individual armies, but no attempt has yet been made to evaluate these effects on the size of the armies raised. The evidence is that for the Great War wastage, the accumulation of deaths and discharges, for the British Army ran with some consistency at 1·5% of the Army's strength each month. This figure fell to 1·2% in quiet periods and rose to 2·0% at the time of the Somme battles and 2·3% in the spring of 1918. About half of the wastage is directly attributable to battle casualties; died, invalided and missing. The wastage rates calculated do not vary in any significant way with the strength of the force deployed.[11] These rates, apparently small, conceal more specific wastages, for from December 1914 a replacement rate of 15% per month was found necessary for infantry. Such reinforcement rates place an even heavier burden on the young and fit age groups and reduce the number of formations which a country can place in the field. In the Second World War wastage rates were much more variable, due to the changing nature of the War as it developed. An annual rate of loss of 10·6% in 1940 fell to 4·6% in 1943 before rising again.[12] Infantry casualties still ran at a high rate, however, and replacement became a particular problem in the Italian campaign from 1943. After D-Day in northern Europe casualties were lighter than had been expected, although heavy enough, but the campaign had been begun in the knowledge that replacements in sight would be insufficient to replace wastage and that formations would have to be broken up in the course of the campaign. Similar remarks could be applied to the British forces in the Far East. The comment regarding the burden carried by the 20–25 year-olds in the Great War thus applies equally to the Second.

One could thus envisage a situation in which a group of men is mobilised and remains in service for a number of years, suffering a wastage of about 10% per year, more in the Great War, less in the Second, and with about 10% 'ineffective' at any one time. After five years, at an annual rate of loss of 10%, 59% of them would still be serving. Each year a further group could be added, perhaps representing men reaching military age, suffering similar rates of wastage as time goes by. The strength of this army would rise very much as depicted in Figures 1.1, 2.3 or 3.3, with the effective increase in total strength each year becoming less as wastage tended to overtake recruitment.

v *Conclusion*

Britain entered the Great War in August 1914 with no experience of developing a mass army and regarding conscription to do so as an alien concept. The following years, to the end of the war, were a period of trial and error as both a mass army and a system of national service were improvised. The simplistic initial idea that men could be recruited, formed up into units, brigades and divisions and marched away to fight was hampered by lack of pre-war preparation and confused by the alternative means used to improvise divisions for the field. Only later was it realised that extensive reinforcement and replacement organisations would have to be created to maintain the formations in the field. Later still was it realised that very large numbers were needed to supply and support those in the firing line. The result was a considerable over-estimate of the number of fighting organisations Britain could support, leading to attempts to keep divisions in the field by any means practicable and with reluctant and delayed disbandment of units and formations to keep the remainder up to strength.

The industrial support which a mass army needed was also under-estimated at first and attempts to increase munitions production were hampered by the enlistment of skilled workers in the early part of the war. With no clear idea as to how many workers were needed, and with what skills, industrial development also took place as an improvisation. Manpower deployment thus took place with no clear idea as to what was and what was not in the national interest. Although military conscription was introduced, the confused policies regarding industrial priorities reduced its effectiveness and cast doubts on how fairly the system was administered. Allied to those who opposed conscription in principle and labour leaders who wished to preserve the negotiated rights of their followers, the effect of conscription was to produce internal dispute and reduce and delay the supply of men to the army.

So far as the Dominions were concerned, loyalty to the mother country demanded that Britain should be supported. Developing senses of nationhood demanded that that support should be offered on the Dominions' own terms. The involvement of the Dominions was therefore less whole-hearted than that of Britain and could not really be expected to be otherwise. Certainly the Dominions could not be expected to submerge their identity and that of their forces into that of Britain, as was at times expected by some British leaders. The development of the forces of the Dominions, and of the manpower of those countries, broadly followed that of Britain with improvisations of similar nature, and to some extent the same sort of internal divisions. Generally the peace-time forces of the Dominions proved to be readily adaptable to provide the foundation for the war-time armies and, perhaps because they were smaller and more easily monitored, the expansions undertaken seem to have proceeded more efficiently than those of Britain. The fighting reputations earned by the troops from the Dominions were such as to increase awareness of separate national identities and marked a significant step along the road to full independence. In India confusion as to what was the real role of the Indian Army, and the lack of an effective system of providing reinforcements, resulted in the country barely being able to support its peace-time forces until the third year of the Great War. Thereafter a very large expansion was undertaken with the ultimate objective of relieving British troops in the outer theatres, allowing them to be concentrated for the defeat of Germany.

The experiences of 1914 to 1918 were absorbed in Britain in the inter-war years and much clearer ideas were developed regarding the overall control of labour needed to facilitate industrial production in a future war. The military development which a future war might need was less clearly thought out and, with economic considerations of greater importance, the role of the British Army remained in doubt for a considerable period. It was very few months before the outbreak of war in 1939 that a role for the army was recognised which bore any great resemblance to the tasks faced in September. When war came the problems of the previous War regarding the allocation of men to industry were largely reduced to the problems of which weapons should be produced and what should be the priorities between them. So far as the army was concerned a supply of men was ensured, limited by the priorities imposed for the distribution of men between the Services and industry. So far as the organisational expansion of the army was concerned the message of the previous war was less clearly observed and the number of men needed to keep a given formation in the field was greatly under-estimated. In consequence more fighting formations were created than could be maintained, with results much as in the previous war. In Britain the political pressures to expand were considerable, as were the pressures to keep formations in being even when it was clear that they could not be kept up to strength. The result was to confuse an already complex situation. In the First World War very large labour and supply organisations had to be built up in France to support the front-line troops and although the manpower demands for this were not repeated between 1940 and 1944 other demands existed. The need to create large bases in the Middle East, Persian Gulf and Far East were very expensive in manpower terms and even when the war moved on from Africa garrisons had to be retained in the redundant theatres. Although as far as possible these garrisons were found from troops it was considered inadvisable to deploy in Europe, the drain on British resources was not eliminated entirely. Thus the number of men needed in the army as a whole remained high relative to the number of formations in contact with the enemy.

In the Dominions the inter-war years were marked by a greater inclination towards spending what funds were available on the creation and improvement of naval and air forces at the expense of the armies. In the Pacific the growing influence of Japan provided a focus for the attention of Australia and New Zealand, and to some extent of Canada. The outbreak of war in Europe in 1939 was therefore regarded even more as a limited liability than it had been in 1914. Only in 1941, with all the appearances of a threat on the doorstep, did the three older Dominions attempt a full expansion of their forces. Under what was believed to be the imminent threat of invasion they over-expanded them and reductions followed as soon as the threat had waned. Indian Army organisation was greatly improved between the wars, even though funds were lacking for equipment to full modern standards. The Imperial Reserve role of at least part of the Army was formally recognised and some movement towards an Army for a Dominion of India took place. The expansion of the Indian Army after 1939 was achieved against the background of the universal shortage of equipment which prevailed. The methods of expansion followed were similar to those used in the earlier war but, whereas they had been found effective when the Indian Army faced Turkish troops in 1918, they were far less effective when the enemy was the Japanese Army of 1941 and 1942. The expansion was thus brought to an end through doubts in London concerning the quality of the new forces and, according to the Indian Army's C-in-C, because of lack of officers, in part a reflection of the British Army's own shortage of men.

The general picture of the development of the Commonwealth armies during both World Wars is one of expansion and development over two or three years until a point was reached when the available supply of men was insufficient to sustain the organisations created and contractions followed. Put this way the problem was one of manpower shortages. But this is to invert the problem. For any one country manpower is a finite resource. Men cannot be created to fit a particular organisational structure. The organisational structure must be created to fit the number of men available. Ultimately the number of men for the army is fixed by the number the Government of the day chooses to allocate between the competing demands of industry and the other two Services. More men for the army can only be found by allocating fewer to the navy, air force or industry. The choice can only be made in terms of the policy which the Government has established regarding the contribution which the nation is going to make to the war. With the number of men established, both as an absolute number immediately available and as an anticipated rate of reinforcement, the organisation follows. If the Government subsequently decides to reduce the number of men available to the army by a partial demobilisation, as happened in Australia and New Zealand in 1943 and 1944, either to release men for industry or because there is no longer public consent for the existing degree of mobilisation, contraction of the organisation naturally follows. However in both World Wars all of the Commonwealth armies, except the mercenary forces in the Great War, were expanded to a greater extent than was justified by the manpower available and organisational contraction ensued piecemeal as the symptoms of this became apparent. The pressures to over-expand are considerable. The authorities responsible for expanding an army are under pressure from their political leaders and the public to show a large return in front-line formations from the investment made in public effort and political will. Allies have to be satisfied that support is whole-hearted, while a country's influence over its Allies in forwarding its own policies is clearly related to its apparent military strength. The result of yielding to those pressures in both World Wars was that some of Britain's leaders were able to deceive themselves that the country was militarily stronger than in fact it was. The necessary reductions had to be made in the course of major campaigns, when commitments had already been accepted, and in the face of strong enemies.

Notes

1 G. Long, *The Final Campaigns*, Australian War Memorial, Canberra, 1963, p. 77.

2 H. Moyse-Bartlett, *King's African Rifles*, Gale and Polden, Aldershot, 1956, p. 568.

3 N. Orpen, *East African and Abyssinian Campaigns*, Purnell, Cape Town, 1968, pp. 219–20.

4 Sri Nandan Prasad, *Expansion of the Armed Forces and Defence Organisation*, Combined Historical Section, Delhi, 1956, p. 88.
   B. Bond, *British Military Policy Between the Two World Wars*, Oxford U. P., 1980, p. 23.

5 D. Lloyd George, *War Memoirs*, II, Odhams, London, Two-vol. edn., 1938, p. 1573.
   R. Blake (Ed.), *Private Papers of Douglas Haig*, Eyre and Spottiswoode, London, 1952, p. 294.

6 Sir William Robertson, *Soldiers and Statesmen*, II, Cassell, London, 1926, p. 10.

7 Sir Arthur Bryant, *The Turn of the Tide*, Collins, London, 1957, p. 539.

8 Sir William Slim, *Defeat into Victory*, Cassell, London, 1956, pp. 535–36.
   Bryant, *Turn of the Tide*, p. 210 (f.n.).
   J. Connell, *Auchinleck*, Cassell, London, 1959, p. 189.
   J. H. A. Sparrow, *Morale*, War Office, London, 1949, pp. 22–3.

9 H. M. D. Parker, *Manpower*, H.M.S.O., London, 1957, p. 495.

10 Orpen, *East Africa and Abyssinia*, p. 222.
   H. J. Martin and N.D. Orpen, *South Africa at War*, Purnell, Cape Town, 1979, p. 346.
   J. C. Smuts, *Jan Christian Smuts*, Cassell, London, 1952, p. 485.

11 War Office, *Statistics of the Military Effort of the Empire*, H.M.S.O., London, 1922, pp. 83–5.

12 Parker, *Manpower*, p. 485.
   Statistical Digest of the War, H.M.S.O., London, 1951, p. 9.

Select bibliography

a. *Documentary sources*

Hansard
Parliamentary Papers
Army Lists – British, Indian, Australian, Canadian, New Zealand
Army Council Instructions
Army Orders
Census Reports: England and Wales, Scotland, Ireland, 1911
                     Australia, 1911 and 1947
                     Canada, 1921 and 1941
                     India, 1911 and 1931
                     New Zealand, 1936
                     South Africa, 1911 and 1936
New Zealand Year Books, 1915–18

Public Record Office Papers:

Cab 2	CID Minutes
Cab 16	Cabinet and CID Committees
Cab 23 and 24	Cabinet Minutes and Memoranda, 1916–39
Cab 53	Chiefs of Staff Committee, 1923–39
Cab 65 and 66	War Cabinet Minutes and Memoranda, 1939–45
Cab 79 and 80	Chiefs of Staff Committee Minutes and Memoranda 1939–45
WO 32 and 33	Reports and correspondence
WO 95	War Diaries, 1914–20
WO 165–79	War Diaries, 1939–46
WO 212	Orders of Battle, 1939–45

India Office Papers:

WS	War Staff reports and correspondence
L/Mil/17/--	Military Department papers

b. *Official histories and other authoritative works*

Bean, C. E. W., *Official History of Australia in the War of 1914–18*, I–VI, Angus and Robertson, Sydney, 1921, 1924, 1929, 1933, 1936, 1942.

Butlin, S. J., *War Economy, 1939–42*, Australian War Memorial, Canberra, 1955.

Butlin, S. J. and Schedvin, C. B., *War Economy, 1942–45*, Australian War Memorial, Canberra, 1977.

Gibbs, N. H., *Grand Strategy*, I, HMSO, London, 1976.

Gillespie, O. A., *The Pacific*, Department of Internal Affairs, Wellington, 1952.

Long, G., *To Benghazi*, Australian War Memorial, Canberra, 1952.

Long, G., *The Final Campaigns* Australian War Memorial, Canberra, 1963.

Lucas, Sir Charles (Ed.), *The Empire at War*, I–V, Oxford U. P., 1921, 1923, 1924, 1925, 1926.

McClyemont, W. G. *To Greece*, Department of Internal Affairs, Wellington, 1959.

Martin, H. J. and Orpen, N. D., *South Africa at War*, Purnell, Cape Town, 1979.

Moberly, F. J., *History of the Great War*, Mesopotamia, I–IV, HMSO, London, 1923, 1924, 1925, 1927.

Nicholson, G. W. L., *Canadian Expeditionary Force, 1914–19*, Queen's Printer, Ottawa, 1962.

Orpen, N. D., *East African and Abyssinian Campaigns*, Purnell, Cape Town, 1968.

Parker, H. M. D., *Manpower*, HMSO, London, 1957.

Prasad, Sri Nandan, *Expansion of the Armed Forces and Defence Organisation*, Combined Historical Section, Delhi, 1956.

Scott, E., *Official History of Australia in the War of 1914–18*, XI, Angus and Robertson, Sydney, 1936.

Stacey, C. P., *Six Years of War*, Queen's Printer, Ottawa, 1955.

Ungerson, B., *Personnel Selection*, War Office, London, 1953.

War Office, *Statistics of the Military Effort of the British Empire during the Great War*, HMSO, London, 1922.

Central Statistical Office, *Statistical Digest of the War*, HMSO, London, 1951.

c. *Biographical works*

Barrow, Sir George, *The Life of General Sir Charles Monro*, Hutchinson, London, 1931.

Birdwood, Field Marshal Lord, *Khaki and Gown*, Ward Lock, London, 1941.

Blake, R. (Ed.), *The Private Papers of Douglas Haig*, Eyre and Spottiswoode London, 1952.

Bond, B. (Ed.), *Chief of Staff: The Diaries of Lieutenant-General Sir Henry Pownall*, I and II, Leo Cooper, London, 1972, 1974.

Bryant, Sir Arthur, *The Turn of the Tide* (Viscount Alanbrooke), Collins, London, 1957.
Bryant, Sir Arthur, *Triumph in the West* (Viscount Alanbrooke), Collins, London, 1959.
Callwell, Sir C. E., *Field Marshal Sir Henry Wilson: His Life and Diaries*, I and II, Cassell, London, 1927.
Cassar, G. H., *Kitchener: Architect of Victory*, Kimber, London, 1977.
Connell, J., *Wavell: Supreme Commander*, Collins, London, 1969.
Connell, J., *Auchinleck*, Cassell, London, 1959.
Godley, Sir Alexander, *Life of an Irish Soldier*, John Murray, London, 1939.
Hancock, W. K., *Smuts*, I and II, Cambridge U.P., 1962, 1968.
Magnus, Sir Philip, *Kitchener: Portrait of an Imperialist*, John Murray, London, 1958.
Maurice, Sir Frederick, *The Life of General Lord Rawlinson*, Cassell, London, 1928.
Morton, D., *The Canadian General Sir William Otter*, Hakkert, Toronto, 1974.
North, J. (Ed.), *The Alexander Memoirs, 1940–45*, Cassell, London, 1962.
Robertson, Sir William, *Soldiers and Statesmen*, I and II, Cassell, London, 1926.
Singleton-Gates, P., *General Lord Freyberg*, Michael Joseph, London, 1963.
Slim, Sir William, *Defeat into Victory*, Cassell, London, 1956.
Spiers, E. M., *Haldane: An Army Reformer*, Edinburgh U.P., 1980.
Terraine, J., *Douglas Haig: The Educated Soldier*, Hutchinson, London, 1963.

d.   Regimental histories – bibliographies

Dornbusch, C. E., *The Canadian Army, 1855–1965*, Hope Farm Press, New York, 1966.
White, A. S., *Bibliography of Regimental Histories of the British Army*, SAHR, 1965.
Australian Second World War Histories are in Long, *Final Campaigns*, Appendix 8.

e.   Doctoral theses

Allison, M. J., 'The National Service Issue, 1899–1914', London, 1975.
Armstrong, G. P., 'The Controversy over Tanks in the British Army, 1919–33', London, 1976.
French, D. W., 'Some Aspects of Social and Economic Planning for War in Great Britain, c.1905–15', London, 1979.
Jacobsen, M. H., 'The Modernisation of the Indian Army, 1925–39', California, Irvine, 1979.
Perry, F. W., 'Manpower and Organisational Problems in the Expansion of

the British and other Commonwealth Armies During the Two World Wars', London, 1981.

Rawson, J. O., 'The Role of India in Imperial Defence Beyond Indian Frontiers and Home Waters, 1919–39, Oxford, 1976.

Summerton, N. W., 'Development of British Military Planning for War Against Germany, 1904–14', London, 1970.

f. *Secondary sources*

Barclay, G. St. J., *The Empire is Marching*, Wiedenfeld and Nicolson, London, 1976.

Beckett, I. F. W. and Simpson, K. (Eds.), *A Nation in Arms*, Manchester U.P., 1985.

Bond, B., *British Military Policy Between the Two World Wars*, Oxford U.P., 1980.

Dennis, P., *Decision by Default*, Routledge and Kegan Paul, London, 1972.

Dunlop, J. K., *The Development of the British Army, 1899–1914*, Methuen, London, 1938.

Gooch, J., *The Plans of War*, Routledge and Kegan Paul, London, 1974.

Howard, M., *The Continental Commitment*, Temple Smith, London, 1972.

Kennedy, P. M. (Ed.), *War Plans of the Great Powers, 1880–1914*, Allen and Unwin, 1979.

Mason, P., *A Matter of Honour*, Peregrine Books, Harmondsworth, 1976.

Preston, R. A., *Canada and Imperial Defence*, U. of Toronto Press, 1967.

Watt, D. C., *Too Serious a Business*, Temple Smith, London, 1975.

Index